Emily Lynell Edwards
Digital Islamophobia

De Gruyter Contemporary Social Sciences

Volume 21

Emily Lynell Edwards

Digital Islamophobia

Tracking a Far-Right Crisis

DE GRUYTER

ISBN 978-3-11-163130-1
e-ISBN (PDF) 978-3-11-103288-7
e-ISBN (EPUB) 978-3-11-103295-5
ISSN 2747-5689

Library of Congress Control Number: 2023941100

Bibliographic information published by the Deutsche Nationalbibliothek
The Deutsche Nationalbibliothek lists this publication in the Deutsche Nationalbibliografie;
detailed bibliographic data are available on the internet at http://dnb.dnb.de.

www.degruyter.com

Contents

Chapter I
Introduction

The House is on Fire: The Far-Right in 1933 & 2022

Among scholars, politicians, technology companies, and everyday citizens there is a renewed fixation and vexation with far-right politics. The increased visibility of far-right digital communities and discourse has generally been treated as a burgeoning societal crisis, or, framed as a reasonable form of reactionary politics addressing a set of imagined catastrophes ranging from the changing demography of nation-states to the supposed breakdown of the nuclear family (Brubaker 2017; Ganesh and Froio 2020). Much ink has been spilled over the last few years regarding the rise of the "alt-right" in the United States (US), invoked by the #GamerGate movement, the 2016 American presidential election, or the violent white supremacist 2017 Unite the Right rally in Charlottesville, Virginia (Bezio 2018; Daniels 2018; Hawley 2019; Nagle 2017; Stern 2019), or by the now countless incidents of physical and digital far-right violence. Comparatively in Germany, the meteoric rise of the far-right anti-immigration party Alternative for Germany (AfD) with its electoral sweep in 2017 has spurred political consternation and new scholarly reflection on the resurgence of far-right political ideologies in the contemporary reunified German state with recurrent instances of violent far-right protests and even the botched "Day of X" coup (Berning 2017; Beauchamp 2022; Havertz 2021; Klikauer 2018).

Particularly significant in both scholarly and popular discussions of the supposed resurgence of far-right political movements in the US, Germany, and beyond, is how digital platforms, social media, and algorithmic technologies have supported the proliferation of these groups and ideologies (Daniels 2018, 61), even as it has been documented that far-right groups have a long history of appropriating digital mediums from message boards to simple websites to organize and connect (Conway, Scrivens, and Macnair 2019). If there is a spirited debate about the origins and precursors to the resurgence of far-right politics in Germany and the US (Bezio 2018; Havertz 2021; Shoshan 2016; Michael 2017), what is clear is that the mushrooming of far-right communities on digital platforms and the spread of far-right hate-speech is not merely a content moderation challenge, but a foundational threat to democracy, a platformed crisis in the making.

Antonio Gramsci, in theorizing the concept of crisis noted that "crisis consists precisely in the fact that the old is dying and the new cannot be born; in this interregnum a great variety of morbid symptoms appear" (1976, 276). In this context

https://doi.org/10.1515/9783111032887-001

of crisis, this book explores the appearance of these morbid symptoms; of the formation of far-right German and American digitally networked communities, engaging in a Transatlantic comparison to shed light on how a particular subsection of these digital communities—far-right Islamophobic users—serve as key manifestations of a more chronic and historic sickness, of racialized nationalism in Germany and the US. Now more virulent and viral than ever. Studying this digital subculture against the context of the larger far-right digital ecosystem reveals the way in which far-right Islamophobic communities are both seeking to enact the continuation of white supremacy and ethnic German homogeneity, as well as to realize a set of reactionary social politics while fostering transnational, global connections with other Islamophobic groups beyond the US and Europe, in Nigeria and India.

With far-right political movements increasingly defined by their digitality, this book examines the networks and digital political discourse that makes up part of the infrastructure of far-right Islamophobic digital communities focusing on the platform Twitter. In both Germany and the US, far-right groups are increasingly seeking to actualize the future of racialized, nationalism from the embers of each of their respective national pasts through Tweets. Today, far-right Islamophobic German and American Twitter users increasingly view themselves as digital cultural warriors, or present-day crusaders, confronting what they imagine as a world beset by crises of globalization, immigration, feminism, and increasing racial pluralism, which is to say, the possible destabilization of patterns and structures of white and ethnic German, patriarchal, Christian hegemony, with Muslim communities imagined as the primary threat (Ganesh and Froio 2020, 724). It is this notion of crisis; cultural crisis, demographic crisis, political crisis, that is advanced as the key frame by far-right digital publics on social media platforms (Ganesh and Froio 2020, 717).

Far-right digitally networked Islamophobic communities are actively engaged in a discursive, digital "war of position" racializing and rhetorically excluding Muslim groups from the boundary of nation on the battlefield of social media platforms (Gramsci 1976), particularly Twitter. And today, these groups are seeking to actualize these racially and religiously exclusionary visions of the future through political activism, organizing, fundraising, and political violence (Awan and Zempi 2017; Perocco 2018; Saylor 2014). But this off-platform activity germinates and takes root in digital spaces, whereby users update historic racialized ideologies and traffic in extremist nostalgia and conspiracies to make networked connections and affectively radicalize sympathetic adherents to the cause (J. Johnson 2018).

Critically, it is the new technological affordances of micro-blogging platforms such as Twitter, that, because of their structure, allow for the spreading and remixing of historic racist conspiracies and far-right ideologies that makes it easier and more seamless for transnational far-right users to connect, collaborate, and grow into formative networked communities. Far-right Islamophobic hate-speech is not merely a national or Western issue, rather, it is a technologically mediated crisis linking Global North and South. Far-right Islamophobic German and American Twitter users increasingly view themselves as symbolically connected to historic far-right movements and crusaders, locked in a civilationalist battle (Brubaker 2017; Huntington 1993). In digital landscapes anti-Muslim beliefs and Islamophobia serves as the "transnational glue" that binds together seemingly disparate users into cohesive and visible far-right networks beyond the US and Europe (Froio and Ganesh 2018, 101)

While far-right, anti-Muslim communities may be emergent in the sense that they are actively re-appropriating digital technologies to engage in new forms of discursive production and movement building, they are still mired within past histories of racialized nationalism, with scholars of the far-right noting that when we historicize contemporary political trends in Germany and the US the resurgence looks more like "a continuation of [a] national story of systemic racism" in both nations (Daniels 2018, 64), carrying forward the past more than breaking with it in any sense.

On the platform Twitter far-right German and American users are actively engaging in a reconstruction of their national pasts through their (re)production of digital content, on a mission to articulate a "usable past" for their own contemporary ideological aims (Moeller 2001; Trachtenberg 1984). Historically this scholarly exercise in articulating a "usable past" has been part of a practice of German and American scholars aiming to make sense of national tragedies including the Holocaust and the Transatlantic Slave Trade, seeking to examine, theorize, and present a coherent national narrative or story to make sense of present socio-culture conditions (Moeller 2001, 20; Trachtenberg 1984, 671; Shank 1997, 97). As skilled digital storytellers, far-right users are actively producing content that recasts historical and contemporary narratives with white Americans and ethnic Germans as besieged victims, imagining one such usable future of the global far-right—a digital cultural war designed to discursively eliminate Muslim communities along with other marginalized groups.

In Germany in particular, the state's history of ethnonationalism and fascist political movements firmly underlies the reemergence of the contemporary Germany digital right. Today, the historic German philosophical theory of the *Volksgeist* (Herder 1800), of a national community bound together through shared spiritual purpose and cultural superiority, presupposing a connection between race, temperament, and cultural identity resonant during the Third Reich, has re-surfaced in present day AfD discourse and in the content produced by far-right German Twitter users (Klikauer 2018; Tansill 1940). From the Third Reich, to the *Gastarbeiter* era where former West Germany saw an influx of predominately Muslim Turkish guest-workers settling in the country (Chin 2007, 108; Triadafilopoulos and Schönwälder 2006), to reunification in 1990, race, religion, and national identity in Germany have always been intertwined. However, since reunification, race has frequently become "repackaged in cultural terms," with racialized discourse situated as merely cultural concerns regarding the growing visibility of Islamic religious practice (Shoshan 2016, 57).

In modern reunified Germany, culture remains the critical field where citizenship and racial membership is mediated and expressed. The AfD in their manifesto state that a common Western European, Christian culture forms the basis for political discourse and political subjectivity in Germany, echoing Herder's treatise written hundreds of years ago ("AfD Grundsatzprogramm Englisch" 2017, 45–46). In this sense then, German historical conceptions of national belonging have come full circle, with contemporary far-right communities on digital platforms re-articulating historic concepts of race, nation, and culture to police the boundaries of the nation-state, responding to present day instances of immigration and demographic change by situating German-Turkish Muslim communities and Muslim immigrants as foreign agents within the state.

Comparatively, in the US, racial, national, and religious belonging has long been defined by economic structuration during eras of settler colonialism, the plantation economy, and industrial capitalism. Mainstream American nationalism has long been defined by discourses of (un)freedom predicated on racializing, disenfranchising, and dehumanizing Black Americans, indigenous communities, Latinx communities, and immigrants to re-affirm the political rights of white citizens (Morgan 1972, 24; Fields 1990). While there is a long history of Muslim immigration to the US going back to the 16th century and accompanying the Transatlantic Slave Trade (GhaneaBassiri 2013), Muslims became a nationally legible racialized community in the 1970s during the Iranian hostage situation and subsequent oil crisis (Love 2017, 87). These political developments dovetailed mediatized representations in American popular culture throughout the 1980s and 1990s which homogenized the Arab world and depicted Muslims as a short-hand for racialized, foreign terroristic figures (Love 2017, 89; Shaheen 2012). Thus, in the US and West more broadly, "modern Islamophobia is preoccupied with the idea that Muslims pose an inner threat to the 'West'" and that Muslim communities are somehow foreign to the body politic (Ekman 2015, 1989), which we can understand as contemporizing a historic pattern of Western Orientalism and civilationalist conflict as identified by Edward Said (1979).

This Orientalization and racialization of Muslim in the US in the 1980s and 1990s is located with a larger racial context of the rise of "color-blind" rhetoric and ideology particularly characteristic of the 1990s and 2000s which coincided with the watershed moment of 9/11 (Bonilla-Silva 2015), and the parallel disappearance of explicit discussion of race or *Rasse* from the German public lexicon (Chin and Fehrenbach, 2009). Despite these public discourses of a transcendence of race in the US in the 1990s and early 2000s and the German shift away from explicit engagements with race towards the obfuscating language of multiculturalism, following the 9/11 terrorist attacks, a new and racialized public political rhetoric manifested that specifically targeted Muslim communities (GhaneaBassiri 2013; Love 2017). In the US, cultural concerns over supposed fundamental differences in a dialectical Eastern Muslim and implicitly American or Western "way of life" were mobilized to racialize and exclude Muslim communities as separate from the nation and subjects of suspicion (GhaneaBassiri 2013, 54, 56).

This period saw a refashioning of a "clash of civilizations" rhetoric that has lately been revived by former president Donald Trump (Haynes 2021; Huntington 1993). However, 9/11 and the subsequent programs of US military intervention abroad and surveillance of domestic Muslim communities accompanied by increased anti-Muslim rhetoric and violence may be understood as a nadir of the Muslim experience in the US (Abbas 2021; Hanes and Machin 2014). Globally speaking, this period and the specific historical manifestation of Islamophobia expressed therein may be defined as part of a longer term "racial project" of racializing Muslim communities in the West (Hafez 2018; Love 2017). Following 9/11, Islamophobic discourse became more mainstreamed, transnationalized, and increasingly formalized in domestic and foreign policies (Mondon and Winter 2017).

Muslim communities in Germany and the US during the height of the global "War on Terror" and thereafter have had their citizenship identities defined by crisis and shifting boundaries of political and religious exclusion (Baker and Shryock 2009; Shryock 2013; Shryock and Lin 2009). In the particular context of American racialized nationalism, Muslim communities are not only affected by these securitization and crisis discourses but are also subject to explicit forms of American racialization whereby historically in the US "social status and indeed citizenship have been generated by assignment to a position in the racial hierarchy" (Garner and Selod 2014, 8). Yet, along with the exportation of American Islamophobia abroad (Bakali and Hafez 2022), the proliferation of new medias has changed how Islamophobia and nationalism are mediated and expressed globally.

In Germany and the US, nations defined by centuries old racial projects, the intersection between Islamophobia and contemporary far-right ethnonationalism collides with various actors from formal political parties, to the state, to media outlets, invested in the process of racializing and Othering Muslim communities. With the advent and proliferation of social media platforms, individual users and adherents of far-right Islamophobic ideologies are now more able to take part in these racial projects themselves through the production of far-right content and the formation of national and transnational networks on platforms such as Twitter, sitting on the couch, smartphone in hand.

Islamophobic Ideology & Making Sense of the Contemporary, Global, Digital Far-Right

The spread of far-right digital communities has increasingly been investigated in both German and American political contexts (Berg 2019; Bezio 2018; Hartzell 2018; Nagle 2017; Miller-Idriss 2020; Morstatter et al. 2018; Stern 2019), with emerging research on the American far-right digital ecosystem focusing on the topic of Muslim immigration and the presence of Islamophobia in German public attitudes and formalized far-right political parties (Ahmed and Pisoiu 2020; Benkler, Faris, and Roberts 2018; Gardner, Karakaşoğlus, and Luchtenberg 2008). Looking at these far-right communities in tandem, deploying a Transatlantic comparison, yields new insights into the transnationalization of far-right Islamophobic content and the critical role everyday users play in mainstreaming far-right hate-speech and ideology online.

There is an extensive history of transnational European far-right cooperation (Albanese and Del Hierro 2016; Macklin 2013), with the exportation of concepts and conspiracies from the French New Right which has influenced the anti-modern, anti-Muslim, and culturalist bent of other Western far-right social movements (Ahmed and Pisoiu 2020; Bar-On 2012; Michelsen and de Orellana 2020). Going back further, there are also historic Transatlantic connections between German and American far-right and Neo-Nazi networks extending into the 1970s (Kahn 2021; Koehler 2014). However, today new media technologies are platforming far-right ideologies and enabling the creation of global networked connections like never before.

And political parties, elite, verified users, and media institutions, while critical loci in the larger far-right ecosystem have hitherto received lopsided attention. Increasingly, everyday, run-of-the-mill, average social media users, particularly those on Twitter, are engaged in the production, dissemination, and mainstreaming of virulent, far-right Islamophobic digital content and ideology. Far-right politics and political communication are undergoing a process of transnationalization *and* banalization due to the affordances of mainstream platforms like Twitter. Tracking these communities, identifying the content of their ideology, and visualizing the contours of their networked connections requires a unique methodological approach combining quantitative data analytic techniques and insights from a robust body of feminist and critical theory to make sense of how race, gender, religion, and national identity are mediated in the far-right imagination by different subnetworks.

Digitally networked communities which emerge on Twitter, from fan groups, to the far-right coalitions which are the subject of this book, may be understood as multiple overlapping digital publics, which Michael Warner has defined as a type of community which "comes into being only in relation to texts and their circulation" (Warner 2002, 50). In platformed digital environments these texts can be posts, messages, or comments. In the case of Twitter, Tweets and hashtags are the key texts in circulation that create discursive, mutable, or "ad hoc" national digital communities on the platform that are made legible through conversations specifically focused on Muslim communities (Bruns and Burgess 2011; Shahin 2020). Scholars studying online hate-movements and communities have conceptualized far-right digital communities drawing on Warner's theory specifically, noting that the openness of digital landscapes and of social media platforms within the larger context of the new media era have increasingly enabled an "opportunity space" for these types of "counter publics" to emerge (Shepherd et al. 2015, 3; Squires 2002).

As a primarily text-driven, micro-blogging platform, Twitter is notable for its circulation of national political discussion and the way it has facilitated the formation of transnational digital political networks (Shahin 2020). The so-called "hashtags revolutions" of the Arab Spring, #MeToo, and the #BlackLivesMatter movement all are recognized as major instances of political activism and communication which grew on and made use of Twitter to platform their messages to a range of lasting results (Howard and Hussain 2013; Jenkins 2013; Rambukkana 2015). And while Twitter has played a major role in progressive and pro-democracy social movements, it has also comparatively platformed far-right views across the globe (Ahmed and Pisoiu 2020; Chaturvedi 2016).

This is because Twitter, unlike comparative social media sites, is "heterogenous" in so far as it allows for more extensive network building due to the structural ease by which actors connect simply by including usernames in Tweets (Zheng and Shahin 2018, 1). Twitter as a social media platform is defined by a series of unique affordances that facilitate the creation of networked public spheres, however, a much more fractious and fragmented public sphere than Jürgen Habermas conceived of in an earlier media era (Bruns and Highfield 2015; Habermas 1991).

The "@," and moreso the "#" mechanisms used on the platform represent a revolution in digital communication and connection (Losh 2014), with the # facilitating the "connecting [of] people with shared interests," even as users may not be followers or friends (Zheng and Shahin 2018, 3), allowing individuals to follow topics, frame messages, and enter into discursive communities at will. Different from other mainstream legacy social media platforms like Facebook and Instagram which are structured on the curation of a list of friends and followers, operating in some sense as "walled gardens" (Murthy, Gross, and McGarry 2016), Twitter has defined itself by an ethos of openness and worked to cultivate the perception that it, unlike its competitors, is the platform for news and political communication, with journalists, academics, writers, and public figures recognized as key "power users" on the platform (Ghaffary 2022).

The home for mainstream political and news conversation online, Twitter also remains more dominant than the new assortment of "alt-tech" social media platforms catering to social conservatives and far-right audiences such as Parler, Gab, Truth Social, and Koo (Dixit 2021; H. Johnson et al. 2022), and more popular than niche sites known for their extremist and graphic content such as 4chan, 8kun, or Kiwi Farms (Hall 2022; Nagle 2017). Even as platforms such as Facebook are increasingly identified as hotbeds for the growth of far-right Islamophobic groups (Törnberg and Nissen 2022; Squire 2018), these groups often remain siloed and private. And on more open platforms which support far-right extremist content production like YouTube (Ekman 2017; Munger and Phillips 2022; Rauchfleisch and Kaiser 2020), much of this information is produced by (micro)influencers, politicians, and media personalities to then be consumed by users or discussed in the comment sections.

Twitter is thus unique both in its hosting of public, political conversations and for its organization whereby elite and everyday users produce content, circulate, and connect, and, where far-right views are increasingly algorithmically amplified under the platform's leadership by billionaire, provocateur, and "free speech" absolutist Elon Musk (Alter 2022; Bond 2022; Huszár et al. 2021). Twitter thus functions as an absolutely critical point in a larger far-right digital landscape for its amplification and platforming of far-right Islamophobic digital content to mainstream audiences, (Huszár et al. 2021; Muis, Klein, and Dijkstra 2020; Vidgen, Yasseri, and Margetts 2022), thereby facilitating the banalization of these ideologies and radicalization of users.

These far-right digitally networked groups on Twitter are powerful counterpublics that come into being for a moment in time through their usage of shared hashtags or texts. As Anatoliy Gruzd and Caroline Haythornthwaite note in the context of Twitter: "[s]ocial media traces are thus an entry point to describing and later understanding and facilitating community interaction" (2013, 3). Hashtags on Twitter thus serve as a particular "trace" to then examine how far-right digitally networked Islamophobic communities on Twitter form, interact, and transmit ideology. In addition to analyzing in a platformed context how these communities are networked, identifying individual users or network actors outside the usual scope of the formerly elite "blue-checked" set within these communities reveals the process by which far-right users construct a "networked self" on Twitter through user biographies and connections with other users (Papacharissi 2010, 309), revealing a transnationalized, heterogenous community of users (Vidgen, Yasseri, and Margetts 2022), as well as a changing cast of user-types (Awan 2014, 2016). Thus, giving us a more substantive scope of the development of far-right digital political movements.

In studying these everyday Twitter users, it is possible to track a resurgence of what Sabina Mihelj and César Jiménez-Martínez have termed the "digitally updated version of banal, everyday nationalism," which, mediated on digital platforms has "provided a fertile environment for the apparent 'resurgence' of nationalism— or, more precisely, for the promotion and spreading of more visible and exclusive forms of nationalism" (2020, 332), and in this case, of increasingly banal forms of Islamophobia that are then linked to other forms of reactionary ideology.

To investigate these communities and parse through their traces requires a multi-scalar methodological approach guided by a commitment to feminist forms of knowledge production which seeks to make visible what has remained hidden (Leurs and Olivieri 2014, XXXI). In other words, combining analytic and visualization methods with feminist grounded theory to make sense of scraped data produced by everyday Twitter users. The foundation of this investigation then begins with the scraping of a series of traces, the detailed collection of Twitter discourse tracking the comparative hashtags #Islamization and ##Islamisierung for over six months during a period of systemic global crisis—the COVID-19 pandemic—which has also paralleled a rise in Islamophobia globally (Apoorvanand 2020; Mahmood 2020).

Hashtags serve as an initial archive of data with which to track and trace a larger community of far-right Islamophobic groups to study dynamics of user interaction, visualize networked connections, and identify the origin of far-right content. The phrases and hashtags of #Islamization and #Islamisierung, utilized in the context of far-right communities, refer to a supposed fear that Muslim immigrants and citizens may render supposedly secular, liberal democracies into conservative Islamic cultural societies (Genova 2015; Perocco 2018), and are a shorthand to enter into a particular and influential far-right subculture that exists right out in the open on Twitter.

Drawing attention to everyday Twitter communication on the comparative hashtags #Islamization and #Islamisierung reveals how average, everyday Twitter users produce and share increasingly extreme Islamophobic content, make transnational connections with other far-right users, and express a disturbing belief in violent conspiracies. Twitter, as a micro-blogging platform ultimately serves as a mainstream site whereby far-right content from external sites is exchanged, circulated, and mainstreamed. If, broadly speaking, new media technologies have facilitated the expression of new forms of "user-generated nationalisms" they also contribute to exclusionary, racially, and religiously bounded forms of national identity (Shahin 2020, 13). And Twitter with all of its affordances increasingly supports the expression of user-generated, global Islamophobia.

A Lay of the Land: Terminology & History

This subsection of Islamophobic networked communities within the larger far-right digital ecosystem illustrates how some of the most virulently racist and outlandish political communication is increasingly mainstreamed. To best understand these dynamics of the mainstreaming of far-right Islamophobic discourse on platforms like Twitter, it is prudent to articulate some operational definitions, particularly of the term "far-right" as we begin to enter into this platformed terrain. Even, as in both national cases defining the far-right is less of an exercise in ideological standardization, rather than a rough attempt in identifying which themes, patterns, and typographies appear on social media, composing and characterizing the larger chimeric far-right network (Crosset, Tanner, and Campana 2018, 944).

In a German context, the far-right refers to a diffuse collection of German individuals who ascribe to (neo)fascist and ethnically nationalist political ideals in the reunified German state. While Germany has a formalized, extreme far-right party, the Die Nationaldemokratische Partei Deutschlands (NPD), this group is electorally marginal (Jesse 2001), and the term far-right is more useful to deploy in a cultural sense. Germans who ascribe to and support (neo)fascist and ethnically nationalist ideologies as evidenced by their engagement in far-right Twitter networks may or may not be formally politically affiliated with the NPD, or the AfD, however, they emphasize a belief in ethnic German nationalism, critique immigration in racialized terms, and hold a position of anti-multilateralism or Euroscepticism (Lees 2018). The fundamental characteristics of the German digital far-right include a core belief in ethnic nationalism; updating ethnonationalist, Nazi-era ideological values and principles for the digital age, with Islamophobia the central crux that links together potentially disparate individuals who may appear more or less extreme. The deluge of far-right German digital content shared and produced on social media platform is but part of a larger trend of the increased visibility of far-right politics in the state.

The electoral successes of the AfD, despite their recent legal troubles (Schumacher 2022), coupled with high-profile instances of vigilante attacks on pro-immigration German politicians, and the embarrassing detection of an extensive network of Neo-Nazis within the German military (Bennhold 2020; Hill 2019), all illustrate the offline ascendency of the German far-right in terms of formal political activity, violence, and social radicalization. Furthermore, during the COVID-19 pandemic, anti-lockdown and vaccine protests were visibly aligned with far-right actors and groups (AP 2021). Collating these on and offline trends, the state has also witnessed a dramatic rise in antisemitic violence, with German Jews pointing towards the troubling emerging cross-over between digital-born COVID-19 conspiracies and far-right hate-speech (DW 2021). Germany is thus home to both historic and contemporary far-right fascist parties, but the cultural shift of the mainstreaming of far-right political rhetoric directly echoing the language and ideology of the Third Reich is how the contemporary far-right has been most successful in winning the on-going "war of position" (Meier 2022; Gramsci 1976). Everyday Germans are increasingly coming into contact with far-right politics not through NDP speeches or AfD rallies, but through social media, on platforms such as Twitter where Islamophobic content and narratives serve as an entry point into other far-right reactionary politics.

Alternatively, in the context of the US, which has a two-party system lacking a nationally recognized far-right party, the far-right refers to a contemporary manifestation of individuals and groups who champion a form of extreme far-right political ideology that features an enthusiastic support of white supremacy, Christian cultural nationalism, and increasingly, a critique of free-market economics and immigration (Hartzell 2018). Indeed, over the past several years from the election of President Donald Trump in 2016 to the 2020 presidential election it has become increasingly difficult to differentiate between mainstream cultural social conservativism, institutional Republican political ideology, and extreme far-right actors.

Trump's "Make America Great Again," henceforth MAGA, style of politics has spurred a formative shift whereby the ideological base of the Republican Party and the larger cultural right, which, already espousing values of gender traditionalism, Christianity, and anti-immigration sentiment, has taken these beliefs to their extreme and logical conclusion. In the US, the difference between far-right and social conservativism is not so much a difference in ideology but in language and rhetorical positioning. Anti-institutionalism, racist discourse, gender traditionalism, and a reactionary nostalgia for an imagined white past in fact define or direct mainstream Republican and socially conservative politics rather than contradict or supplement them (Bezio 2018; Michelsen and de Orellana 2020).

Ultimately, while users who espouse far-right Islamophobic digital discourse can be situated on a continuum of radicalism, all users are ensconced within and contribute to a larger far-right digital ecosystem. For both German and American far-right users, the question of labeling is not related to differences in the fundamental content of their ideology, but rather, the form and structure of their rhetoric and how they spread information, stories, and narratives to resonate with different audiences from suburban mothers to white nationalists, sometimes who are one and the same. Far-right German and American digitally networked Islamophobic communities serve as significant actors in the larger articulation of far-right political activity and movements globally.

A Roadmap for Reading

Digital Islamophobia documents the disturbing emergence of transnational far-right, Islamophobic networks that link together far-right users not only in Germany and the US, but as this investigation will demonstrate, in India and Nigeria, amongst users who see a strategic value in networking with the European and American far-right. These users are all connected by affective yet locally specific forms of racist, xenophobic, anti-Muslim, and gender reactionary (trans)national ideologies, a "choose your own adventure" style of far-right radicalism offering individuals multiple points of entry. Far-right transnationalized Islamophobic digitally networked communities increasingly imagine and mediate Muslim communities as harbingers of national, civilianization, and cultural crisis whether this is in the US, Europe, India, or Nigeria (Froio and Ganesh 2018).

And the circulation of historic and born-digital conspiracies increasingly motivates far-right users across multiple national boundaries to believe in paranoid linkages between Muslim communities, multi-lateral institutions, national governments, and other groups as internal and external enemies of racially, religiously, and ethnically homogenous nation-states. Reconstructing this fragmented far-right media ecosystem using data analytic tools to engage in feminist digital investigation, *Digital Islamophobia* explores complementary topics that animate far-right groups: COVID-19 conspiracies, gender reactionary ideology, and public education. Tracking far-right German and American users on the platform Twitter, this book takes Islamophobic hate-speech as the point of entry to the far-right digital imaginary, identifying the transmission of (mis)information in global, platformed contexts.

Examining Islamophobic digital discourse among German and American digitally networked communities reveals increasingly transnationalized networks of hate that seek to link Muslim communities with other targeted groups: Jews, Black communities, the LGBTQIA+ community, and political progressives as threatening to destabilize an imagined white or ethnic German, Christian, hetero-patriarchal nation-state and the broader cultural imaginary of the West. And for Nigerian and Indian users, anti-Muslim discourse and connection with American far-right groups serves as a strategic means to advocate for national ethnically and religiously exclusionary policies and forms of nationalism in their respective states. In the case of Nigeria, this is the targeting of the predominately Muslim Fulani ethnic group by pro-Biafran coalitions. And in India this is the exclusion and harassment of Muslim Indians in the majority-Hindu Indian state as championed by far-right Hindu nationalists.

Far-right German and American Islamophobic ideology is fundamentally mutable and connected to other ideological positions such as misogyny, gender reactionary ideology, and racism that are also hawked by far-right Twitter users who act as "digital soldiers" for the cause of racialized (trans)nationalism. We see both far-right Hindu nationalists and Christian Nigerians aligned with the Indigenous People of Biafra (IPOB) separatist movement seeking to re-appropriate Western anti-Muslim digital rhetoric for their own aims. Islamophobic discourse is what links German AfD voters, to white American "boy-moms," to Hindu nationalist BJP supporters, to Nigerian IPOB anti-Muslim influencers. Looking through the lens of Islamophobia, we are able to uncover a dynamic and evolving network of users united in their engagement with and production of Islamophobic digital discourse.

The next chapter, "From Homeland, to Heimat, to Hindutva: Profiling Far-Right Islamophobic Transnational Communities on Twitter," outlines the cast of characters, or user-types, who make up far-right Islamophobic German and American networks, which includes an eclectic yet also mundane group of users connected by their shared engagement with #Islamization and #Islamisierung hashtags. We identify a series of users, far-right Hindu nationalists, neighborly racists, MAGA devotees, and white supremacist nationalists that populate far-right landscapes, illustrating both how locally specific nationalist ideologies and family-values conservatism radicalize users and conversely how Islamophobia serves as a shared point of identification and connection amongst a global group of users. White Americans and Hindu nationalists in India and the US increasingly connect together, and conversely German far-right users increasingly re-appropriate American MAGA-style rhetoric for their own ethnonationalist purposes.

The following chapter, "Islamophobia in Play," takes the user-types introduced in the previous chapter and explores how certain narratives and content animates these digital communities through two case studies, examining how Indian users produce Islamophobic content that resonates with white American users, and how German far-right actors manipulate news stories to spread (mis)information about Muslim religious sites. This chapter illustrates how while user types are often nationalistic, similar forms of fear-mongering articulated by Indian Hindu nationalists and German news sites are effective and affective at motivating a diverse group of Twitter users to engage in Islamophobic hate-speech. Tracing and analyzing how Islamophobic content operates in practice reveals the tensions between Twitter's public stance against hate-speech and its content moderation policies which are designed to elide dealing with the endemicity of hate-speech on the platform.

The chapter "Exporting Home-Grown American Islamophobia" takes the study of these communities to the next level, introducing principles of network analysis and a series of social network visualizations, delving into how American Islamophobic digital groups link out to Nigerian and Indian networked communities. This chapter focuses on how far-right, white supremacist, Christian, Islamophobic American politics and policies during the Trump administration collide with anti-Muslim Nigerian and Indian national politics, thus presenting possibilities for the transnationalization of far-right political coalitions in Global North-South contexts.

The subsequent chapter, "Visualizing Networks, (Mis)Information, & Islamophobia in Germany," examines German Islamophobic digital groups through German network visualizations and analyzes two key themes excavated from the graphs; the role fringe media sites play in (re)circulating Islamophobic content and the role individual users play in re-framing real stories with Islamophobic, conspiratorial frames bypassing Twitter's content moderation policies. This chapter emphasizes the insular, nationalized nature of German far-right networks and reflects on opportunities for policy interventions that address Islamophobic hate-speech on the platform in the wake of Elon Musk's tumultuous acquisition of the platform, firing of critical Trust and Safety teams, and gutting of the already weak content moderation policies.

The following chapter "Islamophobia & the Crisis of Conspiracy," brings network actors and structures together through a detailed assessment of the role conspiracies play in far-right ecosystems and the themes that animate far-right communities, focusing on three fundamental political foci: the family, the state, and the pandemic. Beginning with a focus on Islamophobic conspiracies regarding the family and women, this chapter explores how these subjects are situated as mirroring the state to be to be controlled and policed from racial, religious, and sexual degradation. This chapter also explores state-level Islamophobic conspiracies looking at the supposed collusion between Muslim communities and institutional actors at the state level, and how this type of content radicalizes users. This chapter concludes by discussing the interrelation between COVID-19 and Islamophobic conspiracies that reach global proportions against the backdrop of the "state of exception" inaugurated by the pandemic and exploited in far-right messaging (Agamben 2021)

Ultimately, while far-right, anti-Muslim communities, whether they are German, American, Indian, or Nigerian, may seem emergent, they are deeply connected to histories of racial, ethnic, and religious nationalism, histories that manifest in different national contexts. It is the new technological affordances of microblogging platforms such as Twitter that allow for the spreading and re-mixing of historic racist conspiracies and ideologies which create the conditions for transnational collaboration, heralding an evolution from digital denizens waging a civilizationalist, cultural war into the creation of formative and electorally powerful coalitions offline. If the amorphous, networked far-right is indeed waging a war of position on digital platforms, *Digital Islamophobia* aims to be used as a resource in this war as scholars, policymakers, and platforms work together to address the growing crisis of far-right digital extremism.

References

Abbas, Tahir. 2021. "Reflection: The 'War on Terror', Islamophobia and Radicalisation Twenty Years On." *Critical Studies on Terrorism* 14 (4). Routledge: 402 – 4. doi:10.1080/17539153.2021.1980182.

"AfD Grundsatzprogramm Englisch." AfD Manifesto for Germany, 2017. https://www.afd.de/wp-content/uploads/sites/111/2017/04/2017-04-12_afd-grundsatzprogramm-englisch_web.pdf.Agamben, Giorgio. 2021. *Where Are We Now?: The Epidemic as Politics.* Lanham, MD: Rowman & Littlefield Publishers. https://rowman.com/ISBN/9781538157602/Where-Are-We-Now-The-Epidemic-as-Politics.

Ahmed, Reem, and Daniela Pisoiu. 2020. "Uniting the Far Right: How the Far-Right Extremist, New Right, and Populist Frames Overlap on Twitter – a German Case Study." *European Societies,* 1 – 23.

Albanese, Matteo, and Pablo Del Hierro. 2016. *Transnational Fascism in the Twentieth Century : Spain, Italy and the Global Neo-Fascist Network.* Bloomsbury Academic. https://cadmus.eui.eu/handle/1814/45028.

Alter, Charlotte. 2022. "Elon Musk and the Tech Bro Obsession With 'Free Speech.'" *Time,* April 29. https://time.com/6171183/elon-musk-free-speech-tech-bro/.

AP. 2021. "Far Right Protest COVID-19 Restrictions in German Cities." *Euronews.,* March 21, sec. Germany. https://www.euronews.com/2021/03/20/far-right-protest-covid-19-restrictions-in-german-cities.

Apoorvanand. 2020. "How the Coronavirus Outbreak in India Was Blamed on Muslims." *Al Jazeera,* April 18, sec. Opinion. https://www.aljazeera.com/indepth/opinion/coronavirus-outbreak-india-blamed-muslims-200418143252362.html.

Awan, Imran. 2014. "Islamophobia and Twitter: A Typology of Online Hate Against Muslims on Social Media." *Policy & Internet* 6 (2): 133 – 50. doi:10.1002/1944 – 2866.POI364.

Awan, Imran. 2016. "Virtual Islamophobia: The Eight Faces of Anti-Muslim Trolls on Twitter." In *Islamophobia in Cyberspace Hate Crimes Go Viral,* edited by Imran Awan, 23 – 40. Birmingham, UK: Ashgate.

Awan, Imran, and Irene Zempi. 2017. "'I Will Blow Your Face OFF'—VIRTUAL and Physical World Anti-Muslim Hate Crime." *The British Journal of Criminology* 57 (2): 362 – 80.

Bakali, Naved, and Farid Hafez. 2022. "Introduction: Understanding Islamophobia across the Global North and South in the Context of the War on Terror." In *The Rise of Global Islamophobia in the War on Terror Coloniality, Race, and Islam,* edited by Naved Bakali and Farid Hafez. Manchester, UK: Manchester University Press. https://manchesteruniversitypress.co.uk/9781526161758.

Baker, Wayne, and Andrew Shryock. 2009. "Citizenship and Crisis." In *Citizenship and Crisis Arab Detroit After 9/11,* 3 – 32. New York, NY: Russell Sage Foundation.

16 —— Chapter I Introduction

Bar-On, Tamir. 2012. "The French New Right's Quest for Alternative Modernity." *Fascism Journal of Contemporary Fascist Studies* 1 (1): 18–52.

Beauchamp, Zack. 2022. "The Bizarre Far-Right Coup Attempt in Germany, Explained by an Expert." *Vox*, December 9. https://www.vox.com/2022/12/9/23500307/germany-coup-prince-heinrich-qanon.

Benkler, Yochai, Robert Faris, and Hal Roberts. 2018. *Network Propaganda Manipulation, Disinformation, and Radicalization in American Politics*. Oxford, UK: Oxford University Press.

Bennhold, Katrin. 2020. "As Neo-Nazis Seed Military Ranks, Germany Confronts 'an Enemy Within.'" *The New York Times*, July 3. https://www.nytimes.com/2020/07/03/world/europe/germany-military-neo-nazis-ksk.html.

Berg, Lyn. 2019. "Between Anti-Feminism and Ethnicized Sexism. Far-Right Gender Politics in Germany." In *Post-Digital Cultures of the Far Right*, edited by Maik Fielitz and Nick Thurston, 79–92. Bielefeld: transcript-Verlag.

Berning, Carl C. 2017. "Alternative Für Deutschland (AfD) – Germany's New Radical Right-Wing Populist Party." *DICE Report* 15 (4): 16–19.

Bezio, Kristin MS. 2018. "Ctrl-Alt-Del: GamerGate as a Precursor to the Rise of the Alt-Right." *Leadership* 14 (5): 556–66. doi:10.1177/1742715018793744.

Bond, Shannon. 2022. "Elon Musk Said Twitter Wouldn't Become a 'hellscape.' It's Already Changing." *NPR*, October 31, sec. Technology. https://www.npr.org/2022/10/31/1132906782/elon-musk-twitter-pelosi-conspiracy.

Bonilla-Silva, Eduardo. 2015. "The Structure of Racism in Color-Blind, 'Post-Racial' America." *American Behavioral Scientist* 59 (11): 1358–76. doi:10.1177/0002764215586826.

Brubaker, Rogers. 2017. "Between Nationalism and Civilizationism: The European Populist Moment in Comparative Perspective." *Ethnic and Racial Studies* 40 (8): 1191–1226. doi:10.1080/01419870.2017.1294700.

Bruns, Axel, and Jean Burgess. 2011. "The Use of Twitter Hashtags in the Formation of Ad Hoc Publics." In *Proceedings of the 6th European Consortium for Political Research (ECPR) General Conference 2011*, 1–9. United Kingdom.

Bruns, Axel, and Tim Highfield. 2015. "Is Habermas on Twitter?" In *The Routledge Companion to Social Media and Politics*, edited by Axel Bruns, Gunn Enli, Eli Skogerbø, Anders Olof Larsson, and Christian Christensen, 1st ed., 18. New York: Routledge.

Chaturvedi, Swati. 2016. *I Am a Troll: Inside the Secret World of the BJP's Digital Army*. New Delhi: Juggernaut. https://www.abebooks.com/9789386228093/Troll-Secret-World-BJPs-Digital-9386228092/plp.

Chin, Rita. *The Guest Worker Question in Postwar Germany*. Cambridge, UK: Cambridge University Press, 2007.

Chin, Rita, Heide Fehrenbach, Geoff Eley, and Atina Grossman, eds. 2009. "Introduction: What's Race Got to Do With It? Postwar German." In *After the Nazi Racial State: Difference and Democracy in Germany and Europe*, by Rita Chin and Heide Fehrenbach, 1–29. Ann Arbor, MI: University of Michigan Press.

Conway, Maura, Ryan Scrivens, and Logan Macnair. 2019. "Right-Wing Extremists' Persistent Online Presence: History and Contemporary Trends." ISSN: 2468–0486. The Hauge, Netherlands: International Centre for Counter-Terrorism.

Crosset, Valentine, Samuel Tanner, and Aurélie Campana. 2018. "Researching Far Right Groups on Twitter: Methodological Challenges 2.0." *New Media & Society* 21 (4): 939–61.

Daniels, Jesse. 2018. "The Algorithmic Rise of the 'Alt-Right.'" *Contexts* 17 (1): 60–65.

Dixit, Pranav. 2021. "Koo Is Filled With Hate." *BuzzFeed News*, February 23, sec. Tech. https://
www.buzzfeednews.com/article/pranavdixit/koo-muslim-hate-india.

DW. 2021. "Germany Sees Spike in Anti-Semitic Crimes – Reports." *DW*, February 11. https://
www.dw.com/en/germany-sees-spike-in-anti-semitic-crimes-reports/a-56537178.

Ekman, Mattias. 2015. "Online Islamophobia and the Politics of Fear: Manufacturing the Green
Scare." *Ethnic and Racial Studies* 38 (11): 1986 – 2002. doi:10.1080/01419870.2015.1021264.

Ekman, Mattias. 2017. "You Tube Fascism: Visual Activism of the Extreme Right." In *TOTalitarian ARTs:
The Visual Arts, Fascism(s) and Mass-Society*, edited by Mark Epstein, Fulvio Orsitto, and Andrea
Righi, 350 – 73. Newcastle upon Tyne: Cambridge Scholars Publishing.

Fields, Barbara Jeanne. "Slavery, Race and Ideology in the United States of America." *New Left Review*
1, no. 181 (June 1990).

Froio, Caterina, and Bharath Ganesh. 2018. "The Far Right Across Borders Networks and Issues of
(Trans)National Cooperation in Western Europe on Twitter." In *Post-Digital Cultures of the Far
Right: Online Actions and Offline Consequences in Europe and the US*, edited by Maik Fielitz, Nick
Thurston, and Stephen Albrecht, 93 – 104. New York, NY: Columbia University Press.
doi:10.14361/9783839446706.

Ganesh, Bharath, and Caterina Froio. 2020. "A 'Europe Des Nations': Far Right Imaginative
Geographies and the Politicization of Cultural Crisis on Twitter in Western Europe." *Journal of
European Integration* 42 (5): 715 – 32. doi:10.1080/07036337.2020.1792462.

Gardner, Rod, Yasemin Karakaşoğlus, and Sigrid Luchtenberg. 2008. "Islamophobia in the Media: A
Response from Multicultural Education." *Intercultural Education* 19 (2): 119 – 36. doi:10.1080/
14675980801889658.

Garner, Steve, and Saher Selod. 2014. "The Racialization of Muslims: Empirical Studies of
Islamophobia." *Critical Sociology* 41 (1): 1 – 11. doi:10.1177/0896920514531606.

Genova, Nicholas Paul De. 2015. "In the Land of the Setting Sun:: Reflections on 'Islamization' and
'Patriotic Europeanism.'" *Movements: Journal Für Kritische Migrations- Und Grenzregimeforschung* 1
(2). https://kclpure.kcl.ac.uk/portal/en/publications/in-the-land-of-the-setting-sun(af3ee268-ab0b-
4cb5-9384-859630b075f6).html.

Ghaffary, Shirin. 2022. "Why Journalists Can't Just Quit Twitter." *Vox*, December 2. https://
www.vox.com/recode/2022/12/2/23488678/twitter-journalists-quitting-elon-musk-mastodon-post.

GhaneaBassiri, Kambiz. 2013. "Islamophobia and American History Religious Stereotyping and Out-
Grouping Muslims in the United States." In *Islamaphobia in America The Anatomy of Intolerance*,
edited by Carl W. Ernst. New York: Palgrave Macmillan.

Gramsci, Antonio. 1976. *Selections from the Prison Notebooks of Antonio Gramsci*. Edited and translated
by Quintin Hoare and Geoffrey Nowell-Smith. London: Lawrence & Wishart.

Gruzd, Anatoliy, and Caroline Haythornthwaite. "Enabling Community Through Social Media."
JOURNAL OF MEDICAL INTERNET RESEARCH 15, no. 10 (2013).

Habermas, Jürgen. 1991. *The Structural Transformation of the Public Sphere An Inquiry into a Category
of Bourgeois Society*. Translated by Thomas Burger. Cambridge, MA: MIT Press.

Hafez, Farid. 2018. "Schools of Thought in Islamophobia Studies: Prejudice, Racism, and
Decoloniality." *Islamophobia Studies Journal* 4 (2): 210 – 25. doi:https://doi.org/10.13169/
islastudj.4.2.0210.

Hall, Ellie. 2022. "The Notorious Kiwi Farms Is Back Online." *BuzzFeed News*, October 19, sec. Tech.
https://www.buzzfeednews.com/article/elliehall/kiwi-farms-back-online-keffals-campaign-null.

Hanes, Emma, and Stephen Machin. 2014. "Hate Crime in the Wake of Terror Attacks: Evidence From 7/7 and 9/11." *Journal of Contemporary Criminal Justice* 30 (3). SAGE Publications Inc: 247–67. doi:10.1177/1043986214536665.

Hartzell, Stephanie L. 2018. "Alt-White: Conceptualizing the 'Alt-Right' as a Rhetorical Bridge between White Nationalism and Mainstream Public Discourse." *Journal of Contemporary Rhetoric* 8 (1/2): 6–25.

Havertz, Ralf. 2021. *Radical Right Populism in Germany AfD, Pegida, and the Identitarian Movement.* London: Routledge.

Hawley, George. 2019. *Making Sense of the Alt-Right.* New York, NY: Columbia University Press.

Haynes, Jeffrey. 2021. "From Huntington to Trump: Twenty-Five Years of the 'Clash of Civilizations.'" In *A Quarter Century of the "Clash of Civilizations,"* 1st ed., 13. London: Routledge.

Herder, Johann Gottfried. 1800. *Outlines of a Philosophy of the History of Man.* Berlin: Bergman Publishers.

Hill, Jenny. 2019. "German Politician's Murder Raises Spectre of Far-Right Attacks." *BBC*, June 23. https://www.bbc.com/news/world-europe-48716944.

Howard, Philip N., and Muzammil M. Hussain. 2013. *Democracy's Fourth Wave?: Digital Media and the Arab Spring.* Oxford Studies in Digital Politics. New York: Oxford University Press.

Huntington, Samuel P. 1993. "The Clash of Civilizations?" *Foreign Affairs* 72 (3): 22–49. doi:10.2307/20045621.

Huszár, Ferenc, Sofia Ira Ktena, Conor O'Brien, Luca Belli, Andrew Schlaikjer, and Moritz Hardt. 2021. "Algorithmic Amplification of Politics on Twitter." *PNAS* 119 (1): 1–6. doi:https://doi.org/10.1073/pnas.2025334119.

Jenkins, Henry. 2013. "Twitter Revolutions?" In *Spreadable Media Creating Value and Meaning in a Networked Culture*, edited by Henry Jenkins, Sam Ford, and Joshua Green. New York: NYU Press. https://spreadablemedia.org/essays/jenkins/index.html.

Jesse, Eckhard. 2001. "Soll die Nationaldemokratische Partei Deutschlands verboten werden? Der Parteiverbotsantrag war unzweckmäßig, ein Parteiverbot ist rechtmäßig." *Politische Vierteljahresschrift* 42 (4): 683–97. doi:10.1007/s11615–001–0103–0.

Johnson, Hailey, Karl Volk, Robert Serafin, Cinthya Grajeda, and Ibrahim Baggili. 2022. "Alt-Tech Social Forensics: Forensic Analysis of Alternative Social Networking Applications." *Forensic Science International: Digital Investigation*, Proceedings of the Twenty-Second Annual DFRWS USA, 42 (July): 301406. doi:10.1016/j.fsidi.2022.301406.

Johnson, Jessica. 2018. "The Self-Radicalization of White Men: 'Fake News' and the Affective Networking of Paranoia." *Communication, Culture and Critique* 11 (1): 100–115. doi:10.1093/ccc/tcx014.

Kahn, Michelle Lynn. 2021. "The American Influence on German Neo-Nazism: An Entangled History of Hate, 1970s–1990s." *The Journal of Holocaust Research* 35 (2). Routledge: 91–105. doi:10.1080/25785648.2021.1901496.

Klikauer, Thomas. 2018. "Germany's New Populist Party The AfD." *German Politics and Society* 36 (4): 78–97.

Koehler, Daniel. 2014. "The German 'National Socialist Underground (NSU)' and Anglo-American Networks. The Internationalisation of Far-Right Terro." In *The Postwar Anglo-American Far Right: A Special Relationship of Hate*, edited by Paul Jackson and Anton Shekhovtsov, 122–41. Cham, Switzerland: Palgrave Macmillan.

Lees, Charles. 2018. "The 'Alternative for Germany': The Rise of Right-Wing Populism at the Heart of Europe." *Politics* 38 (3): 295–310. doi:10.1177/0263395718777718.

Leurs, Koen, and Domitilla Olivieri. 2014. "Introduction." In *Everyday Feminist Research Praxis: Doing Gender in the Netherlands*, edited by Olivieri Domitilla and Koen Leurs, xxiv–xxxix. Newcastle upon Tyne, UK: Cambridge Scholars Publishing.

Losh, Elizabeth. 2014. "Hashtag Feminism and Twitter Activism in India." *Social Epistemology Review and Reply Collective* 3 (12): 11–22.

Love, Erik. 2017. *Islamophobia and Racism in America*. New York, NY: New York University Press.

Macklin, Graham. 2013. "Transnational Networking on the Far Right: The Case of Britain and Germany." *West European Politics* 36 (1). Routledge: 176–98. doi:10.1080/01402382.2013.742756.

Mahmood, Basit. 2020. "Rise in Anti-Muslim Hate Crimes as Islam Wrongly Blamed for Coronavirus." *Newsweek*, April 18, sec. World. https://www.newsweek.com/islam-muslims-coronavirus-lockdown-ramadan-islamophobia-1498499.

Meier, Anna. 2022. "Germany's White Supremacist Problem—and What It Means for the United States." *Lawfare*, January 30. https://www.lawfareblog.com/germanys-white-supremacist-problem—and-what-it-means-united-states.

Michael, George. 2017. "The Rise of the Alt-Right and the Politics of Polarization in America." *Skeptic*.

Michelsen, Nicholas, and Pablo de Orellana. 2020. "Pessimism and the Alt-Right: Knowledge, Power, Race and Time." In *Pessimism in International Relations Provocations, Possibilities, Politics*, edited by Tim Stevens and Nicholas Michelsen, 119–36. Cham: Springer International Publishing.

Mihelj, Sabina, and César Jiménez-Martínez. 2020. "Digital Nationalism: Understanding the Role of Digital Media in the Rise of 'New' Nationalism." *Nations and Nationalism* 27: 331–46. doi:10.1111/nana.12685.

Miller-Idriss, Cynthia. 2020. *Hate in the Homeland*. Princeton, NJ: Princeton University Press. https://press.princeton.edu/books/hardcover/9780691203836/hate-in-the-homeland.

Moeller, Robert G. 2001. *War Stories: The Search for a Usable Past in the Federal Republic of Germany*. Berkeley, CA: University of California Press.

Mondon, Aurelien, and Aaron Winter. 2017. "Articulations of Islamophobia: From the Extreme to the Mainstream?" *Ethnic and Racial Studies* 40 (3): 2151–79.

Morgan, Edmund S. "Slavery and Freedom: The American Paradox." *The Journal of American History* 59, no. 1 (1972): 5–29. https://doi.org/10.2307/1888384.

Morstatter, Fred, Yunqiu Shao, Aram Galstyan, and Shanika Karunasekera. 2018. "From Alt-Right to Alt-Rechts: Twitter Analysis of the 2017 German Federal Election." In *WWW '18: Companion Proceedings of The Web Conference 2018*. Lyon, France: International World Wide Web Conferences Steering Committee Republic and Canton of Geneva, Switzerland. https://dl.acm.org/citation.cfm?id=3188733.

Muis, Jasper, Ofra Klein, and Guido Dijkstra. 2020. "Challenges and Opportunities of Social Media Research: Using Twitter and Facebook to Investigate Far Right Discourses." In *Researching the Far Right*. Routledge.

Munger, Kevin, and Joseph Phillips. 2022. "Right-Wing YouTube: A Supply and Demand Perspective." *The International Journal of Press/Politics* 27 (1). SAGE Publications Inc: 186–219. doi:10.1177/1940161220964767.

Murthy, Dhiraj, Alexander Gross, and Marisa McGarry. 2016. "Visual Social Media and Big Data. Interpreting Instagram Images Posted on Twitter." *Digital Culture & Society* 2 (2). transcript Verlag: 113–34. doi:10.14361/dcs-2016–0208.

Nagle, Angela. 2017. *Kill All Normies: Online Culture Wars From 4Chan And Tumblr To Trump And The Alt-Right*. London, UK: John Hunt Publishing.

Papacharissi, Zizi. 2010. "Conclusion." In *A Networked Self Identity, Community, and Culture on Social Network Sites*, edited by Zizi Papacharissi, 304–18. New York: Routledge.

Perocco, Fabio. 2018. "Anti-Migrant Islamophobia in Europe. Social Roots, Mechanisms and Actors." *Revista Interdisciplinar Da Mobilidade Humana – REMHU* 26 (53): 25–40.

Rambukkana, Nathan. 2015. "From #RaceFail to #Ferguson: The Digital Intimacies of Race-Activist Hashtag Publics." In *Hashtag Publics The Power and Politics of Discursive Networks*, edited by Nathan Rambukkana, Kindle. New York: Peter Lang.

Rauchfleisch, Adrian, and Jonas Kaiser. 2020. "The German Far-Right on YouTube: An Analysis of User Overlap and User Comments." *Journal of Broadcasting & Electronic Media* 64 (3). Routledge: 373–96. doi:10.1080/08838151.2020.1799690.

Said, Edward W. 1979. *Orientalism*. New York, NY: Vintage Books.

Saylor, Corey. 2014. "The U.S. Islamophobia Network: Its Funding and Impact." *Islamophobia Studies Journal* 2 (1): 99–118.

Schumacher, Elizabeth. 2022. "Germany's Far-Right AfD Can Be Put under Surveillance." *DW*, August 3. https://www.dw.com/en/germanys-far-right-afd-can-be-put-under-surveillance/a-61058359.

Shaheen, Jack G. 2012. *Reel Bad Arabs: How Hollywood Vilifies a People*. Ithaca, NY: Olive Branch Press.

Shahin, Saif. 2020. "User-Generated Nationalism: Interactions with Religion, Race, and Partisanship in Everyday Talk Online." *Information, Communication & Society*, 1–16. doi:10.1080/1369118X.2020.1748088.

Shank, Barry. 1997. "The Continuing Embarrassment of Culture: From the Culture Concept to Cultural Studies." *American Studies* 38 (2): 95–116.

Shepherd, Tamara, Aubrey E. Harvey, Tim Jordan, Sam Srauy, and Kate M. Miltner. 2015. "Histories of Hating." *Social Media + Society*, 1–10. doi:10.1177/2056305115603997.

Shoshan, Nitzan. 2016. *The Management of Hate Nation, Affect, and the Governance of Right-Wing Extremism in Germany*. Princeton, NJ: Princeton University Press.

Shryock, Andrew. 2013. "Attack of the Islamophobes Religious War (and Peace) in Arab/Muslim Detroit." In *Islamaphobia in America The Anatomy of Intolerance*, edited by Carl W. Ernst, 145–74. New York: Palgrave Macmillan.

Shryock, Andrew, and Ann Chih Lin. 2009. "The Limits of Citizenship." In *Citizenship and Crisis Arab Detroit After 9/11*. New York, NY: Russell Sage Foundation.

Squire, Megan. 2018. "Network Analysis of Anti-Muslim Groups on Facebook." In *Social Informatics*, edited by Steffen Staab, Olessia Koltsova, and Dmitry I. Ignatov, 403–19. Lecture Notes in Computer Science. Cham: Springer International Publishing. doi:10.1007/978-3-030-01129-1_25.

Squires, Catherine R. 2002. "Rethinking the Black Public Sphere: An Alternative Vocabulary for Multiple Public Spheres." *Communication Theory* 12 (4): 446–68. doi:10.1111/j.1468-2885.2002.tb00278.x.

Stern, Alexandra Minna. 2019. *Proud Boys and the White Ethnostate: How the Alt-Right Is Warping the American Imagination*. Boston, MA: Beacon Press.

Tansill, Charles Callan. "Racial Theories in Germany from Herder to Hitler." *Thought: Fordham University Quarterly* 15, no. 3 (August 1, 1940): 453–68. https://doi.org/10.5840/thought194015371.

Törnberg, Anton, and Anita Nissen. 2022. "Full Article: Mobilizing against Islam on Social Media: Hyperlink Networking among European Far-Right Extra-Parliamentary Facebook Groups." *Information, Communication & Society*. doi:10.1080/1369118X.2022.2118546.

Trachtenberg, Alan. 1984. "Myth and Symbol." *The Massachusetts Review* 25 (4): 667–73.

Triadafilopoulos, Triadafilos, and Karen Schönwälder. "How the Federal Republic Became an Immigration Country." *German Politics & Society* 24, no. 3 (September 2006): 1–19.

Vidgen, Bertie, Taha Yasseri, and Helen Margetts. 2022. "Islamophobes Are Not All the Same! A Study of Far Right Actors on Twitter." *Journal of Policing, Intelligence and Counter Terrorism* 17 (1). Routledge: 1–23. doi:10.1080/18335330.2021.1892166.

Warner, Michael. 2002. "Publics and Counterpublics." *Public Culture* 14 (1): 49–90.

Zheng, Pei, and Saif Shahin. "Live Tweeting Live Debates: How Twitter Reflects and Refracts the US Political Climate in a Campaign Season." *Information, Communication & Society* 23, no. 3 (2020): 337–57. https://doi.org/10.1080/1369118X.2018.1503697.

Chapter II
From Homeland, to Heimat, to Hindutva: Profiling Far-Right Islamophobic Transnational Communities on Twitter

Introduction

This chapter examines the profiles of individual Twitter users captured in the dragnet of the #Islamization and #Islamisierung hashtags, revealing an eclectic yet banal typography of actors which comprise far-right Islamophobic networks (Crosset, Tanner, and Campana 2018, 944; Gruzd and Haythornthwaite 2013). Studying individual users is one method of entering into the techno-social space of far-right digital communities (Shahin and Dai 2019), which is replete with dead-ends; broken links, suspended accounts, and removed posts. There is a distinctive precarity that underlies the data on Twitter (Bruns and Burgess 2016), more so in the aftermath of Musk's hallowing out of multiple critical technical faculties (Newton and Schiffer 2022)

It is possible, however, to reconstruct part of this fractured ecosystem and access archived content via reconstructive scraping to recover traces of information. These traces, which include affiliations, emojis, hashtags, and other descriptors users deploy to identify themselves provide a rich corpus of data with which to explore the major players that make up this particular subsection of the far-right scene. Far-right digital communities thrive on anonymity in digital spaces, thus, establishing a taxonomy of who's who in these extremist networks is a critical step in identifying the types of people who are at risk of radicalization on and offline.

So, we begin at the intersection of political ideology and social identities, examining how members of far-right communities on Twitter constitute themselves through patterns present in user biographies revealing recurring categories of "networked" identities (Papacharissi 2010, 309). Despite the challenges in identifying authenticity or even authorship in the anonymized context of digital platforms (Crosset, Tanner, and Campana 2018, 940), biographies are a useful form of evidence in user expression of digital identities (Bishop 2018).

Digital identities, while constructed and acted out "online," are still mired within conditions of race, gender, class, and geolocation which inform both user experience and identity in digital and physical spaces. As Radhika Gajjala and Melissa Altman have argued in emphasizing the porosity between online and offline

https://doi.org/10.1515/9783111032887-002

boundaries; even in "virtual environments, participants do not leave their bodies behind" (2006, 2). Digital platforms thus represent another space in which individuals may (re)present themselves to engage in what Sarah Gatson calls the "selfing" project (2011), whereby social media platforms such as Twitter provide the technological infrastructure for users to engage in content creation and the production of identity through the selection of usernames and writing biographies (Gatson 2011, 232).

Anthony Giddens, in discussing the articulation of identity in modern yet early-digital contexts, notes the centrality of autobiography in producing the self (Giddens 1991, 76). Social media platforms, which provide self-confessional, autobiographical affordances offer a unique venue for identity production or performance. Zizi Papacharissi also notes how social media platforms provide users with affordances to re-present and negotiate their identities in the larger context of networked sociality (Papacharissi 2011, 304, 306). Posting digital texts such as Tweets and writing user biographies may be read as a form of everyday discursive digital communication that answers Giddens' provocative series of questions that define the project of the self: "[w]hat to do? How to act? Who to be?" (Giddens 1991, 70). Today, we answer these questions through our engagement in digital media environments.

Exploring these practices of "selfing" (Bishop 2018, 145), this chapter employs the procedures of grounded theory with a feminist, close textual reading to identify a typology of users (S. Ahmed 2004; Lukić and Espinosa 2011; McKee 2003). As these far-right digitally networked terrains are fast-moving environments populated by shifting individuals, deploying a feminist grounded theory approach facilitates multiple and repeated readings of data, thus allowing new themes to emerge through close textual reading (Charmaz and Belgrave 2019, 744). Feminist grounded theory in particular throws into greater relief the way in which users engage in the project of "selfing" in gendered and racialized ways. And while the medium of digital data and deployment of data analytic tools may seemingly invite "exclusionary modes of scientific inquiry" that fail to capture the complex nuances of racialization and gender in digital environments (Leurs 2017, 134), the feminist methodological emphasis on partiality, subjectivity, and the situated nature of information and experience is a corrective (Haraway 1988).

Delving deep into the smaller but rich "n-counts" of biographies and user-created data is one such strategy to avoid big data myopia (Latzko-Toth, Bonneau, and Millette 2017). And this "banal" communication and autobiographical writing on Twitter, when examined closely, reveals the everyday political discussions and selfing conversations that occur on the platform, within the context of the "hashtag publics" constituted around the shared tags of #Islamization and #Islamisierung (Bruns and Burgess 2011; Bishop 2018, 144). While scholars have embarked on similar forms analysis of user-created content and autobiographies on Twitter, looking at political parties and far-right leaders on social media platforms (R. Ahmed and Pisoiu 2020; Caian and Kröll 2015; Ekman 2015; Ganesh and Froio 2020; Morstatter et al. 2018), these quotidian users discussed here shift the lens towards the expression of everyday far-right digital political cultures. Probing and identifying the transnational, mundane qualities that make up German and American far-right Islamophobic networked communities uncovers both processes of radicalization and community formation. Increasingly far-right Islamophobic rhetoric is bleeding out of explicitly political contexts and is used by a diverse, transnational, and yet, average community of users.

Documenting a taxonomy of users that appears through the corpus of Tweets by examining user biographies also reveals new patterns of issues that motivate and unite these users. Furthermore, Imran Awan has emphasized a troubling linkage connecting practices of online Islamophobic hate-speech on Facebook and offline instances of violence, radicalization of users, and the growth of offline hate groups (2016, 17). Digitally mediated forms of Islamophobic discourse and far-right identifications parsed out on digital platforms such as Twitter increasingly lay the groundwork for on-the-ground right-wing political activity and violence.

While some scholars have suggested research on digital communities should move beyond describing and documenting the typographies of digitally networked groups (Couldry and Kallinikos 2017, 156), identifying the collection of users engaged in Islamophobic hate-speech provides a necessary taxonomy for both researchers and policymakers to understand the digital terrain of Islamophobic digital publics. If "hating" may be viewed "as a networked communicative practice'" (Shepard et al. 2015, 5), then identifying the key actors in these networks illustrates how Islamophobic digital discourse is tied to other collaboratively articulated constellations of hate-speech related to race, religion, gender, and sexuality, beliefs that increasingly inform offline violence and far-right political mobilizations in the US, Germany, and beyond.

A Taxonomical Method for Identifying Users

Far-right Islamophobic Twitter users who emerge from a corpus of scraped data engaging with the hashtags #Islamization and #Islamisierung are a diverse collective. The taxonomy of user-types engaged in far-right Islamophobic hate-speech are visualized below in *Table 1,* illustrating similarities in identity, ideology, and shared hashtags that connect far-right users transnationally, linking German and American users as well as white American and Indian users.

Table 1: Chart of German and American User-Types and Sample Codes

American User-Types	White Supremacist Nationalist	MAGA Devotee	Neighborly Racist	Far-Right Hindu Nationalist
American Sample Codes	Pro-White, #WhiteLivesMatter, white, Western Civilization, race-mixing, #redpilled	#MAGA, #TRUMP2020, #TRUMP, #STOPTHESTEAL Patriot, #WWGIWWA, #2ndAmendment, #repilled, #KAG,	Proud mother, proud father, Christian, Christ follower, Wife, Husband, #Prolife, Family, Sports,	American Hindu, Indian American Modi/ MODI, #Hindu, Nationalist, India First, Make India Great Again
German User-Type	Heimat Enthusiast	Transnational Trumpist	Neighborly German Racist	Alleged Anti-Totalitarian
German Sample Codes	Heimat, Vaterland, #DefendEurope, Abendland, #NoEU, #MerkelMussWeg, #Dexit	#MAGA, #MGGA, #TRUMP2020, #AfD, #WWGIWWA, #qanon, #Q	Christ, Kinder, Familie, Vater, Mutter, Verheiratet, Sport, Oma, Opa,	totalitäre Ideologie, Contra Islam, Extremismus, anti-extremism, totalitarianism, #islamkritisch

This chart visualizes the four most common user types from the German and American corpus of Tweets; Heimat Enthusiast, Transnational Trumpist, Neighborly German Racist, and Alleged Anti-Totalitarian and Neighborly Racist, MAGA Devotee, White Supremacist Nationalist, and Far-Right Hindu Nationalist respectively. This categorization of users is not exhaustive but focuses on everyday types of users that emerged from coding the scraped data, revealing but a partial thread of larger networks of Islamophobic digitally networked communities that exist on Twitter and other social media platforms.

The types of Twitter users emerged from a close reading a total of 12, 677 user biographies. Following a feminist grounded theory process, initial patterns or codes in phrases, hashtags, and words were identified and then refined into final thematic categories of the user-type label (Charmaz 2006; Connelly 2013). After identifying semantic patterns through reoccurring words or phrases in memos, such as #MAGA or "Boy-mom," these words were refined into more substantive codes of a user-type label that captured the major thematic qualities of the user, thereby uniting principles of thematic coding with the feminist grounded theory process (Braun and Clarke 2006; Braun et al. 2019). *Table 1* includes major initial codes, words and phrases, that defined the user type. As represented in *Table 1,* the user-type labels are derived from the major themes that constitute and define each user such as pro-white sentiment, a support for a German *Vaterland,* or an identification with Trump and the MAGA movement.

Identifying representative user types showcases the type of dominant actors within these far-right Islamophobic networked digital publics evidencing the ubiquity of Islamophobic hate-speech among various users who identify explicitly with (far)-right political groups such as the AfD as well as more seemingly apolitical users who primarily identify themselves in domestic terms. These user-types illustrate how Islamophobic digital discourse is increasingly mainstreamed across a broad swath of German and American Twitter users, as well as among Indian and Indian American Twitter users.

Across multiple user types there is a strong *trans*national support of former President Donald Trump and the "Make American Great Again" movement, a linguistic short-hand for racialized nostalgia and white grievance accompanied by a support of ethno-economic nationalism (Price 2018). This fetishization and repurposing of MAGA-style rhetoric in German and Indian contexts, to Make Germany Great Again or Make India Great Again, demonstrates its mutability to other national contexts, even if the particular manifestations of racial, ethnic, or religious grievance are re-mixed to align with local histories. Furthermore, paralleling the identification of a transnational group of MAGA users is the strong presence of Christian, "family values" social conservatism, and an ethnicized, religious expression of citizenship and national belonging, qualities that unite German, white American, and Indian and Indian American Hindu nationalist Twitter users.

If one thing is clear from this typography of users, it is that despite the unique characteristics of user-types in each taxonomy, ultimately, similarities across transnational connections appear more salient than differences, evidencing the rise of transnational forms of far-right Islamophobic digitally networked communities crisscrossing Germany, the US, and India. Scholars studying European and American far-right political movements and ideologies in digital spaces have emphasized the transnational rather than national dimensions of such communities (Hafez 2014; Froio and Ganesh 2018b; Caian and Kröll 2015). And here we see some of the strongest emerging linkages do not necessarily illustrate a pan-European far-right Islamophobic movement, but rather, the emerging linkages are increasingly parsed out between Global North and South and across the Atlantic.

From Hindutva to "Boy Moms" to Q-Anon: American Islamophobia

The story of far-right American Islamophobic networked users begins not with the usual suspects; white nationalists or preppy alt-right fascists, but rather with far-right Hindu nationalists in India and in the diaspora, a user-type that is the origin source and frequent central network actor within the context of Islamophobic discussions among white American users. Hindu nationalist Indian and Indian American users are among the most influential network actors and can be categorized under the label of Far-Right Hindu Nationalist. The central defining factor of this sub-group is a strong emphasis on a belief in Hindu nationalism that extends beyond national borders. As Somdeep Sen has noted, extremist Hindu nationalist politics increasingly are manifesting globally in violent attacks perpetuated by Indian Hindu nationalists on Muslims not just in India, but in the US, the United Kingdom (UK), Canada, and Australia (Sen 2022).

On digital platforms like Twitter, Far-Right Hindu Nationalist users are particularly adept at producing affective Islamophobic content that is consumed and recirculated by white American users. Other user-types, the MAGA Devotee, the Neighborly Racist, and the White Supremacists Nationalist, respond enthusiastically to their Tweets and posts. Far-Right Hindu Nationalist users, both Indian Americans and Indians, produce and share racialized Islamophobic content in the form of news stories, Twitter threads, and images that are picked up by Neighborly Racists, then shared among more political MAGA Devotees, and endorsed and exchanged by White Supremacist Nationalists. Far-Right Hindu Nationalists are prolific content creators replicating strategies of the Bharatiya Janata Party's (BJP) digital "troll army" for American contexts (Swati Chaturvedi 2016).

Far-Right Hindu Nationalists support extreme Hindu nationalist politics in India and the MAGA movement in the US. While in some sense the electoral prominence of far-right Hindu nationalist politics in India is a recent phenomenon during the tenure of Prime Minister Modi and the ascendency of India's current far-right governing party, the BJP, which has enacted religiously exclusionary political policies targeting Muslims (Filkins 2019; Waikar 2018), anti-Muslim political ideology and violence has a long historical shadow. Anti-Muslim political violence is imbricated with the creation of the independent states of India and Pakistan in 1947 during the crumbling of Great Britain's formal colonial empire, where Partition was accompanied by population movement and displacement between the two regions against the background of widespread violence (Sanjay Chaturvedi 2002). The experience of Partition "ossified religious affiliation" and rendered various groups in India and Pakistan as either members of newly formed majority or minority communities (King 1999; Roy 2013, 4). Subsequently, even as India remains a religiously diverse nation with the third largest population of Muslim citizens in the world (Diamant 2019), Muslim Indians remain an increasingly vulnerable minority in India.

Muslim Indians have increasingly been targeted for political exclusion and violence in the context of the growing, institutionalized far-right Hindu nationalist movement that seeks to realize India as a religiously homogenous Hindu nation (Harriss 2015), an imagined religious and political category that is evoked as a nostalgic reality even as it lacks a historical basis—echoing here the MAGA movement's fetishistic yet ahistorical desire to make America whiter or "greater" than it ever was in reality. Lately this ideological symbiosis has been evidenced by the electoral support the Hindu nationalist Indian American community has provided to Islamophobic Republican candidates in the US (Sen 2022).

And, increasingly Islamophobic legislation and political discourse in India has paralleled a rise in Islamophobic hate-speech on digital platforms. A majority of Islamophobic hate-speech on Twitter originates from India, with more posts from India than the US and the UK combined (U. Butler 2022). As such, the appearance of the Far-Right Hindu Nationalist user type in the American far-right digital landscape is connected to larger trends of the evolution of Islamophobic hate-speech in digital spaces more broadly. But this is not new. In earlier periods, in the 1990s and early 2000s, Indians abroad used messaging boards or listservs, emphasizing their Hindu nationalist affiliations as a means to connect back affectively and discursively with the Indian homeland (Gajjala 2019, 5; Gittinger 2019; Therwath 2012).

Today, Far-Right Hindu Nationalist users bolster far-right ideology globally by adapting Islamophobic Tweets and news stories from Indian to other national and local contexts (Leidig 2019, 79). The appearance of these users illustrates the emergence of a transnational far-right Islamophobic digitally networked political community connecting India and the US as well as the possible emergence of a national multi-racial far-right coalition connecting Indian Americans and white Americans. Daniel Martinez HoSang and Joseph E. Lowndes have noted the on-the-ground emergence of multi-racial far-right coalitions in the US which are defined primarily by shared fascist ideologies (HoSang and Lowndes 2019). Here, in this digital context, multi-racial far-right coalitions are forged through the shared value of Islamophobia.

Representative of the Far-Right Hindu Nationalist user-type within the dataset is the user @NetizenParo. @NetizenParo initially describes herself with the biography, "Dare because you care [US flag] [Indian flag] War is nvr the first choice. Desire fr peace isn't a sign of weakness [praying hands] Respect is a 2-way street. #Scientist: Show me the data [smiley face]" (NetizenParo 2020b), with a reported location of Texas, USA. @NetizenParo, like many other Far-Right Hindu Nationalist users demonstrates a strong connection between India and the US as evidenced by the national flag Emojis. Post-November 3rd, 2020, the date of the highly contested American presidential election between Trump and Biden (Martin and Burns 2020), her biography is updated to illustrate a sense of political radicalization: "PS: Democracy dies with #FakeNews & #appeasement @NetizenParo #HinduAmerican #Patriot Dare bcoz u care [US flag] [red heart] [Indian flag] Desire fr peace isn't a sign of weakness [praying hands] Respect is a 2-way street. #Scientist: Show me the data [smiley face]" (NetizenParo 2020b). This shift in biography, featuring a play on *The Washington Post's* slogan, "Democracy dies in darkness" (Concha 2017), uses familiar far-right rhetoric of attacking journalists and news organizations while simultaneously asserting her connection to Hindutva, "#HinduAmerican," and her patriotism, "#Patriot."

@NetizenParo's biography stands as representative of several thematic trends present in Twitter biographies of Indian American and Indian Twitter users that began to coalesce under the Far-Right Hindu Nationalist type. Users like @Netizen-Paro situate themselves as objective observers and self-identify as Hindu Americans and or members of the Indian Hindu diaspora. @PurnimaNathis is another such example of a Far-Right Hindu Nationalist user who emphasizes her Hindu American identity and her professionalism while conversely amplifying highly racialized, Islamophobic digital content, describing herself as an "American Hindu. Seen & heard on ABC, CBS, NBC, FOX & NPR. Intellectual Pursuits, Politics, Philosophy, Philanthropy. Independent Free Thinker" (Nath 2012). Unlike many white American-identified Twitter users, these accounts usually do not contain explicitly racist or Islamophobic language or political affiliations—the Islamophobic language and content often appears in the Tweets rather than biographies circulated by these users.

In their online biographies, the Far-Right Hindu Nationalist presents an online-self that is professional, respectable, and objective. Once one delves into the content of this user-type's Tweets and visualizes their position with the network community, it becomes clear that accounts such as @NetizenParo and @Purnima-Nathis disseminate racist Islamophobic Tweets even if their ideological position is not immediately apparent from their biographical description. The articulation and imagining of an exclusionary American national community that omits Muslim immigrants and American Muslims is in this case pioneered by the Far-Right Hindu Nationalist Users. While Hindu nationalist Indian Americans and their far-right Christian white counterparts may differ in terms of their religious affiliations, in fact the religious extremism of these two groups proves complementary with a common perceived enemy—Muslims.

This affiliation between white American Christian conservatives and Hindu nationalists has lately been manifested by the cozy relationship between former President Trump and his then counter-part Prime Minister Modi, with Raj Kumar Singh pointing towards the ideological similarities between Hindutva and white supremacy, specifically the shared rhetoric of Islamophobia targeting Muslim minority communities in the US and India (2021). While scholars have noted in European contexts how Muslims in the far-right imaginary are positioned as a "cultural threat to the West or as security threats" (Froio and Ganesh 2018a, 98), this same process is at work among Far-Right Hindu Nationalist users. Muslims are positioned as culturally and religiously other to a supposed homogenous Hindu Indian nation *and* the US, with the US situated as a site of idealized diversity—but a form of inclusion only extended towards certain patriotic minority communities, here Indian Hindus (Liedig 2019, 78).

While in the US 9/11 marked a watershed moment in terms of the visibility and expression of Islamophobia in domestic and foreign policy and political rhetoric, the Indian state has also increasingly positioned Muslim communities as a securitized and racialized threat, particularly in the aftermath of the 2008 Mumbai terrorist attacks carried out by the Pakistani-based Lashkar-e-Taiba organization (Fair 2011). In the wake of these attacks and long-standing attempts by the Indian government to impose additional security controls on the territory of Jammu and Kashmir, a contested region between India and Pakistan (Jones 2009), Muslim communities in India have increasingly been at risk of targeting via state security apparatuses as not simply terroristic anti-state actors but also racial and religious Others foreign to the Indian body politic (Singh 2019). In this sense then, while in each national context Islamophobia emerges as a result of particular historical conditions, it is mobilized among a broad collection of users in digital landscapes where the nation and its boundaries are reconstituted through user-generated content (Shahin 2020, 13).

Users such as @NetizenParo illustrate the confluence of these dynamics well. In a Tweet, @NetizenParo engages in a discussion with the user @ShowUrJew Prides, stating; "@ShowUrJewPride I honestly think tht all #Democratic #nations need to #fight the agenda of #Islamization. Everyone can see hw #Jews &; #Hindus around the world r being #gaslighted , #history #distorted &; #manipulated &; #FakeNews media being used to push the #Islamofascistagenda.#StopGlobalJihad" (NetizenParo 2020a). Indian and Indian American Hindus and Jews are conceptualized here as victims of the alleged "fake news media" pushing an Islamic agenda that is in essence conceived of as a hybrid religious-fascist-totalitarian ideology, backed by the conspiratorial belief that mainstream news organizations are hiding information or publishing (mis)information. The discourse of the "fake news media," popularized by former President Trump, has historical roots as a propaganda technique deployed by the Nazi regime to position critical German newspapers as *Lügenpresse*, or the lying press, to discredit their reporting, and lately this tactic has been re-popularized by the far-right German anti-Muslim organization Pegida (Noack 2016).

Here @NetizenParo also attempts to frame Hindus and Jews as similarity persecuted minorities, a strategy used by Hindu nationalists to emphasize their supposed parallel persecution and affinity with the Zionist pro-Israeli movement (Anderson 2015, 54). This tactic of comparing one's supposed persecution with the Jewish community is also used within European far-right circles situating secular Europeans as "victims in solidarity with the Jews, portrayed standing side-by-side with Israel against the 'Islamic threat', while Muslims are branded as the fascists ('Islamofascists')" (Hafez 2014, 485). Islamophobic tropes are mutable and allow far-right actors to forward "collective victimhood narratives" among far-right digital communities whereby discourses of imperilment serve as a tool of radicalization in far-right spaces (Boussalis, Craig, and Rudkin 2022; Marcks and Pawelz 2022).

Using the term "jihad" is also an established far-right communicative strategy to racialize and Other Muslims, first popularized in a post-9/11 rhetorical context that saw a renewed American focus on the specter of Muslim terrorist groups during the Iraq War (Aguilera-Carnerero and Azeez 2016). Today, however, its usage by far-right actors not only taps into these historic associations but also hints towards the existence of a global conspiracy. No longer is the concept of jihad used to conjure associations of specific terrorist organizations like Al-Qaeda, but the notion of global jihad invokes a shadowy and fragmented process where any and all Muslim communities in the US and India may be complicit—alongside institutional news medias—in seeking to actualize the Islamization of the state. It is precisely this type of imperilment content produced by @NetizenParo that ultimately resonates with other far-right white American users such as the Neighborly Racist user-type, who finds these notions of global conspiracy affectively priming to support their own personal views of individualized persecution.

Even if evidence of Islamization in one's local community is not materially visible, the stories, content, memes, images, and videos users consume, presented intimately on their screens, collapse the distance between Texas and Sweden, feeding into a belief that supposed Islamization abroad will soon be coming home. Social media technologies and the content circulated on platforms like Twitter are mobilized by a range of actors to create communities of affect (Gajjala 2019, 116). Far-Right Hindu Nationalists engage in affect work here, in this case, making transnational and cross-racial connections through the circulation of Islamophobic Tweets, images, and memes.

Every day, average users like Neighborly Racists are prime consumers of this type of affectively laden content. They are individuals mired within the minutiae of local neighborhood communities, presenting as middle-class, religious, socially conservative, and concerned with protecting "family values" of heterosexual marriage, fixed gender roles, and the racial purity of children all within the confines of the neighborhood. Neighborly Racists are a contemporary, digital manifestation of middle-class white racism that has historic roots in mid-century white supremacist movements which were focused upon issues of residential and school segregation and often have been spearheaded by neighborly mothers and wives. Elizabeth

McRae Gillespie notes the prominence of these far-right racist social movements as the "white supremacist maternalism" of the 1950s-1960s (2018). Today, these patterns of white supremacist maternalism re-emerge, not necessarily on the suburban streets but on the digital streets of social media platforms—on Twitter.

White women affiliated with far-right digital movements today champion an ideological form of "alt-maternalism" (Mattheis 2018). And, in a post-9/11 American context in particular, foreign policy, political rhetoric, and a national culture of "homeland security" has bled into a "politics of everyday life" where domestic spaces are situated as sites in need of securitization through parenting; protecting the white, nuclear family unit means protecting the larger homeland (Fixmer-Oraiz 2019, 14). Muslim communities, as well as a host of other actors, emerge as imagined threats to both state and family, a threat to national security on a structural level and a supposed threat to white women and children.

This Neighborly Racist user-type on Twitter is a familiar figure offline, and on a variety of other social media platforms, such as Facebook and Nextdoor (M. Kelly 2020; Kurwa 2019; Lorenz 2020). These Neighborly Racist users emphasize their identities as mothers, fathers, grandmothers, grandfathers, and local community members. They present as merely concerned neighbors and citizens and have been captured and critiqued in American popular culture through the "Karen" meme, which refers to video recordings of white women, usually middle-aged and middle-classed, harassing Black people in public or residential spaces (Williams 2020). Neighborly Racists engage in comparable forms of casualized online racism, here attempting to police and surveille the digital streets of Twitter from the threatening presence of Muslim communities.

Here, not only do white women engage in this racialized securitization discourse, but white men espouse similar forms of racialized discourses concerning family, Islamophobia, and race that manifests as a form of "alt-paternalism." The male Neighborly Racist primarily emphasizes his identity as a father, husband, or grandfather. Racialized, Islamophobic rhetoric thus always contains a gendered component. The gendering of political discourse appears most forcefully as a project in discussions and critiques of Islam and Muslim communities whereby discussions of women, both white women and Muslim women, children, and education become key sites upon which users engage with Islamophobic political content.

Concerningly, both political ideologies, of social conservativism and far-right politics, increasingly overlap in this context of gender, domesticity, and securitization, similarly emphasizing a mythologized desire for fixed gender dynamics and racial homogeneity, even as commitments to racial homogeneity are implicit and explicit respectively, coupled with a shared belief in white victimization (A. Kelly 2017). Securitization of the white family and reproduction are key aspects of rebuilding white civilization in the context of the far-right imagination (Michelsen and de Orellana 2020). Ultimately, Neighborly Racists demonstrate the way in which Islamophobia is deeply imbricated with other beliefs, including gender reactionary ideology and white natalist politics. Family, traditional gender roles, and children are main points of identification and supposed contention in far-right right spaces where users discuss the effects and alleged dangers of Muslim immigration and Muslim communities as both a civilization and personal, gendered threat.

Representative of the Neighborly Racist user is @Laurale71816951, a user who describes herself as a "Mother to 4 amazing sons! My uterus is sexist! current hobby – playing hide and seek with my kids, hoping they don't find me. Definitely not a snowflake" (Lee 2020). Here, we see @Laurale71816951 defines herself fundamentally as a mother, rejecting the label of a "snowflake," which references a derisive, conservative slang term for liberals as weak, overly emotional, delicate, and easily offended (Schwartz 2017). Comparatively, @Stretcharm40 states he is a "[a] humble follower of Jesus, Presbyterian by conviction,husband,father,anti abortion, marriage between man and woman, and NOT perfect in this life, serving ALL" (Armstrong 2020). Similar to @Laurale71816951, and like many male-identified users, @Stretcharm40 emphasizes a Christian religious affiliation and his role as a husband and father, in addition to asserting explicitly political stances against abortion and for homophobic policies such as "traditional marriage."

These types of users, the Neighborly Racists, appear initially rather politically mundane in their biographies—they do not signal an explicit support of white supremacist politics by including pro-white phrases or hashtags within their biographies like White Supremacist Nationalist Users, nor do they contain Islamophobic language. They are merely garden-variety social conservatives. However, the prevalence of this user-type reveals how extremely vitriolic and at times violent Islamophobic Tweets, images, and news stories resonate and circulate among "everyday" socially conservative Americans, neighborhood mothers, fathers, and grandparents. The distinction between social conservativism and the far-right collapses in terms of the content they consume on mainstream social media.

And children and public education are fertile and affective topics of political conversation for both American and German users across the spectrum of extremism. During the COVID-19 pandemic there has been a renewed focus among far-right groups and socially conversative voters on the topic of education, whether the particular focus was upon school closures or book bans. However, the explosion of far-right activity, discourse, and conspiracies focusing on children and public educational systems in the US is mutable, with the subjects of contention shifting from Muslims to the queer community.

The type of content that is particularly engaging across national borders focuses on sensational stories, such as the Tweet originally from user, @based_belgium, re-Tweeted by @fearless12342, a Neighborly Racist: "[w]hen we where young we did school trips to the local Zoo, or to some sports domain, nowerdays kids visit Mosques in Belgium, and learn how to pray to Allah... #Islamization" (Belgium 2020), which includes a video of a group of people praying at a mosque. This type of content is deliberately stripped of context, with the Twitter user modifying the externally hosted media object and providing their own Islamophobic framing and endorsing the message through her re-Tweet.

And user @fearless12342, while separated from this supposed field trip in Belgium by an ocean, engages with this story as a concerned American mother. She describes herself as a "Wife and mother, American, Fully support #1 A and #2 A [US flag]" (Sunshine 2012). The engagement of users such as @fearless12342 with this content illustrates how Islamophobic political discourse is not limited to a network of far-right extremists who belong to formal far-right political groups and parties but rather, average Americans, who, in their digital communications endorse and amplify Islamophobic political content from across the globe thereby mainstreaming of this type of hate-speech (Mondon and Winter 2017). If, as *Breitbart* founder Andrew Breitbart noted, "politics is downstream from culture" then the presence of these casual networked connections between various users signals the development of a shared far-right cultural discourse that lays the groundwork for formal political movements and policies (Weatherby 2018).

The Neighborly Racist user type is thus both dangerous and banal. These are users like @StaceyM78844177 who is a "[red heart] [US flag] [red heart] BoyMom & Wife [kissing lips] Lover of Tacos & Lazy Sundays [taco] Love my country and fellow Patriots!! #MAGA #KAG #2ndAmendment #Trump2020" (StaceyM78844177 2020), a regular wife and mom who loves tacos and relaxed weekends, but also someone who spends her time online engaging with Islamophobic content. While @StaceyM78844177, as demonstrated by her biography, does not necessarily explicitly support white supremacist nationalist movements, she appears sympathetic to and interested in the same gendered logics of preservation of the white traditional family that motivate white supremacists and nationalists (Hartzell 2018). And a support of MAGA illustrates the porous boundaries between American user-types.

This type of user, the Neighborly Racist, is also the most troubling in the context of online radicalization, as this user demonstrates an increasing convergence between mainstream social conservatism in the US and the increasingly ascendent and violent far-right. Here, engagement with Islamophobic content is an indicator or risk factor in radicalization. Savannah Badalich in discussing trends of far-right radicalization of white women on platforms such as Twitter notes a beginning step for users is to include gender traditionalist phrases in their biographies with users then algorithmically primed to engage with increasingly more extreme far-right accounts (Badalich 2019, 56), and this is the same for Islamophobic content.

Engagement with Islamophobic digital content and connection with other users who produce this form of hate-speech is one such way to visibilize the process of radicalization, the appearance of networked connections between these users-types is aligned with the recognition of the influence communities hold over individuals, who become primed and supported to adopt more extremist views over time (Wang et al. 2022). This process of radicalization becomes readily apparent with @fearless12342, who updates her biography to read "Pro-White and anti-communist" (Sunshine 2012). Neighborly Racist users increasingly "relay far right ideology without claiming to belong to any far right groups" ultimately "provid[ing] improved visibility and enhanced legitimacy" for far-right political ideologies to leach into public discourse and policy (Crosset, Tanner, and Campana 2018, 944), expressed through seemingly anodyne messengers.

Comparatively, the MAGA Devotee is a more explicitly political user and an enthusiastic, fervent supporter of President Trump and the MAGA movement—evidenced by their usage of the #MAGA or #Trump2020 hashtags. This type of user demonstrates the next step of radicalization and is characterized by consumption and circulation of far-right conspiracies. The conspiratorial bent of these users fits within a larger trend in American (far) right political movements that has long haunted American society from anti-Catholic and anti-Masonic conspiracies in the 19th century, to Red Scare conspiracies circulated by the John Birch Society during the Cold War, to early internet conspiracies of the New World Order (Oliver and Wood 2014; Stewart 2002). Richard Hofstadter wrote infamously of the "paranoid style" of American politics and that has never been more true today—with the platformed structure of Twitter and other social media sites providing an optimal structure for the memetic reproduction of viral conspiracies, each story gaining new credence and vitality through its cultural replication (Milner 2016). It is this memetic reproduction of Islamophobic conspiracies circulated among MAGA Devotees and other networked actors that speaks to the appearance of the morbid symptom of far-right political culture online, these viral conspiracies infecting and radicalizing an ever-greater group of users.

The user @jrconse is a clear representative example of the interconnections between MAGA supporters, conspiratorial thinking, and Islamophobia. @jrconse describes himself as an "American dad, husband, Grampa, Catholic, USAF (ret) #2 A #MAGA [US flag] #WWG1WGA #WakeUpAmerica #manners Take back control of our children's education now" (jrconse 2020). This biographical description echoes many of the unifying user traits of the Neighborly Racist user, such as an emphasis on traditional gender roles, Christianity, and a preoccupation with issues of children and their education. We see these themes emerge through @jrconse's placement of dad, husband, and Grampa as the first identifiers in his biography followed by his religious adherence to Catholicism, but also conspiratorial hashtags and a fetishization of racialized nostalgia.

These MAGA users illustrate too the collapsing of a division between contemporary alternative conservative movements, mainstream Republican politics, and the far-right (Coppins 2018). MAGA or MGGA, in the US and Germany, ultimately functions as a racialized, political reaction to particular "cultural aspects of modernity [such as] state-sanctioned legal equality, liberalism, socialism, social democracy, and multiculturalism" (Bar-On 2012, 26), and seeks to realize an "alternative modernity," first theorized by the French New Right (Bar-On 2012). Some of these now well-worn conspiracies and ideological positions including the Great Replacement Theory were initially articulated by French New Right thinkers such as Renaud Camus, who explicitly railed against the alleged replacement of white French and European populations with immigrants from majority-Muslim countries (Froio 2018). For Americans, these conspiratorial emphases on Islamophobia, anti-feminism, anti-social justice movements, and anti-immigration constitute the bedrock of right-wing political ideology—even as parts of them originate genealogically from abroad.

This desire for an idealized, white past fundamentally purports a fantasy for a nostalgic historic period that also selectively edits out immigrants, Muslims, and communities of color more broadly (Santa Ana and González de Bustamante 2012, 279). For both Neighborly Racists and MAGA Devotees this form of racialized nostalgia is characterized as either implicit or explicit respectively, with MAGA Devotees making this argument for racialized nostalgia explicit in the usage of hashtags such as #MAGA; to make American great *again* like it once was—with Muslim communities a particular target. These users increasingly identify with digital-born racialized fantasies or conspiracy theories—specifically Q Anon—as an attempt to address and fight back against their own supposed victimization at the hands of liberal elites, and their alleged partners, Muslim communities and global institutions, to remake and realize society in its past, idealized form.

Many users who signaled a support for MAGA or MGGA also expressed support for the Q Anon conspiracy theory and movement by including phrases such as "#WWGI1GA" or "Q" in their biographies. "Q" refers to a supposed high-level military/government official who is providing information about Trump's supposed fight against the "deep state" in the form of anonymous posts on the platform 8kun, and " ##WWGI1GA" refers to "where we go one, we go all" a slogan that purports support for following the Q Anon movement, users often also include phrase such "Q-Army" as well (Planck 2020). These are all hashtags which, in the aftermath of the 2021 Capitol Insurrection, explicitly signal the conspiracy community as potentially violent—with members of this digital army turning real on January 6, 2021.

While this conspiracy group is fragmented and fluid (LaFrance 2020), its relevance here is its Christian, religious undertones and focus on children; it purports that there is a cabal of elites who sexually abuse children, torture them, and drink their blood that is alleged to possess the "chemical adrenochrome" (Friedberg 2020). This emphasis on children and blood drinking has clear historic overlap to earlier antisemitic conspiracy theories that suggested Jews were engaged in "blood libel" rituals (Friedberg 2020). As such, the MAGA Devotees are identifiable not only through their intense support of Trump but also through their enthusiasm for historic far-right antisemitic conspiratorial tropes that are re-mixed on social media platforms in increasingly more virulent and violent forms, increasingly implicating Muslim communities as gendered threats to white women and children (Allington and Joshi 2018; van Prooijen 2017).

Children in danger, of either death, sexual violence, or religious conversion, is a connective theme that runs across users and national contexts as a conservational topic. While the threatening figures may change; Democrats, Muslims, or Hollywood elites, the foundational conspiracy of children in danger remains a potent symbol in far-right circles who are particularly concerned with the proliferation and protection of the white, patriarchal family unit. Both @jrconse and @Laurale71816951, MAGA Devotees and Neighborly Racists respectively, re-Tweeted the same Tweet about the supposed Islamic conversion of Belgian children, illustrating similar forms of engagement focused upon European and American children, all linked in whiteness. Ultimately, showing these linkages demonstrates how a "boy-mom" can evolve into a Q Anon supporter and MAGA adherent.

MAGA Devotees all represent the correlation between a belief in racialized, gendered conspiracies, a support of Trump, and Islamophobic content. Their appearance and engagement within the corpus of scraped Tweets also emphasizes their concern with the topic of Muslim immigration as part of a conspiratorial global threat. Farid Hafez notes this same trend among far-right European communities that:

> ...the imaginary of the Muslim has become an enemy on a global scale, connected to leftist thought (Marxists)...Subsequently, this construction of the powerful, conspiratorial Islamic threat has become a regular feature in far-right ideology (2014, 492).

As such, for Trump supporters engaging with Islamophobic digital discourse on Twitter, the lines between mainstream Republic conservativism, Islamophobia, and conspiracy are increasingly blurred. And on social media platforms like Twitter, the "Overton window" of mainstream right-wing political discourse has shifted, with digital-born conspiracies and racist online rhetoric not simply becoming more common but increasingly informing policy making (Astor 2019). We also witness politicians from former President Trump to local officials in a variety of states parrot and re-circulate digital-born Islamophobic hate-speech (Allam and Ansari 2018).

And taking these socially conservative beliefs concerning racial homogeneity, traditional gender roles, and Islamophobia to their natural conclusion, we find the White Supremacist Nationalist user. White Supremacist Nationalist users identify themselves explicitly as white nationalists and white supremacists in their biographies by the inclusion of pro-white statements. All different branches of white supremacist and nationalist movements and affiliations are fundamentally linked by an "underlying logic [of] pro-white rhetoric, ideologies" (Hartzell 2018, 9), whether the establishment of a white racial state is explicit or implicit.

The political ideologies of white supremacy and re-surgent racialized nationalism parallels here a more universalized belief of securing a white, Western civilization. Neighborly Racists or MAGA Devotees, like all members of the far-right, are distinguished by their "rhetoric[al] attempts to construct an 'alternative' political ideology using key tenets of white nationalism as its foundation" (Hartzell 2018, 11), however, not everyone crosses the rhetorical threshold of explicitly using pro-white language. The question here is not of the different policy preferences between these users, but how they frame their ideological positions and identities through language on digital platforms such as Twitter. MAGA Devotees and Neighborly Racists, while emphasizing many of the same key themes as White Supremacist Nationalists, do not explicitly use whiteness as an identifier as they construct their networked identities within their biographies. This difference, while nuanced, is an important distinction when considering processes of radicalization. As Ashley Mattheis has noted "there is a leap that must be made between mainstream racialized world views and white supremacist hate" (2018, 153). The question is, what precipitates this leap? In this case, it is engagement with racist, Islamophobic discourse as a gateway to more extremist white supremacist beliefs.

White Supremacist Nationalist users distinguish themselves from mainstreamed, racialized socially conservative views through an emphasis on racial, religious, civilizationalist conflict. In considering the tensions between the conception of a common Western civilization and the nationalist affiliations of far-right groups, Rogers Brubaker has noted that; "'the nation' is not disappearing, but 'the nation' is being re-characterized in civilizational terms" (2017, 1211). In this sense, civilizational conflict, racialized nationalism, and transnational far-right movements operate on complementary tracks. @real_sindorei, for example, identifies themselves as a "truth seeker, defender of western civilization and white people" (Sindorei 2020). Another user, @BLcxQcHRxw2 fC0 V describes themselves as "Pro white and that all that matters" (Angrywhiteguy [angry face][angry face] 2020).

Within these examples there is a clear emphasis on the concept of a white Christian civilization that is allegedly under threat from Muslims, immigrants, Jews, feminists, members of the LGBTQIA+ community, liberals, Communists, and cosmopolitan, cultural elites. The engagement of these users with Islamophobic Tweets emphasizes that for White Supremacist Nationalists, Muslims pose a racial and cultural threat to "whiteness" and an imagined Western civilization. @hawkwindsean makes this trend quite explicit with his biography; "Anglo [English flag] a slave to globalism ,a witness to white erasure. The invasion continues" (SeeILatin crossFlag of EnglandID2020Transhumanism 2011). This is a persistent emphasis on a supposed white genocide or an invasion, itself a digital-born conspiracy (Wilson 2018, 28).

Even so, recurring phrases and individually coded themes sediment into a focus on family, traditional gender roles, and global conspiracies that suggest connections across potentially disparate groups, such as white nationalists and seemingly suburban "apolitical" mothers and fathers. Ultimately, we see there is a distinctive sense of one's nation or "civilization" being under attack and a view that national patriotism is a form of identity under threat of victimization or marginalization in society. As the German typography of users demonstrates, German users are motivated by similar ideological foci, emphasizing a belief in ethnonationalism, even as they enthusiastically re-appropriate symbols and rhetoric from the American MAGA movement.

Germany First: The Ubiquity of German Islamophobia

In articulating a German taxonomy of users, several unique user-types emerged from coding that both paralleled and diverged from the American user types, illustrating some particular elements unique to far-right German political identifications. The user types fall into four types: Heimat Enthusiasts, Alleged Anti-Totalitarians, Neighborly (German) Racists, and the Transnational Trumpists. Unlike the American user taxonomy, the German Twitter users do not show a clear linear path of possible radicalization from socially conservative to AfD voter to (Neo) Nazi, for example. However, this taxonomy of users demonstrates how far-right Islamophobic content is circulated and reveals that Islamophobia is mainstreamed in German political discourse in so far as a broad range of users, often with no far-right political identification, engage with virulent, racialized content.

One such recurring user is the Heimat Enthusiast. *Heimat* refers to "homeland" in German, but users of this persuasion also reference *Heimat* in a broader sense of an imagined Western European civilization. This user is defined by their patriotic support of Germany and their sense of passionate support of a German *Heimat* or *Vaterland* (fatherland). This user, who is a fervent supporter of the German nation must be contextualized against the German nation's contemporary "heightened anxieties about nationalist sentiment and politics in the postwar period" (Shoshan 2016, 203). This is to say, that intense national patriotism in Germany in the contemporary period is always read against the historical backdrop of the Third Reich and WWII.

These Heimat Enthusiasts demonstrate a form of geographical, cultural, and political possession towards their homeland that mirrors American possessive logics of whiteness of physical space and culture (Bonds 2019; Lipsitz 1998). Heimat Enthusiasts presuppose a strong connection to Western Europe as a cultural, racial, and religious concept but go on to assert a total rejection of transnational European integration, referring here to the integration of European Union (EU) member states. The hashtag #Dexit frequently appears among these users, which refers to a possible German exit of the EU similar to Great Britain's "Brexit" (DW 2019).

This attempt to both "defend Europe" against Muslim immigrants, while also rejecting EU multilateralism is both potent and contradictory in the context of the steady weakening of the EU as a result of Great Britain's removal from the bloc and the now lukewarm threat of a French departure as a result of the rising or lingering influence of Marine Le Pen's far-right anti-immigration anti-EU National Rally Party in France (Dijkstra, Poelman, and Rodríguez-Pose 2019). Germany, as a founding EU member state, has been viewed on the continent as holding the EU framework together against a rising tide of European far-right populism in the late 2010s (Mikhina, Mikhin, and Shulezhkova 2018). As such, the appearance of anti-EU sentiment within these user biographies suggests the possible resurgence of far-right German ethnonationalism and a rejection of EU integration as a framework because it allegedly weakens national sovereignty.

These individual impulses expressed in user biographies point towards a larger anti-EU sentiment that has been brewing since the 2015 Syrian Refugee crisis when millions of Syrians fled their homeland as a result of the brutal and still on-going Syrian Civil War (Rabinovich 2017). Millions of Syrians crossed the Mediterranean Sea and physically walked to Europe to claim asylum. The inability of the EU to cope with this humanitarian crisis and enact a standardized, humane process of entry for asylum seekers resulted in a catastrophe of asylum seekers drowning in the Mediterranean and languishing in border camps as they attempted to seek safe haven (Momigliano 2017). The entry of Syrian refugees into Germany spurred an upswing in anti-immigration populist political support for the AfD, particularly after former Chancellor Merkel accepted nearly one million asylum seekers into the country (Berning 2017). For many Germans, opposition to further EU integration and welcoming immigration policies went hand in hand, with increased rhetoric that the German *Heimat* was in some way under attack—by either Muslim Syrian immigrants or Brussels cosmopolitans. Thus, we see these overlapping impulses of Islamophobia, ethnonationalism, and Euroscepticism collide in the form of the Heimat Enthusiast.

The Heimat Enthusiast is well represented by user @DerPatriot444 who describes himself with the biography; *"Deutschland meine Heimat! NO ISLAM! Unser Deutschland zuerst! Deutsch und frei wollen wir sein!"* (National 2020). Which translates to "Germany is my homeland, 'NO ISLAM!,' our Germany first, German and we're going to stay free!" Such a biography is typical of the Heimat Enthusiast who asserts both a sense of German nationalism as well as an approval for the imported lexicon of President Trump, evidencing a symbiosis between German and American far-right rhetoric, without any engagement of the cognitive dissonance of championing a set of foreign politics and slogans to support a nationalist cause. Most critically, among these types of users there is a recurrent positioning of Islam as a foreign element—this is to say that Islam and Muslim communities are not situated as part of a Western European or German homeland. Such a position is not merely racist, but historically revisionist, erasing Germany's long history of immigration and settlement of Muslim Turkish communities in the state from the mid-20th century onward (Münz and Ulrich 1998; Şen 2003).

A similar type of Heimat Enthusiast is user is @Nutzer_019 who states "HEIMAT-UND KULTURLIEBHABEND, AUSLÄNDER JA, ABER ZU VIEL IST ÜBERFREMDUNG. #TIERSCHÜTZER #MENSCHENRECHTLER" (#Widukind 2021). This translates to "Lover of Homeland and Culture, foreigners yes, but too much is over-foreignization. #AnimalRights #HumanRights." Alexa Lenz has noted that the rehabilitation of the Nazi-era term *Überfremdung* once used to describe a supposed infiltration of "alien" races and Jews in Germany in the 1930s is now increasingly used in mainstream conservative German political discourse (2017). Lenz notes that:

> [t]he word "Überfremdung" works...by implying that there is an abundance of strangers invading the 'German race.' What seems to have changed, however, is the definition of the outgroup or the enemy. Promoted by PEGIDA [Patriotic Europeans Against the Islamicisation of the Occident] and the AfD, the new threat are Muslim immigrants and the idea of the "Islamization" of the Western culture. Thus, this becomes a powerful example for the political myth of the clash of civilizations between Islam and the West (2017).

As Lenz chronicles in her discussion of the terminology of the phrase *Überfremdung*, the Heimat Enthusiast user-type articulates this exact claim to an ethnically pure, Christian German homeland and situates Muslim immigrants and Islam more broadly as alien to Europe and Germany, demonstrating clear rhetorical historical continuities to the racialization and Othering of Jews in the 1930s. In Western Europe today, the far-right situates "Islam as a threat to 'the spiritual foundations of the West'" (Hafez 2014, 484), which, for both German and American users appears as both spiritual *and* cultural in the contemporary context.

If Heimat Enthusiasts seem preoccupied with policing the boundaries of the German national body historically on Twitter through their postings, then the Neighborly German Racist is devoted to policing the boundaries of the racial and religious German body politic through a focus on local issues. These users, named in conjunction with their American counterparts, emphasize their affiliation with traditional gender roles and frame their concerns over society as benignly middle-class and neighborly, focused on children, schooling, and community issues. In practice, however, these users engage with highly racialized and explicitly Islamophobic Tweets, images, memes, and news stories.

One such user that represents this categorization is @rosmarietoggwe1, who describes herself as; *"Verheiratet, erwachsene Kinder, bin für die Familie, gegen Kindstötung im Mutterleib, vertraue auf Gott. Bitte bleibt mir mit Gender vom Leib!"* (Toggweiler 2020), which translates to "Married, with grown children, I'm for family, against abortion, and a believer in God. Get that gender away from me!" As an anti-abortion, Christian @rosmarietoggwe1's inadvertently pithy comment of "get that gender away from me" likely refers here to her opposition to contemporary feminist and queer movements that emphasize a right to one's gender identity expression (J. Butler 2011). Similar to the American Neighborly Racist, the Neighborly German Racist represents the connection between socially conservative values of family, Christianity, and traditional gender roles alongside anti-feminist and Islamophobic political positions (Törnberg and Törnberg 2016).

Concern over socially conservative issues related to abortion, gender expression, and Christianity operate in a similar fashion in German as in American far-right circles, they are a means to police the boundaries of national community. Some users within this category make the connection between the patriarchal family unit, traditional gender roles, and Islamophobia more explicit in their biographies. User @letstalkabout4 states in her biography, *"Ich mache mir große Sorgen um meine Kinder & die Länder [German flag][Austrian flag] [blue heart] die ich liebe! Der ISLAM und die Unbedarftheit unserer Politiker sind der Grund meiner Sorge!"* (letstalkabout4 2020), or "I'm very worried about my children and the lands I love! Islam and the naivete of our politicians are my greatest worries!" Here we see a direct and explicit linkage between far-right ideology, ethnic nationalism, Islamophobia, and the patriarchal family unit.

Users who espouse socially conservative values in their biographies and emphasize their roles as mothers or fathers frequently cast the religion of Islam as a threat to children and the local neighborhood community. Children for both German and American Twitter users are motivating affective symbols within Islamophobic online discourse, who like white American women and ethnic German women, are seen as in need of protection by far-right political movements from the supposed sexual or religious violence of Muslim men (Benkler, Faris, and Roberts 2018; Boulila and Carri 2017).

For both Americans and Germans, virulent forms of racialized nationalism are mediated through the family. Natalie Fixmer-Oraiz in discussing the linkages between post-9/11 homeland security culture and maternalism in the US, notes that "[h]omeland security culture refers to a vision of nation and national belonging that celebrates nativism, nationalism, indiscriminate patriotism, and an adherence to resurging conservatism and normative 'family values'" (2019, 21). In this sense, both male and female identified users situate their identities as mothers and fathers as pivotal to securing the American and German homeland from a culturalized Muslim threat, thereby "perform[ing] citizenship through domesticity" (Fixmer-Oraiz 2019, 4), and now performing citizenship online through the circulation of Tweets, posts, videos, images, and memes of children in potential crisis of religious conversion.

Domesticity is racialized, politized, and mediated through user-biographies and performed virtually in these digitally networked communities as users emphasize their identities as mothers, fathers, husbands, and wives. To engage in this securitization of the homeland one no longer has to fight on the frontlines, but merely engage in socially mediated practices of "selfing," producing content, and sharing posts, information, and stories. Just as progressive online social movements work to circulate affective stories and content to mobilize sympathetic constituencies (Edwards et al. 2021, 17), far-right white supremacist, Hindu nationalist, and German nationalists deploy the same strategies. Far-right Islamophobic users are mobilized in the project of user-generated nationalism and are energized by their participation (Shahin 2020). Seemingly individuated, solitary acts of engaging online; sharing Tweets, adding #ContraIslam to one's biography, suddenly become religiously, culturally, and political significant—part of a (digital) war designed to save ethnic German, white American, and Western civilization from the imagined enemy of Muslim community.

These conspiratorial and apocalyptic leanings of the larger far-right become particularly evident in the Transnational Trumpist user-type, who supports German ethnonationalism and is preoccupied with themes of domesticity but evinces a full-throated support of MAGA or MGGA, led by the far-right party the AfD. @Orlanetta demonstrates this form of intense ethicized nationalism and a transnational support of Trump; "I [red heart] Trump – the greatest President in history! #DrainTheSwamp #AmericaFirst #Trump2020 #AfD *#MerkelMussWeg #ClimateRe-*

alism #Entgrünifizierung" (Orli 2020), including a hodgepodge of hashtags referencing Trumpist phrases, #DrainTheSwamp referring to corruption in Washington D.C., and support for the AfD.

Other types of Transnational Trumpists are explicit and extreme in their support of American imported conspiratorial beliefs such as @MetelingS, who describes themselves as a *"Patriot....für Deutschland Fan AFD Trump Urban Salvini Le Pen Israel 5G soll verboten werden allgemein Musik Politik News Politik & Staat"* (Christina 2020), which translates to "Patriot for Germany, fan of the AfD, Trump, Urban, Salvini, Le Pen, Israel, 5G should be totally forbidden, music, political news, politics and state." The names in the biography refer to a series of far-right authoritarian leaders including Trump, Viktor Orbán of Hungary, and Marine Le Pen of France.

Critically, the far-right imaginary is defined by conspiratorial racialized thinking that ranges in focus from fearmongering about immigration to cautioning against 5G technology. This refers to an emergent conspiracy that 5G, which facilitates the functionality of broadband cellular networks, either causes cancer, is a cover for spying on citizens, or is part of an imagined evil plot led by Microsoft founder and philanthropist Bill Gates whereby Gates has included microchips in the COVID-19 vaccine that will be activated by 5G technology to surveille citizens (Bruns, Harrington, and Hurcombe 2020; Evstatieva 2020).

Many users also profess support for the Q Anon conspiracy theory of which Trump is a key actor and hero, and the frequent appearance in a German corpus of Tweets for support of Q Anon or the #WWG1WGA is notable and evidences a transnational connection beyond formal far-right political movements into a more complex, fragmented, and transnationalized digital network of violent conspiracy movements. The user @galgo_lady illustrates this trend with her biography that states *"Aufmerksam und kritisch. #WWG1WGA #AfD #Qanon #followthewhiterabbit #redpill #patriot"* (galgo_lady 2020). Which translates to "alert and critical," and goes on to references a series of hashtags related to the Q Anon movement and the American far-right "pill-based" awakening (Chapelan 2021).

Transnational far-right conspiracy communities and Islamophobic digitally networked communities share a common vocabulary even if they are literally speaking in different languages. And these phrases, referencing the famous pill scene from *The Matrix* (1999) and the white rabbit from Lewis Caroll's *Alice in Wonderland Story* (1865) that riffs on Alice's falling into a different dimension and Neo's consumption of the pill as metaphors of far-right awakening illustrates the complex cultural language traded by far-right communities in digital spaces. To become conversant in these far-right spaces requires users not necessarily to learn German or English but to become fluent in an ever-shifting vocabulary of cultural symbols, text, and images. Far-right politics are mediated not through manifestos but through memes.

And this is even among ostensibly apolitical actors, such as the German Alleged Anti-Totalitarian. Here it is key to note that the absence of explicit (Neo) Nazi users within the corpus of Tweets is not surprising in so far as due to Germany's history of Nazism, the post-war reunified state has articulated a series of strict laws governing hate-speech compared to other free speech models of Western European democracies and the US (Delcker 2020). The explicit advocacy of (Neo) Nazism with the German Twittersphere thus is less common than American discussion of white nationalism on mainstream platforms like Twitter.

German national laws decree that companies with over two million users must adhere to certain national laws and regulations, one of which is the 2017 Network Enforcement Act, which requires social media companies such as Twitter to remove and take down hate-speech that is "manifestly unlawful" on their platforms within 24 hours after it is flagged (Bundestag 2017). For these reasons, while quantitatively there may be less hate-speech and explicit support for Nazism, this is not to say it does not exist. It is merely more implicit and nuanced, or occurring within more private digital spaces, such as in encrypted messaging platforms. The Alleged Anti-Totalitarian user is a clear example of how far-right German actors strategically describe themselves and produce far-right content that slips through the cracks of content moderation policies and federal laws.

Alleged Anti-Totalitarian users describe themselves in their biographies as against totalitarianism or against extremism, which, perhaps seemingly suggests their political moderation. However, these users emphasize Islam as a totalitarian political, cultural, and religious ideology. Hans-George Betz has described this discursive tactic among Western European far-right groups as waging a war against "Green Totalitarianism" (2016). Users of this category describe themselves in a similar form as @LeeGesundemitte; *"Kein Unterschied zwischen Rechts,– & Linksradikalen, radikalen Humanisten & radikalen Moslems"* (Spiegelvorhalter 2020). This translates to "there's no difference between right and left radicals, radical humanists, and radical Muslims," emphasizing a false equivalence between various political factions and "radical" Islam.

These users also style themselves as political moderates rather than far-right extremists. @Fermodes emphasizes their supposed moderation in a profile that states, *"Bin weder Extremist, noch Radikaler und erst recht kein Nazi – ich bin einfach nur politisch Rechts angesiedelt. #deutschland #AfD #grundgesetz #verfassung"* (Der Erwachte (ツ) 2020), which translates to "I'm neither an extremist nor a radical and certainly not a Nazi, I am simply politically right-wing #Germany #AfD #BasicLaw #Constitution." Suggesting here that this user views a support for ethnonationalist political policies as not extreme or evidence of (Neo) Nazi sympathies but simply a position of social conservativism.

Many users also explicitly state that they view Islam as a totalitarian ideology, such as user @R1chtungsweiser, a prolific poster, who uses his profile to rail against Islam; *"Der Islam ist eine totalitäre Ideologie und hat in Europa nichts verloren. Stoppt die Islamisierung unserer Heimat. Selber denken, Meinungen hinterfragen."* (Richtungsweiser 2020). This translates to, "Islam is a totalitarian ideology and has no place in Europe. Stop the Islamization of our homeland. Think for yourself and ask questions." What unites this user type is a consistent insistence upon their supposed political moderation and supposed disdain for all extremist beliefs while featuring frequent appearances of militant anti-Muslim language.

These types of users are in many ways similar to Far-Right Hindu Nationalists who preface increasingly radical positions with seemingly unobjectionable positions of supporting "truth," the "rule of law," or "facts." Even as users may eschew overtly radical language in their biographies, their engagement with Islamophobic digital discourse reveals their political affiliation and support for far-right ideologies. In this sense then, users ensconced within a far-right digital ecosystem while identifiable into a cohesive typology, are also a diverse collective that only becomes legible through the lens of Islamophobia.

Conclusion

In analyzing the way in which these users present their "networked" selves via autobiographies to identify patterns and similarities (Papacharissi 2010, 309), we see several emergent ideological trends that unite these seemingly disparate users together—primarily a support for socially conservative politics, traditional gender roles, MAGA-style politics, and violent conspiracy theories with the shared value of Islamophobia knitting them together into an interconnected community. American and German Twitter users engaged in Islamophobic hate-speech fall into a total of eight categories respectively: White Supremacist Nationalists, MAGA Devotees, Neighborly Racists, Far-Right Hindu Nationalists, and Heimat Enthusiasts, Transnational Trumpists, Neighborly German Racists, and Alleged Anti-Totalitarians. This taxonomy reveals both the Global North-South and Transatlantic transnationalization of far-right Islamophobic networks as well as the way in which these groups are affectively motivated by the topics of gender, family, and education in their communications, localizing national issues.

Through an examination of these actors, we see how far-right digitally networked communities engage in fetishizing an idealized, nostalgic white racial and ethnic German past defined by racial homogeneity and gender traditionalism, of which Muslims as citizens and immigrants are a great disrupter. This is the fundamental theme that unites German, American, and Indian users of all political persuasions and user types—a desire to return to an imagined ethnically and religiously pure racial past. This form of racialized nostalgia is not merely discursively exclusionary—it is explicitly connected to the contemporary political affiliations of users to violent conspiracy groups such as Q Anon and the MAGA movements that increasingly seek to make the "past" a reality through political activity or violence, whether that is through the 6,720 reported instances of anti-Muslim discrimination reported to the Council on American-Islamic Relations (CAIR) or the more than 900 documented individual instances of anti-Muslim hate-crimes in Germany over the year 2020 (Daily Sabah 2021; V. O. A. News 2022). In the next chapter, we see how these beliefs grow, evolve, and fester out in the open, linking together users across racial and geographic boundaries.

References

Aguilera-Carnerero, Carmen, and Abdul Halik Azeez. 2016. "'Islamonausea, Not Islamophobia': The Many Faces of Cyber Hate Speech." *Journal of Arab & Muslim Media Research* 9 (1): 21–40. https://doi.org/10.1386/jammr.9.1.21_1.

Ahmed, Reem, and Daniela Pisoiu. 2020. "Uniting the Far Right: How the Far-Right Extremist, New Right, and Populist Frames Overlap on Twitter – a German Case Study." *European Societies*, 1–23.

Ahmed, Sara. 2004. *Differences That Matter Feminist Theory and Postmodernism.* Cambridge, UK: Cambridge University Press.

Allam, Hannah, and Talal Ansari. 2018. "Republican Officials Have Been Bashing Muslims. We Counted." *BuzzFeed News*, April 10, 2018, sec. USNews. https://www.buzzfeednews.com/article/hannahallam/trump-republicans-bashing-muslims-without-repercussions.

Allington, Daniel, and Tanvi Joshi. 2018. "'What Others Dare Not Say': An Antisemitic Conspiracy Fantasy and Its YouTube Audience." *Journal of Contemporary Antisemitism*, 1–53. https://doi.org/10.26613/jca/3.1.42.

Anderson, Edward. 2015. "'Neo-Hindutva': The Asia House M. F. Husain Campaign and the Mainstreaming of Hindu Nationalist Rhetoric in Britain." *Contemporary South Asia* 23 (1): 45–66.

Angrywhiteguy [angry face][angry face]. 2020. "Profile." Twitter. August 16, 2020. https://twitter.com/BLcxQcHRxw2fC0V.

Armstrong, Alistair. 2020. "Profile." Twitter. August 16, 2020. https://twitter.com/Stretcharm40.

Astor, Maggie. 2019. "How the Politically Unthinkable Can Become Mainstream." *The New York Times*, 2019. https://www.nytimes.com/2019/02/26/us/politics/overton-window-democrats.html.

Awan, Imran. "Islamophobia on Social Media: A Qualitative Analysis of the Facebook's Walls of Hate." *International Journal of Cyber Criminology* 10, no. 1 (2016): 1–20. https://doi.org/10.5281/zenodo.58517.

Badalich, Savannah. 2019. "Online Radicalization of White Women to Organized White Supremacy." Master's Thesis, New York: Columbia University.

Bar-On, Tamir. 2012. "The French New Right's Quest for Alternative Modernity." *Fascism Journal of Contemporary Fascist Studies* 1 (1): 18 – 52.

Belgium, Based. 2020. "When We Where Young We Did School Trips to the Local Zoo, or to Some Sports Domain, Nowerdays Kids Visit Mosques in Belgium, and Learn How to Pray to Allah... #Islamization." Twitter. August 16, 2020. https://twitter.com/based_belgium/statuses/ 1294978111180812289.

Benkler, Yochai, Robert Faris, and Hal Roberts. 2018. *Network Propaganda Manipulation, Disinformation, and Radicalization in American Politics.* Oxford, UK: Oxford University Press.

Berning, Carl C. 2017. "Alternative Für Deutschland (AfD) – Germany's New Radical Right-Wing Populist Party." *DICE Report* 15 (4): 16 – 19.

Betz, Hans-George. 2016. "Against the 'Green Totalitarianism': Anti-Islamic Nativism in Contemporary Radical Right-Wing Populism in Western Europe." In *Europe for the Europeans : The Foreign and Security Policy of the Populist Radical Right*, edited by Christina Schori Liang, 33 – 54. London and New York: Routledge.

Bishop, Sophie. 2018. "Fetishisation of the 'Offline' in Feminist Media Research." *Feminist Media Studies* 18 (1): 143 – 47. https://doi.org/10.1080/14680777.2018.1407120.

Bonds, Anne. 2019. "Race and Ethnicity II: White Women and the Possessive Geographies of White Supremacy." *Progress in Human Geography.* https://doi.org/10.1177/0309132519863479.

Boulila, Stefanie C, and Christiane Carri. 2017. "On Cologne: Gender, Migration and Unacknowledged Racisms in Germany." *European Journal of Women's Studies* 24 (3): 286 – 93. https://doi.org/ 10.1177/1350506817712447.

Boussalis, Constantine, Callum Craig, and Aaron Rudkin. 2022. "Collective Victimhood Narratives in Far-Right Communities on Telegram." SocArXiv. https://doi.org/10.31235/osf.io/bgk96.

Braun, Virginia, and Victoria Clarke. 2006. "Using Thematic Analysis in Psychology." *Qualitative Research in Psychology* 3: 77 – 101.

Braun, Virginia, Victoria Clarke, Nikki Hayfield, and Gareth Terry. 2019. "Thematic Analysis." In *Handbook of Research Methods in Health and Social Sciences*, edited by Pranee Liamputtong, 843 – 60. Singapore: Springer.

Brubaker, Rogers. 2017. "Between Nationalism and Civilizationism: The European Populist Moment in Comparative Perspective." *Ethnic and Racial Studies* 40 (8): 1191 – 1226. https://doi.org/10.1080/ 01419870.2017.1294700.

Bruns, Axel, and Jean Burgess. 2011. "The Use of Twitter Hashtags in the Formation of Ad Hoc Publics." In *Proceedings of the 6th European Consortium for Political Research (ECPR) General Conference 2011*, 1 – 9. United Kingdom.

Bruns, Axel, and Jean Burgess. 2016. "Methodological Innovation in Precarious Spaces: The Case of Twitter." In *Digital Methods for Social Science*, edited by Helene Snee, Christine Hine, Yvette Morey, Steven Roberts, and Hayley Watson, 17 – 33. London, UK: Palgrave Macmillan.

Bruns, Axel, Stephen Harrington, and Edward Hurcombe. 2020. "'Corona? 5G? Or Both?': The Dynamics of COVID-19/5G Conspiracy Theories on Facebook." *Media International Australia.* https://doi.org/10.1177/1329878X20946113.

Bundestag. 2017. *Act to Improve Enforcement of the Law in Social Networks (Network Enforcement Act).* https://www.bmj.de/SharedDocs/Gesetzgebungsverfahren/Dokumente/NetzDG_engl.pdf? __blob=publicationFile&v=2.

Butler, Judith. 2011. *Gender Trouble: Feminism and the Subversion of Identity.* New York, NY: Routledge.

Butler, Umar. 2022. "Islamophobia in the Digital Age: A Study of Anti-Muslim Tweets." Victoria: Islamic Council of Victoria. https://doi.org/10.25916/GC0A-X327.

Caian, Manuela, and Patricia Kröll. 2015. "The Transnationalization of the Extreme Right and the Use of the Internet." *International Journal of Comparative and Applied Criminal Justice* 39 (4): 331–51. https://doi.org/10.1080/01924036.2014.973050.

Chapelan, Alexis. 2021. "'Swallowing the Red Pill': The Coronavirus Pandemic and the Political Imaginary of Stigmatized Knowledge in the Discourse of the Far-Right." *Journal of Transatlantic Studies* 19 (3): 282–312. https://doi.org/10.1057/s42738-021-00073-2.

Charmaz, Kathy. 2006. *Constructing Grounded Theory: A Practical Guide Through Qualitative Analysis.* Thousand Oaks, CA: SAGE Publications.

Charmaz, Kathy, and Linda Liska Belgrave. 2019. "Thinking About Data With Grounded Theory." *Qualitative Inquiry* 25 (8): 743–53. https://doi.org/10.1177/1077800418809455.

Chaturvedi, Sanjay. 2002. "Process of Othering in the Case of India and Pakistan." *Tijdschrift Voor Economische En Sociale Geografie* 93 (2): 149–59.

Chaturvedi, Swati. 2016. *I Am a Troll: Inside the Secret World of the BJP's Digital Army.* New Delhi: Juggernaut. https://www.abebooks.com/9789386228093/Troll-Secret-World-BJPs-Digital-9386228092/plp.

Christina. 2020. "Profile." Twitter. 36 2020. https://twitter.com/MetelingS.

Concha, Joe. 2017. "The Washington Post: 'Democracy Dies in Darkness.'" *The Hill*, February 22, 2017. https://thehill.com/homenews/media/320619-the-washington-post-democracy-dies-in-darkness.

Connelly, Lynne M. 2013. "Grounded Theory." *MEDSURG Nursing* 22 (2): 124–27.

Coppins, McCay. 2018. "Trump Already Won the Midterms Even If Republicans Lose the House on Tuesday, It's Unlikely That the President's Grip on His Party Will Loosen Anytime Soon." *The Atlantic*, November 6, 2018. https://www.theatlantic.com/politics/archive/2018/11/trump-won-midterms-changing-republican-party/574987/.

Couldry, Nick, and Jannis Kallinikos. 2017. "Ontology." In *The SAGE Handbook of Social Media*, edited by Jean Burgess, Alice Marwick, and Thomas Poell. London: SAGE Publications.

Crosset, Valentine, Samuel Tanner, and Aurélie Campana. 2018. "Researching Far Right Groups on Twitter: Methodological Challenges 2.0." *New Media & Society* 21 (4): 939–61.

Daily Sabah. 2021. "Over 900 Anti-Muslim Attacks Recorded in Germany in 2020." *Daily Sabah*, February 8, 2021, sec. Europe. https://www.dailysabah.com/world/europe/over-900-anti-muslim-attacks-recorded-in-germany-in-2020.

Delcker, Janosch. 2020. "Germany's Balancing Act: Fighting Online Hate While Protecting Free Speech." *Politico*, October 1, 2020. https://www.politico.eu/article/germany-hate-speech-internet-netzdg-controversial-legislation/.

Der Erwachte (ツ). 2020. "Profile." Twitter. May 24, 2020. https://twitter.com/der_erwachte.

Diamant, Jeff. 2019. "The Countries with the 10 Largest Christian Populations and the 10 Largest Muslim Populations." *Pew Research Center*, April 1, 2019. https://www.pewresearch.org/fact-tank/2019/04/01/the-countries-with-the-10-largest-christian-populations-and-the-10-largest-muslim-populations/.

Dijkstra, Lewis, Hugo Poelman, and Andrés Rodríguez-Pose. 2019. "The Geography of EU Discontent." *Regional Studies* 54 (6): 737–53. https://doi.org/10.1080/00343404.2019.1654603.

DW. 2019. "AfD Demands Radical EU Reforms to Avoid Germany's 'Dexit.'" *DW*, January 13, 2019, sec. News.

Edwards, Emily, Sarah Ford, Radhika Gajjala, Padmini Ray Murray, and Kiran Vinod Bhatia. 2021. "Shaheen Bagh: Making Sense of (Re)Emerging 'Subaltern' Feminist Political Subjectivities in Hashtag Publics through Critical, Feminist Interventions." *New Media & Society*. https://doi.org/10.1177/14614448211059121.

Ekman, Mattias. 2015. "Online Islamophobia and the Politics of Fear: Manufacturing the Green Scare." *Ethnic and Racial Studies* 38 (11): 1986–2002. https://doi.org/10.1080/01419870.2015.1021264.

Evstatieva, Monika. 2020. "Anatomy Of A COVID-19 Conspiracy Theory." *NPR*, July 10, 2020. https://www.npr.org/2020/07/10/889037310/anatomy-of-a-covid-19-conspiracy-theory.

Fair, C. Christine. 2011. "Lashkar-e-Taiba beyond Bin Laden: Enduring Challenges for the Region and the International Community." U.S. Senate, Foreign Relations Committee.

Filkins, Dexter. 2019. "Blood and Soil in Narendra Modi's India." *The New Yorker*, 2019. https://www.newyorker.com/magazine/2019/12/09/blood-and-soil-in-narendra-modis-india.

Fixmer-Oraiz, Natalie. 2019. *Homeland Maternity: US Security Culture and the New Reproductive Regime.* Urbana, Chicago, and Springfield, IL: University of Illinois Press.

Friedberg, Brian. 2020. "The Dark Virality of a Hollywood Blood-Harvesting Conspiracy." *Wired* (blog). July 31, 2020. https://www.wired.com/story/opinion-the-dark-virality-of-a-hollywood-blood-harvesting-conspiracy/.

Froio, Caterina. 2018. "Race, Religion, or Culture? Framing Islam between Racism and Neo-Racism in the Online Network of the French Far Right." *Perspectives on Politics* 16 (3): 696–709. https://doi.org/10.1017/S1537592718001573.

Froio, Caterina, and Bharath Ganesh. 2018a. "The Far Right Across Borders Networks and Issues of (Trans)National Cooperation in Western Europe on Twitter." In *Post-Digital Cultures of the Far Right: Online Actions and Offline Consequences in Europe and the US*, edited by Maik Fielitz, Nick Thurston, and Stephen Albrecht, 93–104. New York, NY: Columbia University Press. https://doi.org/10.14361/9783839446706.

Froio, Caterina, and Bharath Ganesh. 2018b. "The Transnationalisation of Far Right Discourse on Twitter Issues and Actors That Cross Borders in Western European Democracies." *European Societies* 21 (4): 513–39.

Gajjala, Radhika. 2019. *Digital Diasporas Labor and Affect in Gendered Indian Digital Publics.* Lanham, MD: Rowman & Littlefield Publishers.

Gajjala, Radhika, and Melissa Altman. 2006. "Producing Cyber-Selves through Technospatial Praxis: Studying through Doing." In *Health Research in Cyberspace*, edited by Pranee Liamputtong, 1–17. Hauppauge, New York: Nova Publishers.

galgo_lady. 2020. "Profile." Twitter. April 7, 2020. https://twitter.com/galgo_lady.

Ganesh, Bharath, and Caterina Froio. 2020. "A 'Europe Des Nations': Far Right Imaginative Geographies and the Politicization of Cultural Crisis on Twitter in Western Europe." *Journal of European Integration* 42 (5): 715–32. https://doi.org/10.1080/07036337.2020.1792462.

Ganesh, Bharath, and Caterina Froio. "A 'Europe Des Nations': Far Right Imaginative Geographies and the Politicization of Cultural Crisis on Twitter in Western Europe." *Journal of European Integration* 42, no. 5 (2020): 715–32. https://doi.org/10.1080/07036337.2020.1792462.

Gatson, Sarah. 2011. "Self-Naming Practices on the Internet: Identity, Authenticity, and Community." *Cultural Studies Critical Methodologies* 11 (3): 224–35. https://doi.org/10.1177/1532708611409531.

Giddens, Anthony. 1991. *Modernity and Self-Identity: Self and Society in the Late Modern Age.* Redwood City, CA: Stanford University Press.

Gillespie, Elizabeth McRae. 2018. *Mothers of Massive Resistance: White Women and the Politics of White Supremacy.* Oxford, UK: Oxford University Press.

Gittinger, Juli L. 2019. *Hinduism and Hindu Nationalism Online.* New York: Routledge.

Gruzd, Anatoliy, and Caroline Haythornthwaite. 2013. "Enabling Community Through Social Media." *JOURNAL OF MEDICAL INTERNET RESEARCH* 15 (10).

Hafez, Farid. 2014. "Shifting Borders: Islamophobia as Common Ground for Building Pan-European Right-Wing Unity." *Patterns of Prejudice* 48 (5): 479 – 99.

Haraway, Donna. 1988. "Situated Knowledges: The Science Question in Feminism and the Privilege of Partial Perspective." *Feminist Studies* 14 (3): 575 – 99.

Harriss, John. 2015. "Hindu Nationalism in Action: The Bharatiya Janata Party and Indian Politics" 38 (4): 712 – 18. https://doi.org/10.1080/00856401.2015.1089826.

Hartzell, Stephanie L. 2018. "Alt-White: Conceptualizing the 'Alt-Right' as a Rhetorical Bridge between White Nationalism and Mainstream Public Discourse." *Journal of Contemporary Rhetoric* 8 (1/2): 6 – 25.

HoSang, Daniel Martinez, and Joseph E. Lowndes. 2019. *Producers, Parasites, Patriots Race and the New Right-Wing Politics of Precarity.* Minneapolis, MN: University of Minnesota Press. https://www.upress.umn.edu/book-division/books/producers-parasites-patriots.

Jones, Reece. 2009. "Agents of Exception: Border Security and the Marginalization of Muslims in India – Reece Jones, 2009." *Environment and Planning D: Society and Space* 27 (5): 879 – 97. https://doi.org/10.1068/d10108.

jrconse. 2020. "Profile." Twitter. May 1, 2020. https://twitter.com/jrconse.

Kelly, Annie. 2017. "The Alt-Right: Reactionary Rehabilitation for White Masculinity." Eurozine. September 15, 2017. https://www.eurozine.com/the-alt-right-reactionary-rehabilitation-for-white-masculinity/.

Kelly, Makena. 2020. "Inside Nextdoor's 'Karen Problem.'" The Verge. June 8, 2020. https://www.theverge.com/21283993/nextdoor-app-racism-community-moderation-guidance-protests.

King, Richard. 1999. "Orientalism and the Modern Myth of 'Hinduism.'" *Numen* 46 (2): 146 – 85.

Kurwa, Rahim. 2019. "Building the Digitally Gated Community: The Case of Nextdoor." *Surveillance & Society* 17 (1/2): 111 – 17. https://doi.org/10.24908/ss.v17i1/2.12927.

LaFrance, Adrienne. 2020. "The Prophicies of Q." *The Atlantic*, June 2020. https://www.theatlantic.com/magazine/archive/2020/06/qanon-nothing-can-stop-what-is-coming/610567/.

Latzko-Toth, Guillaume, Claudine Bonneau, and Melanie Millette. 2017. "Small Data, Thick Data: Thickening Strategies for Trace-Based Social Media Research." In *The SAGE Handbook of Social Media Research Methods*, edited by Luke Sloan and Quan-Haase, 199 – 214. Los Angeles, CA: SAGE Publications.

Lee, Laura. 2020. "Profile." Twitter. August 16, 2020.

Leidig, Eviane Cheng. 2019. "Immigrant, Nationalist and Proud: A Twitter Analysis of Indian Diaspora Supporters for Brexit and Trump." *Media and Communication* 7 (1): 77 – 89. https://doi.org/10.17645/mac.v7i1.1629.

Lenz, Alexa. 2017. "'Völkisch' and 'Überfremdung' Different Enemies, Same Fascist Ideology?" *Public Seminar* (blog). July 14, 2017. https://publicseminar.org/2017/07/volkisch-and-uberfremdung/.

letstalkabout4. 2020. "Profile." Twitter. March 27, 2020. https://twitter.com/letstalkabout4.

Leurs, Koen. 2017. "Feminist Data Studies: Using Digital Methods for Ethical, Reflexive and Situated Socio-Cultural Research." *Feminist Review* 115: 130 – 54.

Lipsitz, George. 1998. *The Possessive Investment in Whiteness How White People Profit from Identity Politics.* Philadelphia, PA: Temple University Press.

Lorenz, Taylor. 2020. "Upper East Side Mom Group Implodes Over Accusations of Racism and Censorship." *The New York Times*, June 9, 2020. https://www.nytimes.com/2020/06/09/style/ues-mommas-facebook-group-racism-censorship.html.

Lukić, Jasmina, and Adelina Sánchez Espinosa. 2011. "Feminist Perspectives on Close Reading." In *Theories and Methodologies in Postgraduate Feminist Research Researching Differently*, edited by Rosemarie Buikema, Gabriele Griffin, and Nina Lykke. New York, NY: Routledge.

Marcks, Holger, and Janina Pawelz. 2022. "From Myths of Victimhood to Fantasies of Violence: How Far-Right Narratives of Imperilment Work." *Terrorism and Political Violence* 34 (7): 1415–32. https://doi.org/10.1080/09546553.2020.1788544.

Martin, Jonathan, and Alexander Burns. 2020. "Biden Wins Presidency, Ending Four Tumultuous Years Under Trump." *The New York Times*, November 7, 2020.

Mattheis, Ashley. 2018. "Shieldmaidens of Whiteness: (Alt) Maternalism and Women Recruiting for the Far/Alt-Right." *Journal for Deradicalization* 17: 128–62.

Mckee, Alan. 2003. *Textual Analysis : A Beginner's Guide.* Thousand Oaks, CA: SAGE Publications.

Michelsen, Nicholas, and Pablo de Orellana. "Discourses of Resilience in the US Alt-Right." *International Policies, Practices and Discourses* 7, no. 3 (2019): 271–87.

Mikhina, Olga, Artem Mikhin, and Svetlana Shulezhkova. 2018. "'Wir Schaffen Das!' (Angela Merkel as a Linguistic Persona)." In *Current Issues of Linguistics and Didactics: The Interdisciplinary Approach in Humanities and Social Sciences*, 50:4. Web.

Milner, Ryan M. 2016. "Introduction: The Rise of Memetic Media." In *The World Made Meme: Public Conversations and Participatory Media*, edited by Ryan M. Milner. The MIT Press. https://doi.org/10.7551/mitpress/9780262034999.003.0001.

Momigliano, Anna. 2017. "Italian Forces Ignored a Sinking Ship Full of Syrian Refugees and Let More than 250 Drown, Says Leaked Audio." *Washington Post*, May 9, 2017, sec. WorldViews. https://www.washingtonpost.com/news/worldviews/wp/2017/05/09/italian-forces-ignored-a-sinking-ship-full-of-syrian-refugees-and-let-more-than-250-drown-says-leaked-audio/.

Mondon, Aurelien, and Aaron Winter. 2017. "Articulations of Islamophobia: From the Extreme to the Mainstream?" *Ethnic and Racial Studies* 40 (3): 2151–79.

Morstatter, Fred, Yunqiu Shao, Aram Galstyan, and Shanika Karunasekera. 2018. "From Alt-Right to Alt-Rechts: Twitter Analysis of the 2017 German Federal Election." In *WWW '18: Companion Proceedings of The Web Conference 2018.* Lyon, France: International World Wide Web Conferences Steering Committee Republic and Canton of Geneva, Switzerland. https://dl.acm.org/citation.cfm?id=3188733.

Münz, Rainer, and Ralf E. Ulrich. 1998. "Changing Patterns of Immigration to Germany, 1945–1997." Berkley Center for German and European Studies.

Nath, Purnima. 2012. "Profile." Twitter. 2012. https://twitter.com/PurnimaNath.

National, Deutsch. 2020. "Profile." Twitter. March 26, 2020. https://twitter.com/DerPatriot444.

NetizenParo. 2020a. "@ShowUrJewPride I Honestly Think Tht All #Democratic #nations Need to #fight the Agenda of #Islamization. Everyone Can See Hw #Jews & #Hindus around the World r Being #gaslighted , #history #distorted & #manipulated & #FakeNews Media Being Used to Push the #Islamofascist Agenda. #StopGlobalJihad." Twitter. April 27, 2020. https://twitter.com/NetizenParo/statuses/1254896282834997251.

NetizenParo. 2020b. "Profile." Twitter. November 3, 2020.

Newton, Casey, and Zoe Schiffer. 2022. "Elon Musk Ignored Twitter's Internal Warnings about His Paid Verification Scheme." *The Verge*, November 14, 2022. https://www.platformer.news/embed.

Noack, Rick. 2016. "The Ugly History of 'Lügenpresse,' a Nazi Slur Shouted at a Trump Rally." *Washington Post*, October 24, 2016. https://www.washingtonpost.com/news/worldviews/wp/2016/10/24/the-ugly-history-of-luegenpresse-a-nazi-slur-shouted-at-a-trump-rally/.

Oliver, J. Eric, and Thomas J. Wood. 2014. "Conspiracy Theories and the Paranoid Style(s) of Mass Opinion." *American Journal of Political Science* 58 (4): 952–66.

Orli, Wusel. 2020. "Profile." Twitter. March 21, 2020. https://twitter.com/Orlanetta.

Papacharissi, Zizi. 2010. "Conclusion." In *A Networked Self Identity, Community, and Culture on Social Network Sites*, edited by Zizi Papacharissi, 304–18. New York: Routledge.

Planck, Samuel. 2020. "Where We Go One, We Go All: QAnon and Violent Rhetoric on Twitter." *Locus: The Seton Hall Journal of Undergraduate Research* 3 (11): 1–17.

Price, Bryan D. 2018. "Material Memory: The Politics of Nostalgia on the Eve of MAGA." *American Studies* 57 (1/2): 103–15. https://doi.org/10.1353/ams.2018.0027.

Prooijen, Jan-Willem van. 2017. "Conspiracy Theories as Part of History: The Role of Societal Crisis Situations." *Memory Studies* 10 (3): 323–33. https://doi.org/10.1177/1750698017701615.

Rabinovich, Itamar. 2017. "The Syrian Civil War as a Global Crisis." *Sphere of Politics / Sfera Politicii* 25 (1/2): 44–48.

Richtungsweiser. 2020. "Profile." Twitter. May 23, 2020. https://twitter.com/R1chtungsweiser.

Roy, Haimanti. 2013. *Partitioned Lives: Migrants, Refugees, Citizens in India and Pakistan, 1947–65.* Oxford, UK: Oxford University Press.

Santa Ana, Otto, and Celeste González de Bustamante, eds. 2012. "Can American Learn to Think Globally? We Don't at Our Own Risk." In *Arizona Firestorm: Global Immigration Realities, National Media, and Provincial Politics*, by Otto Santa Ana and Celeste González de Bustamante, 277–90. Rowman & Littlefield Publishers.

Schwartz, Dana. 2017. "Why Trump Supporters Love Calling People 'Snowflakes.'" *GQ*, February 1, 2017. https://www.gq.com/story/why-trump-supporters-love-calling-people-snowflakes.

SeeILatin crossFlag of EnglandID2020Transhumanism. 2011. "Profile." Twitter. 2011. https://twitter.com/hawkwindsean.

Şen, Faruk. 2003. "The Historical Situation of Turkish Migrants in Germany." *Immigrants & Minorities* 22 (2–3): 208–27. https://doi.org/10.1080/0261928042000244835.

Sen, Somdeep. 2022. "Hindu Nationalists Now Pose a Global Problem." *Al Jazeera*, September 26, 2022. https://www.aljazeera.com/opinions/2022/9/26/violent-hindu-extremism-is-now-a-global-problem.

Shahin, Saif. 2020. "User-Generated Nationalism: Interactions with Religion, Race, and Partisanship in Everyday Talk Online." *Information, Communication & Society*, 1–16. https://doi.org/10.1080/1369118X.2020.1748088.

Shahin, Saif, and Zehui Dai. 2019. "Understanding Public Engagement With Global Aid Agencies on Twitter: A Technosocial Framework." *American Behavioral Scientist* 63 (12): 1–24.

Shepherd, Tamara, Aubrey E. Harvey, Tim Jordan, Sam Srauy, and Kate M. Miltner. "Histories of Hating." *Social Media + Society*, 2015, 1–10. https://doi.org/10.1177/2056305115603997.

Shoshan, Nitzan. 2016. *The Management of Hate Nation, Affect, and the Governance of Right-Wing Extremism in Germany.* Princeton, NJ: Princeton University Press.

Sindorei. 2020. "Profile." Twitter. August 16, 2020. https://twitter.com/real_sindorei.

Singh, Raj Kumar. 2021. "Hindutva and Donald Trump: An Unholy Relation." In *The Anthropology of Donald Trump*. Routledge.

Singh, Ujjwal Kumar. 2019. "Law, State and Right-Wing Extremism in India." *Journal of Policing, Intelligence and Counter Terrorism* 14 (2): 280–97. https://doi.org/10.1080/18335330.2019.1667518.

Spiegelvorhalter. 2020. "Profile." Twitter. March 26, 2020. https://twitter.com/LeeGesundemitte.

StaceyM78844177. 2020. "Profile." Twitter. June 1, 2020. https://twitter.com/StaceyM78844177/statuses/1267557213138153472.

Stewart, Charles J. 2002. "The Master Conspiracy of the John Birch Society: From Communism to the New World Order." *Western Journal of Communication* 66 (4): 423 – 47. https://doi.org/10.1080/10570310209374748.

Sunshine, Fearless. 2012. "Profile." Twitter. *Twitter* (blog). 2012. https://twitter.com/fearless12342.

Therwath, Ingrid. 2012. "Cyber-Hindutva: Hindu Nationalism, the Diaspora and the Web." *Social Science Information* 51 (4): 551 – 77. https://doi.org/10.1177/0539018412456782.

Toggweiler, Rosmarie. 2020. "Profile." Twitter. April 2, 2020. https://twitter.com/rosmarietoggwe1.

Törnberg, Anton, and Petter Törnberg. 2016. "Combining CDA and Topic Modeling: Analyzing Discursive Connections between Islamophobia and Anti-Feminism on an Online Forum." *Discourse & Society* 27 (4): 401 – 22.

V. O. A. News. 2022. "US Muslims See Rise in Islamophobia." VOA. May 10, 2022. https://www.voanews.com/a/us-muslims-see-rise-in-islamophobia-/6565523.html.

Waikar, Prashant. 2018. "Reading Islamophobia in Hindutva: An Analysis of Narendra Modi's Political Discourse." *Islamophobia Studies Journal* 4 (2): 161 – 80. https://doi.org/10.13169/islastudj.4.2.0161.

Wang, Emily L., Luca Luceri, Francesco Pierri, and Emilio Ferrara. 2022. "Identifying and Characterizing Behavioral Classes of Radicalization within the QAnon Conspiracy on Twitter." arXiv. http://arxiv.org/abs/2209.09339.

Weatherby, Lief. 2018. "Politics Is Downstream from Culture, Part 1: Right Turn to Narrative." *The Hedgehog Review*, March 5, 2018. https://hedgehogreview.com/web-features/infernal-machine/posts/politics-is-downstream-from-culture-part-1-right-turn-to-narrative.

#Widukind[blue heart] [rainbow] [German flag] [Israeli flag][Armenian flag][Taiwanese flag][Wallis and Futana' [Indian flag] [Greek flag][flame][snowman] [globe][statue of liberty]. 2021. "Profile." Twitter. March 21, 2021. https://twitter.com/Nutzer_019.

Williams, Apryl. 2020. "Black Memes Matter: #LivingWhileBlack With Becky and Karen." *Social Media + Society* 6 (4): 2056305120981047. https://doi.org/10.1177/2056305120981047.

Wilson, Andrew F. 2018. "#whitegenocide, the Alt-Right and Conspiracy Theory: How Secrecy and Suspicion Contributed to the Mainstreaming of Hate." *Secrecy and Society* 1 (2): 1 – 47.

Chapter III
Digital Islamophobia in Play

Introduction

Now familiar as we are with the players on the stage, it is critical to examine in greater detail how far-right digitally networked communities come together through shared consumption and circulation of place-based stories within the seemingly despatialized context of digital environments. Through studying the processes of "selfing" that these users practice (Gatson 2011), we have started to identify how a range of users from white suburban moms, to Indian Americans, to AfD voters are all invested in complementary racial projects. Now, we can examine how these actors interact around shared narratives, shedding light on the way in which local, national, global, and civilizationalist stories are re-fashioned by far-right actors in different contexts to appeal to particular user sensibilities.

On any social media platform discourse moves at an electric speed, and Twitter is no different. What is viral one day is forgotten the next. However, as Henry Jenkins has noted in his discussion of networked cultures and social movements, the "capacity of everyday people to circulate information and opinion online" can be "key in shaping and mobilizing public opinion" (2013). Conversations and stories on Twitter circulated can sediment, signaling larger political and cultural changes, with the affective engagement of individual users online sparking feelings of deep political connectivity (Jenkins 2013).

Such is the case of formalized political and socio-cultural movements born on the platform through hashtags, ranging from the Arab Spring (Howard and Hussain 2013), to the #BlackLivesMatter movement (Garza 2014), to #MeToo (Suk et al. 2021). While there continues to be disagreement over whether these movements achieved off-platform change or were merely flashes of "slacktivism" (Gladwell 2010), of interest to us here is not formalized social media campaigns, but rather, as Jenkins has also noted, how this "capacity to circulate" may be deployed both "effectively and spontaneously toward political ends" (2013), and, *affectively*. Just as parsing everyday digital discourse provides a window into the processes of identity construction among far-right communities, analyzing everyday digital discourse sheds light on the formulation of political, socio-cultural far-right public ideologies more broadly.

As such, in this chapter we look back to two viral conversations that implicated various users within the dynamic far-right mediated ecosystem as case studies of how everyday users engage with both content and one another across geograph-

https://doi.org/10.1515/9783111032887-003

ical divides. American far-right Islamophobic networks are in fact both heavily nationalized and influenced by Hindu nationalist Indian politics abroad, a politics
that is re-fashioned to resonate with racialized domestic concerns in the US. Comparatively, while far-right German audiences remain insular, actors within the German Twitter-scape re-purpose and circulate local and urban stories for their own
political ends. Both processes, of the transnationalization and nationalization of
American and German far-right networks, are facilitated through Twitter's platformed structure, which allows for the creation of multi-scalar affective publics
(Fraser 1990; Papacharissi 2015a; 2015b). Local issues become civilizationalist
level clashes and national politics abroad heralds sinister neighborhood changes
at home.

Just as Twitter creates a space for place-based user-generated nationalisms to
emerge (Shahin 2020), it facilitates the circulation of content in the broader context
of what Marcus Owens calls the "despatialized dynamics of cyberspace" (2019). Affect may be "sticky" in these viral stories traded on Twitter (Ahmed 2013), but
place also has a similar clinging quality, as far-right communities barter stories
and conspiracies amongst one another, with these two dynamics at tension—the
flattening quality of Twitter to serve the depoliticized, generic "public conversation" (Twitter 2022), as if there is one digital public, and the fundamental place-
based nature of far-right ideological movements where home and heartland feature heavily into belief and discourse.

Twitter may frame itself as a platform catering to a singular digital public,
however, it is more accurate to view the platform as a staging ground for multiple,
oscillating networks and counter-publics (Florini 2019), publics that come into
being through the shared circulation of affective content. As Michael Warner
has argued, "[t]he more punctual and abbreviated the circulation, and the more
discourse indexes the punctuality of its own circulation, the closer a public stands
to politics" (2002, 68). Twitter, defined by its structuration of content in 280 characters or less, is particularly close to politics, even when the purpose of the company is articulated through the seemingly de-politized, prosaic description of being
focused on "what's happening and what people are talking about right now" (Twitter 2022).

These far-right counter-publics may also be thought of as political enclaves,
borrowing from Catherine Squire's exploration of the "Black Public Sphere"
(2002), here emphasizing the way in which far-right networked communities
mimic discursive and political tactics of other groups. The rhetorical connections
forged within these far-right virtual enclaves on Twitter ultimately generate
what in offline contexts have been called "complicated, coalitional subjectivities"
of social movements (Chávez 2011, 14). Peeking into these enclaves by studying
how users interact and share content helps us understand how far-right rhetoric

is repurposed and redeployed across a range of audiences, and, reveals the way in which spaces from the nation to the neighborhood become mutable yet central materials in the construction of far-right Islamophobic digital coalitions on the seemingly despatialized platform of Twitter.

As such, in this chapter we examine two cases, extending the practice of close textual feminist reading to make sense of viral conversations on Twitter by employing thematic analysis, investigating the traces left behind by these groups. Engaging in thematic analysis of discourse involves identifying the themes that lurk beneath the surface of the data (Braun et al. 2019, 846), looking for patterns which indicate meaning or significance (Braun and Clarke 2006, 79). In this case, the patterns that emerge in these viral Twitter threads have to do with spaces; local and national. And the application of a feminist lens in particular assists us in detangling the overlap of race, gender, and geographies, both real and imagined, virtual and material, that characterize both contemporary far-right digital conversations and historic projects of racial nationalism (Bonds 2019, 779).

Just as digital discourse and communities may influence off-online public opinion and electoral politics, the imagined local, national, and transnational communities invoked and policed by far-right groups on Twitter, while mediated virtually on the platform, invoke real communities and places (Anderson 1991). Notions of homeland and hearth figure heavily into far-right social movements and digital discussion; for far-right communities, racialist, patriarchal claims of possession of physical spaces, women and children, and political power are mutually constitutive (Kelly 2017; Lipsitz 1995; Michelsen and de Orellana 2020). And these claims are mediated on Twitter through the circulation of content. Even as far-right populist politics increasingly taken on a civilizationalist tone (Brubaker 2017), these discourses of possession and its parallel, dispossession, garner affect through the mechanism of place. Far-right actors utilize place-based settings from the neighborhood to the nation to appeal to and connect to other users, flattening ideological and spatial distances between an eclectic coalition of sympathetic actors.

The possessive racial geographies enacted by Indian, American, and German users on Twitter illustrate how social media platforms can function simultaneously to both collapse distances between groups and re-embed the historic trifecta of race/nation/culture that constitutes racialized nationalism (Eriksen 2007, 7). As Bharath Ganesh and Caterina Froio note regarding Twitter in particular, Twitter is a unique virtual space where far-right "imaginative geographies" are circulated and posed as in crisis (2020, 720). And this is precisely the case among far-right Islamophobic communities. However, this imaginative circulation is not just limited to European or specifically national contexts; local, national, and global imaginative geographies collide on Twitter, repurposed to speak to a range of audiences. With the scene laid, the following section examines how spaces are situated by a collection of users attending particularly to the gendered dimensions of viral stories.

Saffronization, Islamophobia, & Whiteness: Hindu Nationalism Abroad & American Far-Right Politics at Home

How does content produced by Far-Right Hindu Nationalist Twitter users located in India become circulated by American white far right actors? Or, put another way, why do Indian legal polices such as the CAA-NRC passed in New Delhi interest white suburbanites in Arkansas? Here, we see how a discussion of Indian citizenship policies, seemingly geared towards Indian national users, resonates with and circulates among a far-right white American audience. The vibrant far-right Indian Twitter-sphere or enclave (K. V. Bhatia 2022), while ostensibly focused on domestic issues and policies in relation to actualizing Hindu nationalism at home, is in fact highly connected to a subsection of American white far-right actors and influencers. Through the repurposing of global Islamophobic tropes that play on Orientalist imaginings of the Muslim world through a civilizationalist lens (Said 1979), Indian Hindu nationalist Twitter users are able to produce content that resonates with both a domestic Indian national digital public and a white American far-right audience, both instrumentalizing place and transcending it.

Hindu nationalists and white American far-right users similarly imagine Muslims as both a global and national threat, destabilizing society on all levels. While the particular nation under threat may change, from India to the US, these users coalesce around a racialized representation of Muslims as fomenting disorder and chaos globally, threatening both Western white and Eastern Indian Hindu civilization. In this case, the historical origins of Hindu nationalism as a form of "'Aryan supremacy'" are relevant "not only in India and in the global Hindutva diaspora [but in] the more recent alt-right" (Sahgal 2020, 20). Thus, the rhetoric and ideology developed and circulated by Hindu nationalists that advances a notion of a pure Hindu nation stretching back to the supposed antecedents of an Aryan civilization (Sahgal 2020, 30), also creates linkages to American far-right communities invested in similar projects of racialist historical revisionism.

Contemporary forms of Indian "saffronisation," which refer to the BJP's enactment of right-wing policies designed to advance a Hindu nationalist agenda particularly in the sector of education, promoting a Hindu-nationalist version of history, culture, and society in opposition to the secular founding of the Indian state, predominate on social media as well (A. Bhatia 2020; Hayat and Abbasi 2021), and operate complementary to American white nationalist aims. As Chetna Khandelwal has noted, anti-immigrant far-right Indian and American Twitter networks enact parallel masculinist possessive logics over geography, community, and education (2022). It is precisely this "saffronised" nationalist content that engages white American far-right users, even as this groups is seeking conversely to realize comparative programs of Christian religious and white nationalist homogeneity.

Content that brings together white American and Indian nationalist users originates from this "saffronised" perspective, from users like @Saffron_Tweeter, an Indian Twitter user who seeks to "...make Sanatan Rashtra a reality" (Saffron Tweeter 2020). Referencing here Sanatan Rashtra, a religious organization that seeks to advance a variety of causes including eliminating the use of English to "purify" discourse in India and establishing a "Hindu Rashtra" that is "guided by the Principles of Dharma" while allegedly remaining open to all castes and religions (Khandelwal 2022). The organization suggests secularism is inconsequential in India, with the term added to the Indian constitution in 1976 as part of the 42nd amendment (Singh 2022). With these traces, we get a sense of the ideological situation of @Saffron_Tweeter as ensconced firmly within project of Hindutva. @Saffron_Tweeter is but one in an army of Hindu nationalist and BJP supporting "trolls" who engage in sophisticated forms of digital coordination as highly motivated everyday users (Chaturvedi 2016; Jaffrelot and Verniers 2020; Purohit 2022b).

The content though, that @Saffron_Tweeter produces bringing various users together, while intensely focused on the Indian national political situation emphasizes a civilationalist lens. @Saffron_Tweeter posts "Islam is not a religion, nor is it a cult. In its fullest form, it is a complete, total, 100 % system of life," going on to say, "Islam has religious, legal, political, economic, social, and military components #Islamization" (Saffron Tweeter 2019b). @Saffron_Tweeter also deploys the hashtags "# #Need_For_CAA_NRC" along with "#Islamization" (Saffron Tweeter 2019a), referring to the Citizenship Amendment Act (CAA) and National Registry of Citizens (NRC) two policy initiatives passed by Prime Minister Modi's BJP led national government.

@Saffron_Tweeter's Tweets about the possible Islamization of society are not in and of themselves surprising, given the way in which far-right actors, BJP supporters, and pro-CAA-NRC coalitions mobilized on Twitter during passage of these policy amendments in late 2019 (Dash et al. 2022). However, the resonance of @Saffron_Tweeter's posts with a white American audience suggests that what appeared to be a national Indian digital political conversation focused on the pro and anti-CAA-NRC movements, in fact held affective salience beyond pro-CAA-NRC constituencies at home and in the Indian diaspora. In deploying hashtags like #Need_For_-CAA_NRC and #Islamization together, far-right Hindu nationalist users utilize themes that resonate not only with nationalized Indian audiences, but American far-right publics as well, illustrating how Islamophobic tropes are flexible in translocal applications (Leidig 2019).

The CAA-NRC refers to a series of anti-Muslim policy interventions initiated by the BJP-led Indian government. The Citizenship Amendment Act (CAA), passed in December 2019 requires individuals in India to produce a series of approved legal documents to prove their citizenship, however, non-Muslim immigrants and refugees from Pakistan, Bangladesh, and Afghanistan and undocumented, non-Muslim Indian citizens are exempt from such requirements (Laliwala 2020). In doing so, the CAA effectively discriminates against both Muslims and working-class Indians who do not possess legal documentation to prove their citizenship status. Conversely, the NRC refers to the National Registry of Citizens which the BJP moved to implement statewide in India, after initially executing the registry in the state of Assam against the backdrop of tensions between undocumented Bangladeshi migrants lacking documentation, Bengali Muslims, and indigenous Assamese populations (Gajjala et al. 2023). Passage of the CAA combined with nation-wide implementation of the NRC to register citizens essentially functioned to exclude Muslim Indians from the state polity on a national level (K. Bhatia and Gajjala 2020, 6287). The CAA-NRC is the culmination of the BJP's adherence to a form of "exclusionary religious nationalism that imagines India as a solely Hindu country" and actualizes this through processes of legal Saffronization (E. Edwards and Ford 2021)

The passage of the CAA-NRC in India sparked massive national and transnational protests by Indians, student groups, and other allied coalitions, in particular, a collective of working-class, Muslim Indian women in Delhi named the "Women of Shaheen Bagh" who viewed these policies as discriminatory towards Muslims and a fundamental threat to India's secular constitution (Bhatia and Gajjala 2020, 6294). And while forms of transnational digital protests blossomed on Twitter linking American, UK, and Indian digital collectives united in their opposition to the CAA-NRC and Islamophobic governmental policies (E. Edwards et al. 2020; Khandelwal 2022), this period was also characterized by the fostering of pro-CAA-NRC Indian and American white far-right networks united in their opposition to the presence and inclusion of Muslim communities in society—whether the US or India, New Delhi or Arkansas.

Just as anti-CAA-NRC Twitter publics emerged circulating affective, gendered content, in this case, images of working-class Muslim Indian mothers and grandmothers peacefully protesting in New Delhi that appealed to national and global audiences (Edwards et al. 2021, 4), far-right Islamophobic networks on Twitter instrumentalized the CAA-NRC as a form of content which trafficked in similar placed-based forms affect. As Somdeep Sen has argued in discussing the fall-out from the passage of the CAA-NRC "the scourge of Hindu nationalism has gone global" (2022). It has re-surfaced among white American far-right nationalists who enter into Indian nationalist Twitter-scapes lending support to the cause.

@Saffron_Tweeter in fact sources parts of their Islamophobic content from Western Christian, far-right writers, Tweeting: "[o]pen, free, democratic societies are particularly vulnerable... 'When politically correct, tolerant, and culturally diverse societies agree to Muslim demands for their religious privileges, some of the other components tend to creep in as well' #Islamization..." (Saffron Tweeter 2019d), quoting from a book entitled, *Slavery, Terrorism & Islam: The Historical Roots and Contemporary Threat* (2005), which bills itself as a "documented response to the relentless anti-Christian propaganda that has been generated by Muslim and marxist [sic] groups and by Hollywood film makers" (Hammond 2005). The book is authored by South African-born Christian missionary Peter Hammond, who has written various Islamophobic texts and, critically, published with American vanity Christian press, Xulon Publishing, owned by a Christian conservative media conglomerate Salem Media Group (Hammond 2015).

Salem Media Group is a "conservative media juggernaut" which supports the production of Christian conservative books, films, podcasts, and radio and has peddled in American election and voter (mis)information (Kang and Hsu 2022). As such, within a single Tweet, we can see the confluence of constituencies brought together—South African Evangelicals, Hindu nationalists, and American Christian conservatives—all united through the shared value of Islamophobia. We also see the emergence of transnational linkages posited between Muslim communities, the film industry in Hollywood, and "marxists" that figure centrally in far-right thinking.

@Saffron_Tweeter, deploying arguments made by Hammond, positions Muslim societies as the opposite of Western nations—that Western nations are supposedly "politically correct," tolerant, and culturally diverse. Thereby suggesting that Muslim nations are regressive, intolerant and highly religious, implicitly aligning India with what is imagined as the Christian democratic West. While this Tweet simply regurgitates well-worn racialized tropes about Muslims in the form of contemporary "cultural racism" that harkens back to historic forms of Orientalism, Islamophobia, and civilizationalist rhetoric familiar in European political contexts (Buettner 2016), what is different here is that Indian Hindu nationalists are actively repurposing this rhetoric to speak to sympathetic American audiences abroad as well as Indian coalitions at home.

@Saffron_Tweeter also strategically presents a series of decontextualized and unverified statistics regarding violence, terrorism, and Muslim communities in various regions outside of South Asia that resonate not only with Indian users but white Americans as well who are affectively motivated by the same rhetoric of homeland securitization and fears of demographic change, Tweeting: "[a]t 40 %, nations experience widespread massacres, chronic terror attacks, and ongoing militia warfare, such as in: Bosnia – Muslim 40 % Chad – Muslim 53.1 % Lebanon – Muslim 59.7% #Islamization #Need_For_CAA_NRC 13/n" (Saffron Tweeter 2019a). Naturally, these unfounded statistics also do not engage with the historic source of potential state-destabilization in majority Muslim-nations; Western imperialism (Abu-Lughod 2013). Rather, @Saffron_Tweeter suggests that as the percentage of Muslims in countries grows, states experience more violence, thereby attempting to justify the passage of the CAA-NRC and the exclusion of Muslims from Indian civic life as an issue of national security.

Within the context of this Tweet, @Saffron_Tweeter effectively collapses distances between India, the US, and Bosnia. The imagined geographies of Bosnia and Lebanon as majority-Muslim violent, war-torn locations become fodder in the argument for supporting the CAA-NRC. And, invoking the specter of violence in these societies allows far-right actors to conveniently manifest and present violence and invasion as if not visible in one's local community or nation, as then lurking on the edges of their borders. The presence of Muslim communities in other societies or instances of terrorism abroad become relevant and motivating to domestic coalitions who imagine themselves as part of a larger collective, of Western, or we may say Aryan civilization.

The strategic oscillation between various national contexts and collapsing of boundaries thus facilitates the emergence of transnational far-right coalitions that do not fully dispense with nationalist politics but re-apply them at will. As Rogers Brubaker has noted in discussing the emergence of far-right populist political movements in Europe and the US, "the civilizational overlay of nationalist rhetoric is increasingly pronounced, and the semantics of self and other are rearticulated in broadly civilizational rather than narrowly national terms" (2017, 1211). This is particularly apparent on platforms such as Twitter where far-right users situate themselves and one another through civilationalist terms even as nationalist rhetoric and assertation of exclusionary boundaries remains pronounced. The notion of Western civilization has itself become mutable, with Hindu nationalists destabilizing historic articulations of West and East by asserting that ideology, here of religious and racialization nationalism, is a more powerful than physical location.

And if far-right American and Indian national communities are increasingly engaging with one another across "cultural and political space" (Brubaker 2017, 1211), then the site of the home and family become an important locator as well, imagined on a nationalized scale through the rhetoric of demography. @Saffron_Tweeter, in their last Tweet in a long thread states "...their [Muslim] birth rates dwarf the birth rates of Christians, Hindus, Buddhists, Jews, and all other believers. Muslims will exceed 50% of the world's population by the end of this century #Islamization #ISupportCAA_NRC 21/21" (Saffron Tweeter 2019c). Here, suggesting that Muslim immigration will change the racial and religious composition of nations. In this case, @Saffron_Tweeter situates the family as a specific site of contention. For far-right Hindu nationalists both the home and nation are in need of securitization, and in this case, the policy prescription is through the passage of the CAA-NRC, which in its design sought to ease access to citizenship for Hindu migrants and disenfranchise Muslim Indians within the state.

So, while this type of content @Saffron_Tweet is producing focuses explicitly on Indian citizenship policy and the CAA-NRC, we see that discussion and mediation of Indian nationalism is intertwined with historic Islamophobic tropes and civilizationalist rhetoric that destabilizes existing conceptions between West/East. Just as Sabina Mihelj and César Jiménez-Martínez have noted in discussing how new media technologies facilitate greater "affective individual engagement with nationalism [to] form a myriad of 'niche' or 'bespoke' nationalisms" (2020, 339), these far-right actors on Twitter, through individual consumption and engagement with Islamophobic hate-speech are forming a particular and powerful form of bespoke *trans*nationalism. This form of bespoke Islamophobic transnationalism articulated across Indian and American Twitter networks is produced through these series of everyday, mundane practices and discourses which then form the basis of imagined far-right geographies online (Mihelj and Jiménez-Martínez 2020, 342).

Here we have explored an illustrative fragment of the type of content produced by far-right Hindu nationalists and its strategic oscillation between Indian national contexts, external states, and larger imaginative concepts of Eastern and Western civilization, and seen how themes of home(land) securitization, terrorism, and demographic change dominate, finding purchase with users across multiple national publics on Twitter. But the question remains, if the Hindu nationalist, pro-CAA-NRC, BJP-supporting Indian Twitter-sphere is the domestic audience for such content, who comprises the American national coalition? And, how does this type of content travel from Indian BJP trolls to white American far-right audiences ostensibly not involved with the specificities of Indian citizenship policy? Why is it that users like @HembG, now since suspended, who love Jesus Christ, the USA, and Trump (HembG 2020), or @snadp, who are American patriots that are "Pro-Life" and "Love Capitalism" (Laurel 2020), are interested in and engaged by far-right Hindu nationalist content?

If Hindu nationalist Indian Twitter users are the producers and origin sources of racialized Islamophobic discourse on Twitter, then far-right white American micro-influencers act as the information brokers across these seemingly disparate enclaves. Micro-influencers on Twitter do not merely operate to hawk products to audiences which perceive them as more authentic (Park et al. 2021), rather, micro-influencers can be powerful political messengers and can even inspire their followers to take material action (Alampi 2019). Organic far-right American micro-influencers, unverified yet active users with respectable followings, are the actors which introduce domestic white American audiences to discourses of far-right Hindu nationalism to bolster American Islamophobia.

This transmission of content occurs through users like @jrambo727, a #Christian #MAGA supporter who has over 5,000 followers (jrambo727 2020), a much larger reach than @Saffron_Tweeter's 2,000. Or through even more established accounts like @ClaraLKatzenmai who spreads this content even further to an audience of over 38,000 followers pushing the boundaries of a micro-influencer designation (Anger and Kittl 2011, 3). This is a much larger community than the population of Flippin, Arkansas, 1,343, she locates herself in. @ClaraLKatzenmai describes herself as, "[X] PATRIOT stands with our greatest ever President TRUMP. I LOVE AMERICA. https://t.co/JvLiNWE4BQ WE NEED TO STAND UNITED #MAGA #KAG [X]" (ClaraLKatzenmai 2020), linking in her biography to her Gab account, illustrating the importance of cross-platform symbiosis between "alt-tech" and mainstream platforms among far-right actors in a contemporary platformed media ecosystem (Johnson et al. 2022).

The social media platform Gab bills itself as an alternative to Twitter under the guise of allowing total free speech due to an absence of moderation policies, and as such, it has become a haven for white supremacists, misogynists, and Holocaust deniers who have been permanently banned from Twitter for violating its hate-speech policies (Canales 2021). However, while in its Securities and Exchange Commission filing, the company stated it had 1,157,000 users (Gab 2020), other estimates place its active userbase at 100,000 (Lee 2021), whereas Twitter has roughly 229,000,000 active users (Perez 2022). While @ClaraLKatzenmai may now be suspended from Twitter, she was a prolific poster, not only bolstering content from far-right Hindu nationalists, but circulating election conspiracy theories during the January 6th insurrection, coming in as one of the top 10,000 most frequent posters on this topic (Brown 2020).

Looking at how these far-right American and Indian network actors interact; we see not only the confluence between a series of global crises including the passage of the CAA-NRC and subsequent protests in December 2019 and comparatively the contestation of the 2020 American presidential election, but we also see how reactionary ideologies overlap; Trumpism in the US and Hindu nationalism in India which collide in digital spaces like Twitter. We also begin to see hints of the broader platformed media ecology far-right actors operate within. If Reddit, for example, serves as the "front-page" of the Internet where extremist content from sites such as 4chan and 8kun surfaces (Lagorio-Chafkin 2018; Zannettou et al. 2017), Twitter, rather, functions imperfectly as the Internet's digital town square, as suggested by its newest majority-stakeholder Elon Musk (E. Edwards 2022), with multiple raucous enclaves and counter-publics all congregating therein.

However, this is a public square which functions less like Jürgen Habermas' conceptualization of the public sphere as a space where public opinion is mediated by a limited group of elite professionals (2006, 416), and more like the fractious, oscillating (counter-)publics discussed by Sarah Florini wherein "material affordances are combined with culturally specific communicative practices that create a space for both intragroup discussion and direct counter-public debate" and often involve off-platform migration and movement (2019, 73). The national and local publics which emerge on Twitter are unlike the Habermasian public which is both conceived as singular and attached to a mode of liberal democratic politics which does not neatly fit in with new political practices of transnational digital activism and coalition building (Bruns and Highfield 2015, 124).

Twitter platforms a cacophony voices, facilitating the formulation of far-right *trans*nationalisms that imagine and mediate affective geographies and a shared political ideology with unique local expressions. Looking below the surface of content, a single viral Tweet thread reveals a confluence of platforms and industries that lurk behind conversations circulated on mainstream social media platforms—such as Gab and Salem Media Group. And Twitter as a mainstream social media site is a critical space for groups to come together and form these transnational connections. While there is a growing network of nationally specific alt-tech social media sites, such as the American-dominated Gab and Parler, or the Indian microblogging platform Koo with a larger user-base of BJP-supporters (Bhat 2021), Twitter remains a key part of the larger online far-right infrastructure that encourages multiple nationalist far-right groups to come together and forge transnational networked connections, with users then filtered back to external extremist platforms.

Far-right Islamophobic hate-speech, even when couched in nationally specific contexts, resonates beyond national borders. While Islamophobic far-right digitally networked communities may be invested in projects of racial and religious nationalism, they are also glocal communities. Stories and content become de-spatialized in digital contexts and re-circulated to emphasize an affective proximity of imperilment where myths of "Islamic terrorism" abroad in India or Bosnia are indicative of potential future domestic attacks. With the US "'ground zero'" for the implementation of Hindutva abroad (Purohit 2022a), these bonds that are fostered between white Americans and Indian Hindu nationalists both in India and in diaspora signal the necessity of not simply examining Islamophobia hate-speech in digital spaces as a transnational crisis, but beginning to situate Islamophobic domestic policies, here in India with the case of the CAA-NRC, as constitutive of a larger global turn towards the articulation of a far-right civilationalist populist political movement. In as the next section, we examine the way in which German far-right ethnonationalist networks on Twitter circulate Islamophobic hate-speech, repurposing local stories. Tapping into not civilizationalist frames but utilizing localized associations and historic rhetoric of racializing urban spaces as sites of religious, ethnic diversity and violent crime.

Der Islamischen Republik Deutschland (IRD): Mosques & Misinformation

On March 26th, 2020 @Netzdenunziant Tweeted, "Eine weitere Aufnahme der islamischen Machtdemonstration aus Duisburg. Der Muezzin der Merkez-Moschee beglückt die weltoffene Nachbarschaft der Islamischen Republik Deutschland (IRD) mit seinem Ruf zum Gebet. #NichtMeinDeutschland #Islamisierung" (Klarname 2020), which translates to, "[a]nother recording of the Islamic demonstration of power from Duisburg. The Muezzin of Merkez-Mosques pleases the liberal-minded neighborhood of the Islamic Republic of Germany with his call to prayer." The Tweet features a video of a minaret in the city Duisburg with the original content sourced from user @AbiAltun, who identifies themselves as affiliated with the mosque in Duisburg (ALtun 2015). This video of the mosque is disembedded from its original context by German micro-influencer @Netzdenunziant, who describes themselves as an "Überzeugter AfD-Wähler" or "enthusiastic AfD-voter" (Klarname 2018), with over 8,000 followers.

In this single Tweet we are transported to a particular neighborhood in the German city of Duisburg that serves as the space through which far-right actors make a larger argument about the supposed Islamization of the entire German nation. Here, neighborhood-level changes herald the coming of the Islamic Republic of Germany. Far-right users in the German Twitter-sphere are strategic in their presentation of local issues as evidence of supposed nation-level religious and demographic changes, triangulating multiple spaces; neighborhoods, cities, and the larger state, to focus upon visible and aural expresses of religiosity in German society, whether the call to prayer or the physical architectural presence of mosques. If far-right American and Indian users feverishly trade Islamophobic viral conspiracies that take place abroad, German users flip the script, disembedding local stories from regional contexts to nationalize German political discourse on Twitter.

While this viral Tweet plays upon long-standing European Islamophobic rhetoric focused on protesting the establishment of mosques (Betz 2013), it also emphasizes a supposed foreign physical and aural encroachment upon local Christian German communities by Muslims cast as foreigners in the state, and, conversely, suggests the natural, ethnic German right to public and local spaces at the expense of other communities. This local-national figuring stretches back in German history to the articulation of a German *Heimat* that became a "mediating concept between local life and abstract nation" (Confino 2000; Sutherland 2011, 1). Today, we witness a similar strategic mediation between local context and nation-state on social media through the sometimes subtle and often explicit invocation of the *Heimat.*

A key part of this assertion of ethnonationalism, of ethnic German possession of space and state, is the articulation of a linkage between what is termed *weltoffene,* "cosmopolitan," and of racial and religious diversity as being the antithesis of the German nation. We see this here with the hashtag *#NichtMeinDeutschland,* "not my Germany." The historical connection of cosmopolitanism with Jewish communities has been used in service of antisemitic persecution during the Nazi period (Sznaider 2015), which associated Jewish communities with notions of "rootlessness and disloyalty" and thus not merely outside the imagined and material community of the state but a potential destabilizing threat to its continuity and cohesiveness (Sutherland 2011, 1). Today, Nazi-era charges of cosmopolitanism are repurposed to Other and racialize contemporary Muslim communities within the state (Mandel 2008). Within the short space of a Tweet, these histories and ideologies collide, deployed to target Muslims in Duisburg and the larger German nation.

Far-right German communities on Twitter are adept at crafting narratives of local spaces under siege to affectively invoke the notion of a nation under attack if not in one's local neighborhood, then just miles away. Enter Duisburg. A single city but a form of code within the far-right German lexicon for a complex, racialized media narrative that brings together anti-immigrant sentiment, Islamophobia, racism, and rhetorics of crime and disorder. Duisburg, located at the conjunction of the Rhine and Ruhr rivers, is a relatively nondescript city in Western Germany, a former steel town caught up in larger national processes of deindustrialization and in the 2017 federal German election, a surprising bastion of AfD support (Hospers 2004, 148; Staudenmaier 2017). In many ways, much like the decaying, deindustrialized cities and towns of the American Rustbelt, former Democratic areas that swung heavily for President Trump in the 2016 American presidential election (McQuarrie 2017).

Duisburg is a political symbol not only as it represents these larger trends of German deindustrialization, but since the early 2000s the city has grown increasingly diverse with a substantial population of Turkish immigrants located in the Marxloh neighborhood (Ehrkamp 2003). Since the 2010s, particularly in the aftermath of the Syrian Refugee Crisis 2015 and the increased political prominence of the AfD on the national German scene, Duisburg became a frequent topic of discussion even in the mainstream German media. Due to its growing immigrant population and percentage of citizens with a *Migrationshintergrund,* a legal-category with racial and ethnonationalist overtones that refers to German citizens with foreign parentage (Rühlmann and McMonagle 2019), frequently Turkish-Germans, Duisburg become a media symbol of what former President Frank-Walter Steinmeier noted in his visit to the neighborhood as "the country's problems – with migration, with structural change" (Schumacher 2018).

Duisburg's Marxloh has been termed the "most dangerous neighborhood in Germany," or a "no-go" zone (Schumacher 2018). The phrase "no-go zone" has been deployed by American Republican politicians in recent years to falsely and luridly allege certain areas in the US were controlled by Muslims implementing Sharia law, such as in Dearborn, Michigan (Bowe 2018). The demographics of Marxloh, a neighborhood where 64 % of residents have a *Migrationshintergrund* has received the most emphasis in the media (Schumacher 2018), associating both immigrants and Turkish-Germans with exaggerated stories of crime and economic decay. Duisburg and Marxloh in particular have been cast as a city and neighborhood out of control where *"[f]rauen sind auf der Straße nicht mehr sicher"* (Wüllenweber 2018), or where (white) women are no longer safe on the streets. Even as such rhetoric has been documented as both highly racialized and false by on-the-ground reporting of conditions in Marxloh (Wüllenweber 2018), this designation persists. Choosing to highlight Duisburg and this particular mosque, which when it opened in 2008 was the largest mosque in the country (Reuters 2008), taps into these larger gendered and racialized anti-immigrant and anti-Muslim discourses.

Tweeting about Duisburg not only illustrates an explicit attempt to tap into these historic racialized discourses of national imperilment, of the pretension voiced by former Interior Minister Horst Seehofer that "Islam does not belong to Germany" (Staudenmaier 2018), but it is an example of the similar ways in which American rhetoric and racialized ideologies, of the white possessive claim towards space, public and private, is similarly expressed in Germany (Sullivan 2006, 10). Assertions of an ethnically homogenous, Christian German *Heimat* are expressed through material environments but also become visible and legible through the digital landscape of Twitter. Just as American far-right coalitions engage with Islamophobic content that imagines Islamic invasion abroad, German users see Duisburg and Marxloh as stand-ins for the larger German nation. Places, both real and imagined, become affectively symbolic within far-right German circles, and these assertions of the interconnectivity between land, culture, and ethnicity once presupposed by German philosopher Johann Gottfried Herder (1800) during early articulations of the German ethnostate have resurfaced in digital environments (Brubaker 1994). For far-right German users, all politics is local just as all local issues are national.

The Far-Right Gone Global: Islamophobia and Transnational Racial Possessives

Communities on Twitter may not be separated by physical borders, but far-right actors located in a variety of state settings congregate on the platform to articulate particular claims to space, whether that is the nation or the neighborhood. And they do so through the articulation of possessive racial geographies not only in the US, but also in Germany and India. Far-right actors, whether asserting a claim to homeland, *Heimat,* or Hindutva articulate a possessive yet quotidian claim towards delineating what Judith Weisenfeld has theorized as "religio-racial" boundaries (2017), in this case of the physical, imagined, and digital state.

Anne Sullivan in discussing everyday expressions of white supremacy notes that in American contexts "white people tend to act and think as if all spaces— whether geographical, pyschical, linguistic, economic, spiritual, bodily, or other-wise—are or should be available for them to move in and out of as they wish" (2006, 10), and this applies to digital platforms like Twitter. Here, far-right users cir-culate spatial content to both bolster their own religio-racial claims to the nation, whether the US, Germany, or India, as well as to create cross-coalitional civilation-alist subjectivities, strategically excluding and racializing Muslims.

We see the logics of racialized possession at work in German contexts through discussion of the Duisburg Mosque and by Hindu nationalist users who argue in support of the CAA-NRC. Sonia Sikka has argued that expressions of Islamophobia in India should be understood as a form of racism that has ideological and histor-ical parallels to expressions of white supremacy in the US and German Nazi-era forms of ethnonationalism and culturalized racism (Sikka 2022). This is to say that if we can understand Islamophobia as operating in transnational contexts as a racialized "global project" (Bonds 2019, 2), its expressions are then naturally "grounded in specific places" whereby these spaces (Bonds 2019, 2), while unique and distinct, become disembedded on Twitter and transnationalized.

Racialized possessive geographies motivate users across a political spectrum and while the land in question may differ from user to user, nation to nation (Sul-livan 2006), operationally, possessive racialized geographies manifest on the flat space of Twitter. Increasingly far-right actors see themselves as linked in battle with compatriots and thereby view themselves as having either a claim or invested interest in what's going on in Arkansas or New Delhi or Duisburg. The converse of this dynamic then, is that Muslim communities are imagined as both a homoge-nous and globally suspect group, and Hindu Indians, white Americans, and ethnic Germans are imagined as united together.

In this way, Islamophobic discourse on Twitter in practice is defined by the expression of transnational racial possessive logics, which previously have been deployed to describe the relationship between global structures of white supremacy, settler colonialism, and land (Moreton-Robinson 2015), but here illuminate the digital civilationalist conflict raging on mainstream social media platforms. And in this case, it is Indian Hindu nationalists who increasingly are the producers of Islamophobic digital content and seek to emphasize the notion of a united Western civilization, with the West referring less to a geographical area than an imagined cultural, racial community, including the US, Europe, and India—a common Aryan civilization.

In this illustrative example of these dynamics, of the expression of transnational racial possessives, is @BhushanLalKoul2 who posts "[i]f you thought #Islamization of #Europe was just a myth made up by #right_wing conspiracy theorists, you are dumb, deaf and blind. Here is #Rome by the way. Your beloved vacation destination. #maga #coronavirus #AfricaDay @secretnstrange9 @pdkamath @Lots_Of_Fun_69   @Cold_Peace_   https://t.co/SKU9B09dDa" (BhushanLalKoul2 2020). @BhushanLalKoul2 has since been suspended and the content of the account scrubbed, but the post speaks to the way in which far-right Hindu nationalists aim to racialize Muslim communities, but not necessarily in India, but abroad in Europe, highlighting patterns of North African immigration to Italy. Hindu nationalist Islamophobia is racialized and informed by a global ideology of anti-Black racism, articulating this ideological argument by hijacking a hashtag, #AfricaDay, which refers to the yearly celebration of the founding of the Organisation of African Unity, now the (AU), on the continent in 1963 and more broadly the history and culture of the continent (Shahid 2022). Here, Rome becomes a symbol for the supposed Islamization of Europe writ large, and a possible harbinger of Islamization in India.

Tagging the post with #maga when discussing this supposed Islamization of Rome and also mentioning it in the context of a vacation destination also implicitly suggests that while Europe, and Rome in particular, may be the geographical setting discussed here, this conversation is fundamentally directed outward, not to Romans, Italians or Europeans, but Indians and white Americans, likely middle-classed, socially conversative, for whom a trip to Europe is not out of the question as a family vacation. In this case here, Indian far-right actors on Twitter transform Europe into a symbol of racialized disorder and chaos.

Perhaps even more critically than the deployment of rhetorics of place in the content is the way in which actors like @BhushanLalKoul2 act as connectors between various far-right nationalist discourses in Europe, the US, and India, made evident through strategic "@"ing which can be understood as a way in which peripheral, non-verified users create discursive pressures and bring various actors together through Twitter's affordances (E. Edwards and Stephens 2023). Tagging a series of users including a MAGA micro-influencer @secretnstrange9 with over 15,000 followers (Secret Strangers Wife 2019), @pdkamath, a supporter of the Hindu nationalist paramilitary organization the RSS Swayamsevak (Kamath 2008), and finally the account of Jeff M. Smith, a research fellow specializing in the region of South Asia at the right-wing conservative think-tank the Heritage Foundation with roughly 54,000 followers (J. M. Smith 2011), all further underscores the transnational dimension of Islamophobic digitally networked publics, as users begin investing in religio-racial projects at home and abroad.

The flattening quality of Twitter and its propensity to disembed discourse is precisely connected to what Anthony Giddens has theorized as the disembedding or "'lifting out' of social relations from local contexts…and their restructuring across indefinite spans of time-space" (Giddens 1990, 21). Twitter, in particular, due to its structuration compared to the affordances of the long-form blog, invites communication to occur in limited forms of text which, as a byproduct, has produced communicative styles which are less nuanced, more extreme, and of course, more open and less siloed (Ott 2017). Twitter thus not only disembeds localized or nationalized social relations across various networks, but it lifts spaces out of their local contexts and allows them to be restructured and redeployed for a variety of ideological purposes.

In earlier years, we could point towards progressive activist use of Twitter to disembed local political relations to forge transnational, affective coalitions that were often correlated to physical places. During the 2010 #ArabSpring, Tahrir Square in Egypt was broadcast across the world (Tufekci 2017), in 2014 there was the #BringBackOurGirls campaign focusing on bringing home Nigerian schoolchildren, named the Chibok girls, stolen by the terrorist group Boko Haram in Chibok, Nigeria (Chiluwa and Ifukor 2015), and more recently in 2021 we have seen the trending hashtag #ShaheenBagh referencing a neighborhood in South Delhi where Muslim Indian women staged a peaceful sit-in protest against passage of the CAA-NRC (K. Bhatia and Gajjala 2020). In all of these cases, places have figured centrally into political communication and digital activism on Twitter, often amongst progressive, pro-democracy, and feminist networks. In each of these cases as well, these spaces were disembedded, lifted out of their local contexts in Egypt, Nigeria, and India, and mediated and discussed by networks of sympathetic supporters and digital activists, becoming transnational protest movements.

These same dynamics of affective disembedding are at work on the platform, but deployed not by progressive digerati, rather here utilized by everyday, casual, far-right users, whether BJP-supporting trolls or AfD micro-influencers. But, as this chapter has shown, far-right actors on Twitter do not need formal and widely adopted campaigns to be effective or affective. Instead, just as we have seen the turn in digital advertising towards more subtle, strategic marketing led by micro-influencers whose currency is authenticity and everydayness (Alampi

2019), this trend is visible in political communication too. Making racialized Islamophobia increasingly banal, or we may say authentic, catering to both existing far-right audiences and the broader public who may be sympathetic to far-right messaging but turned off from explicit, extreme rhetoric and language (Askanius and Keller 2021, 2536). And instead of any hashtag or symbol, place-based rhetoric walks a line of not explicitly running afoul of content moderation policies.

Physical spaces figure centrally into the far-right imagination, their community, and desired policies, and this is true on Twitter not in spite of the platform's propensity to disembed discourse and location, but because of it. The application of possessive religio-racial geographies may be unique in various national contexts of the US, India, and Germany, but in racializing spaces, far-right actors in fact open-up nationalized "enclaves" to sympathetic ideological partners to engage in transnational support of their racial projects (Florini 2019).

The expression and articulation of Islamophobic ideology is thus not merely an issue in Western democracies, or an increasingly disturbing feature of far-right Hindu nationalist politics in India, but it is a platformed and technological phenomenon undergirded in particular by Twitter's technical affordances of disembedding, which are increasingly mimicked by emergent tech platforms, such as Koo, which has lately become immensely popular with Brazilian users (Mehta 2022). And while major tech industry leaders such as Mark Zuckerberg extoll the development of the metaverse and Web3 as an idealized, digital utopia, free from the shackles of borders, a new untapped frontier (Yao 2022), this techno-optimistic naïveté has been shattered during the age of Web2 (Nakamura 2002).

User-generated nationalisms and user-generated religio-racial identities continue to emerge in digital spaces (Shahin 2020), produced by everyday, average users. And if place and space still matter even in platformed digital environments like Twitter, then what does the discursive terrain of these communities look like? Employing data analytic techniques to visualize the discursive networked contours of these communities sheds light on the way in which certain actors build supply chains of hate-speech on Twitter and beyond.

References

Abu-Lughod, Lila. 2013. *Do Muslim Women Need Saving?* Cambridge, MA: Harvard University Press.

Ahmed, Sara. 2013. *The Cultural Politics of Emotion.* New York: Routledge. https://doi.org/10.4324/9780203700372.

Alampi, Amanda. 2019. "The Future Is Micro: How to Build an Effective Micro-Influencer Programme." *Journal of Digital & Social Media Marketing* 7 (3): 203–8.

ALtun, Abdullah (Abbi). "Profile." Twitter, 2015. https://twitter.com/AbiAltun.

Anderson, Benedict. 1991. *Imagined Communities: Reflections on the Origin and Spread of Nationalism.* New York: Verso.

Anger, Isabel and Christian Kittl. "Measuring influence on Twitter." International Conference on Knowledge Management and Knowledge Technologies (2011).

Askanius, Tina, and Nadine Keller. 2021. "Murder Fantasies in Memes: Fascist Aesthetics of Death Threats and the Banalization of White Supremacist Violence." *Information, Communication & Society* 24 (16): 2522–39. https://doi.org/10.1080/1369118X.2021.1974517.

Betz, Hans-George. 2013. "Mosques, Minarets, Burqas and Other Essential Threats: The Populist Right's Campaign against Islam in Western Europe." In *Right-Wing Populism in Europe: Politics and Discourse,* edited by Ruth Wodak, Majid KhosraviNik, and Brigitte Mral, 71–87. London: Bloomsbury Publishing.

Bhat, Prashanth. 2021. "Platform Politics: The Emergence of Alternative Social Media in India." *Asia Pacific Media Educator* 31 (2): 269–76. https://doi.org/10.1177/1326365X211056699.

Bhatia, Aditi. 2020. "The 'Saffronisation' of India and Contemporary Political Ideology." *World Englishes* 39 (4): 568–80. https://doi.org/10.1111/weng.12494.

Bhatia, Kiran, and Radhika Gajjala. 2020. "Examining Anti-CAA Protests at Shaheen Bagh: Muslim Women and Politics of the Hindu India." *International Journal of Communication* 14: 6286–6303.

Bhatia, Kiran Vinod. 2022. "Hindu Nationalism Online: Twitter as Discourse and Interface." *Religions* 13 (8): 739. https://doi.org/10.3390/rel13080739.

Bonds, Anne. 2019. "Race and Ethnicity II: White Women and the Possessive Geographies of White Supremacy." *Progress in Human Geography.* https://doi.org/10.1177/0309132519863479.

Bowe, Nathan. 2018. "Stopping into Detroit Lakes, Newberger Ready to Take on Klobuchar." *Detroit Lakes Tribune,* July 11, 2018, sec. News. https://www.dl-online.com/news/stopping-into-detroit-lakes-newberger-ready-to-take-on-klobuchar.

Braun, Virginia, and Victoria Clarke. 2006. "Using Thematic Analysis in Psychology." *Qualitative Research in Psychology* 3: 77–101.

Braun, Virginia, Victoria Clarke, Nikki Hayfield, and Gareth Terry. 2019. "Thematic Analysis." In *Handbook of Research Methods in Health and Social Sciences,* edited by Pranee Liamputtong, 843–60. Singapore: Springer.

Brown, Travis. 2020. "Top-10k-Tweet-Counts.Csv." GitHub. 2020. https://gist.github.com/travisbrown/01b315f63b78de7474fc64968c4fe66b.

Brubaker, Rogers. 1994. *Citizenship and Nationhood in France and Germany.* Cambridge, MA: Harvard University Press.

Brubaker, Rogers. 2017. "Between Nationalism and Civilizationism: The European Populist Moment in Comparative Perspective." *Ethnic and Racial Studies* 40 (8): 1191–1226. https://doi.org/10.1080/01419870.2017.1294700.

Bruns, Axel, and Tim Highfield. 2015. "Is Habermas on Twitter?" In *The Routledge Companion to Social Media and Politics,* edited by Axel Bruns, Gunn Enli, Eli Skogerbø, Anders Olof Larsson, and Christian Christensen, 1st ed., 18. New York: Routledge.

Buettner, Elizabeth. *Europe after Empire: Decolonization, Society, and Culture.* Cambridge, UK: Cambridge University Press, 2016. http://ebookcentral.proquest.com/lib/nyulibrary-ebooks/detail.action?docID=4465179.

BhushanLalKoul2. "If You Thought #Islamization of #Europe Was Just a Myth Made up by #right_wing Conspiracy Theorists, You Are Dumb, Deaf and Blind. Here Is #Rome by the Way. Your Beloved Vacation Destination. #maga #coronavirus #AfricaDay @secretnstrange9

@pdkamath @Lots_Of_Fun_69 @Cold_Peace_ Https://T.Co/SKU9B09dDa." Twitter, May 25, 2020. https://twitter.com/BhushanLalKoul2/statuses/1264928961223634946.

Canales, Katie. "What Is Gab? The Far-Right Social Media Site That Google and Apple Banned and That Is Still Gaining Thousands of New Users after Twitter and Facebook Deplatformed Trump." *Business Insider,* January 11, 2021. https://www.businessinsider.com/what-is-gab-social-media-platform-free-speech-first-amendment-2021-1.

Chaturvedi, Swati. 2016. *I Am a Troll: Inside the Secret World of the BJP's Digital Army.* New Delhi: Juggernaut. https://www.abebooks.com/9789386228093/Troll-Secret-World-BJPs-Digital-9386228092/plp.

Chávez, Karma R. 2011. "Counter-Public Enclaves and Understanding the Function of Rhetoric in Social Movement Coalition-Building." *Communication Quarterly* 59 (1): 1–18. https://doi.org/10.1080/01463373.2010.541333.

Chiluwa, Innocent, and Presley Ifukor. 2015. "'War against Our Children': Stance and Evaluation in #BringBackOurGirls Campaign Discourse on Twitter and Facebook." *Discourse & Society* 26 (3): 267–96. https://doi.org/10.1177/0957926514564735.

ClaraLKatzenmai. "Profile." Twitter, July 25, 2020. https://twitter.com/ClaraLKatzenmai.

Confino, Alon. 2000. *The Nation as a Local Metaphor Wurttemberg, Imperial Germany, and National Memory, 1871–1918.* Chapel Hill, NC: University of North Carolina Press. https://uncpress.org/book/9780807846650/the-nation-as-a-local-metaphor/.

Dash, Saloni, Dibyendu Mishra, Gazal Shekhawat, and Joyojeet Pal. 2022. "Divided We Rule: Influencer Polarization on Twitter during Political Crises in India." *Proceedings of the International AAAI Conference on Web and Social Media* 16 (May): 135–46.

Edwards, Emily. 2022. "Musk Is Right: Twitter Should Be Treated like a Public Square." *The Drum,* April 27, 2022. https://www.thedrum.com/opinion/2022/04/27/musk-right-twitter-should-be-treated-public-square.

Edwards, Emily, Oladoyin Olubukola Abiona, Sarah Ford, Olayombo Tejumade Raji-Oyelade, Radhika Gajjala, and Riddhima Sharma. 2020. "Shaheen Bagh: Making Sense of (Re)Emerging 'Subaltern' Feminist Political Subjectivities in Hashtag Publics (Through a Mess of Computational Humanities Data Analyses)." In. Virtual.

Edwards, Emily, and Sarah Ford. 2021. "Women of Shaheen Bagh in Transnational Digital Publics." *Journal of Feminist Studies in Religion* 37 (2): 163–66.

Edwards, Emily Lynell, and David F Stephens Jr. 2023. "(Hash)Tagging Intersection(Ality): Black and Palestinian Experiences on Twitter." *Communication, Culture and Critique,* April, 1–8. https://doi.org/10.1093/ccc/tcad013.

Ehrkamp, Patricia. 2003. "Turkish Immigrants' Politics of Belonging: Identity, Assimilation Discourse, and the Transformation of Urban Space in Duisburg-Marxloh, Germany." Minneapolis: University of Minnesota. https://elibrary.ru/item.asp?id=6709946.

Eriksen, Thomas Hylland. 2007. "Nationalism and the Internet*." *Nations and Nationalism* 13 (1): 1–17. https://doi.org/10.1111/j.1469-8129.2007.00273.x.

Florini, Sarah. 2019. *Enclaves and Counter-Publics: Oscillating Networked Publics.* New York: NYU Press. https://doi.org/10.18574/nyu/9781479892464.003.0003.

Fraser, Nancy. 1990. "Rethinking the Public Sphere: A Contribution to the Critique of Actually Existing Democracy." *Social Text* 25/26: 56–80.

Gab. 2020. "GAB AI Inc Annual Report." Gab. https://www.sec.gov/Archives/edgar/data/1709244/000110465920067852/annual_report.pdf.

Gajjala, Radhika, Emily Lynell Edwards, Debipreeta Rahut, Ololade Margaret Faniyi, Bedadyuti Jha, Jhalak Jain, Aiman Khan, and Saadia Farooq. 2023. "Transnationalising Dadis as Feminist Political/Activist Subjects." *Feminist Encounters: A Journal of Critical Studies in Culture and Politics* 7 (1): 08. https://doi.org/10.20897/femenc/12886.

Ganesh, Bharath, and Caterina Froio. 2020. "A 'Europe Des Nations': Far Right Imaginative Geographies and the Politicization of Cultural Crisis on Twitter in Western Europe." *Journal of European Integration* 42 (5): 715–32. https://doi.org/10.1080/07036337.2020.1792462.

Garza, Alicia. 2014. "A Herstory of the #BlackLivesMatter Movement." *The Feminist Wire*, October 7, 2014.

Gatson, Sarah. 2011. "Self-Naming Practices on the Internet: Identity, Authenticity, and Community." *Cultural Studies Critical Methodologies* 11 (3): 224–35. https://doi.org/10.1177/1532708611409531.

Giddens, Anthony. 1990. *The Consequences of Modernity.* Redwood City, CA: Stanford University Press.

Gladwell, Malcolm. 2010. "Small Change." *The New Yorker*, September 27, 2010. https://www.newyorker.com/magazine/2010/10/04/small-change-malcolm-gladwell.

Habermas, Jürgen. 2006. "Political Communication in Media Society: Does Democracy Still Enjoy an Epistemic Dimension? The Impact of Normative Theory on Empirical Research." *Communication Theory* 16 (4): 411–26. https://doi.org/10.1111/j.1468-2885.2006.00280.x.

Hammond, Peter. 2005. *Slavery, Terrorism, and Islam The Historical Roots and Contemporary Threat.* Maitland, FL: Xulon Press.

Hammond, Peter. 2015. "What Islam Isn't." Virtue Online. 2015. https://virtueonline.org/what-islam-isnt-dr-peter-hammond.

Hayat, Muhammad, and Saira Abbasi. 2021. "Rise of Hindutva Mind-Set and Saffronisation of Indian Society" 9 (February): 9–21.

HembG. "Profile." Twitter, July 25, 2020. https://twitter.com/HembG.

Herder, Johann Gottfried. 1800. *Outlines of a Philosophy of the History of Man.* Berlin: Bergman Publishers.

Hospers, Gert-Jan. 2004. "Restructuring Europe's Rustbelt: The Case of the German Ruhrgebiet." *Intereconomics* 39 (3): 147–56. https://doi.org/10.1007/BF02933582.

Howard, Philip N., and Muzammil M. Hussain. 2013. *Democracy's Fourth Wave?: Digital Media and the Arab Spring.* Oxford Studies in Digital Politics. New York: Oxford University Press.

Jaffrelot, Christophe, and Gilles Verniers. 2020. "The BJP's 2019 Election Campaign: Not Business as Usual." *Contemporary South Asia* 28 (2): 155–77. https://doi.org/10.1080/09584935.2020.1765985.

Jenkins, Henry. 2013. "Twitter Revolutions?" In *Spreadable Media Creating Value and Meaning in a Networked Culture*, edited by Henry Jenkins, Sam Ford, and Joshua Green. New York: NYU Press. https://spreadablemedia.org/essays/jenkins/index.html.

Johnson, Hailey, Karl Volk, Robert Serafin, Cinthya Grajeda, and Ibrahim Baggili. 2022. "Alt-Tech Social Forensics: Forensic Analysis of Alternative Social Networking Applications." *Forensic Science International: Digital Investigation*, Proceedings of the Twenty-Second Annual DFRWS USA, 42 (July): 301406. https://doi.org/10.1016/j.fsidi.2022.301406.

Johnson, Hailey, Karl Volk, Robert Serafin, Cinthya Grajeda, and Ibrahim Baggili. "Alt-Tech Social Forensics: Forensic Analysis of Alternative Social Networking Applications." *Forensic Science International: Digital Investigation*, Proceedings of the Twenty-Second Annual DFRWS USA, 42 (July 1, 2022): 301406. https://doi.org/10.1016/j.fsidi.2022.301406.

jrambo727. "Profile." Twitter, February 25, 2020. https://twitter.com/jrambo727.

Kamath, PD. "Profile." Twitter, 2008. https://twitter.com/pdkamath.

Kang, Cecilia, and Tiffany Hsu. 2022. "The Rise of a Conservative Radio Juggernaut." *The New York Times*, October 17, 2022, sec. Technology. https://www.nytimes.com/2022/10/17/technology/salem-media-charlie-kirk-sebastian-gorka.html.

Kelly, Annie. 2017. "The Alt-Right: Reactionary Rehabilitation for White Masculinity." Eurozine. September 15, 2017. https://www.eurozine.com/the-alt-right-reactionary-rehabilitation-for-white-masculinity/.

Khandelwal, Chetna. 2022. "Networked Social Movements: A Critical Interrogation of Pro and Anti-Immigration Twitter Discourse in India and the USA." Master's Thesis, University of Calgary: Arts. https://doi.org/10.11575/PRISM/39722.

Klarname, Markus. "Eine Weitere Aufnahme Der Islamischen Machtdemonstration Aus Duisburg. Der Muezzin Der Merkez-Moschee Beglückt Die Weltoffene Nachbarschaft Der Islamischen Republik Deutschland (IRD) Mit Seinem Ruf Zum Gebet. #NichtMeinDeutschland #Islamisierung." Twitter, March 26, 2020. https://twitter.com/Netzdenunziant/status/1243047780437725186.

Klarname, Markus. "Profile." Twitter, 2018. https://twitter.com/Netzdenunziant.

Lagorio-Chafkin, Christine. 2018. *We Are the Nerds: The Birth and Tumultuous Life of Reddit, the Internet's Culture Laboratory*. Paris: Hachette.

Laliwala, Sharik. "Facing Bias, India's Muslims Are Rallying behind Its Secular Constitution, Not Radical Islam." *Quartz India*, February 20, 2020. https://qz.com/india/1805237/caa-nrc-make-indian-muslims-back-constitution-not-radical-islam/.

Laurel. "Profile." Twitter, July 25, 2020. https://twitter.com/snadp.

Lee, Micah. 2021. "Inside Gab, the Online Safe Space for Far-Right Extremists." *The Intercept*, March 15, 2021. https://theintercept.com/2021/03/15/gab-hack-donald-trump-parler-extremists/.

Leidig, Eviane Cheng. 2019. "Immigrant, Nationalist and Proud: A Twitter Analysis of Indian Diaspora Supporters for Brexit and Trump." *Media and Communication* 7 (1): 77–89. https://doi.org/10.17645/mac.v7i1.1629.

Lipsitz, George. 1995. "The Possessive Investment in Whiteness: Racialized Social Democracy and the 'White' Problem in American Studies." *American Quarterly* 47 (3): 369–87. https://doi.org/10.2307/2713291.

Mandel, Ruth. 2008. *Cosmopolitan Anxieties: Turkish Challenges to Citizenship and Belonging in Germany*. Durham, NC: Duke University Press.

McQuarrie, Michael. 2017. "The Revolt of the Rust Belt: Place and Politics in the Age of Anger." *The British Journal of Sociology* 68 (S1): S120–52. https://doi.org/10.1111/1468-4446.12328.

Mehta, Ivan. 2022. "Indian Social Network Koo Gains Popularity in Brazil but Faces Moderation Challenges." *TechCrunch*, November 22, 2022. https://techcrunch.com/2022/11/22/indian-social-network-koo-gains-popularity-in-brazil-but-faces-moderation-challenges/.

Michelsen, Nicholas, and Pablo de Orellana. 2020. "Pessimism and the Alt-Right: Knowledge, Power, Race and Time." In *Pessimism in International Relations Provocations, Possibilities, Politics*, edited by Tim Stevens and Nicholas Michelsen, 119–36. Cham: Springer International Publishing.

Mihelj, Sabina, and César Jiménez-Martínez. 2020. "Digital Nationalism: Understanding the Role of Digital Media in the Rise of 'New' Nationalism." *Nations and Nationalism* 27: 331–46. https://doi.org/10.1111/nana.12685.

Moreton-Robinson, Aileen. 2015. *The White Possessive Property, Power, and Indigenous Sovereignty*. Minneapolis, MN: University of Minnesota Press.

Nakamura, Lisa. 2002. *Cybertypes: Race, Ethnicity, and Identity on the Internet*. New York, NY: Routledge.

Ott, Brian L. 2017. "The Age of Twitter: Donald J. Trump and the Politics of Debasement." *Critical Studies in Media Communication* 34 (1): 59–68. https://doi.org/10.1080/15295036.2016.1266686.

Owens, Marcus. 2019. "Rupture: The Crisis Of Liberal Democracy By Manuel Castells." *Society + Space* (blog). September 9, 2019. https://www.societyandspace.org/articles/rupture-the-crisis-of-liberal-democracy-by-manuel-castells.

Papacharissi, Zizi. 2015a. "Affective Publics and Structures of Storytelling: Sentiment, Events and Mediality." *Information, Communication & Society* 19 (3): 307–24. https://doi.org/10.1080/1369118X.2015.1109697.

Papacharissi, Zizi. 2015b. *Affective Publics: Sentiment, Technology, and Politics.* Oxford, UK: Oxford University Press.

Park, Jiwoon, Ji Min Lee, Vikki Yiqi Xiong, Felix Septianto, and Yuri Seo. 2021. "David and Goliath: When and Why Micro-Influencers Are More Persuasive Than Mega-Influencers." *Journal of Advertising* 50 (5): 584–602. https://doi.org/10.1080/00913367.2021.1980470.

Perez, Sarah. 2022. "Twitter Says It Overcounted Its Users over the Past 3 Years." *TechCrunch* (blog). April 28, 2022. https://techcrunch.com/2022/04/28/twitter-says-it-overcounted-its-users-over-the-past-3-years-by-as-much-as-1-9m/.

Purohit, Kunal. 2022a. "The Deep, Disturbing Reach of India's Hindutva Agenda in Diaspora." *South China Morning Post*, October 15, 2022, sec. This Week in Asia. https://www.scmp.com/week-asia/people/article/3195976/uk-mob-violence-exposes-deep-disturbing-reach-indias-hindutva.

Purohit, Kunal. 2022b. "A Thread on How Hindutva Has Gone Global:" Twitter. October 16, 2022. https://twitter.com/kunalpurohit/status/1581840079022346243.

Reuters. 2008. "Germany Opens Its Biggest Mosque." *Reuters*, October 26, 2008, sec. World News. https://www.reuters.com/article/uk-germany-mosque-idUKTRE49P29A20081026.

Rühlmann, Liesa, and Sarah McMonagle. 2019. "Germany's Linguistic 'Others' and the Racism Taboo." *Anthropological Journal of European Cultures* 28 (2): 93–100. https://doi.org/10.3167/ajec.2019.280209.

Saffron Tweeter, Hogward Professor. "At 40%, Nations Experience Widespread Massacres, Chronic Terror Attacks, and Ongoing Militia Warfare," Such as in: Bosnia – Muslim 40% Chad – Muslim 53.1% Lebanon – Muslim 59.7% #Islamization #Need_For_CAA_NRC 13/n." Twitter, December 20, 2019. https://twitter.com/Sudharshan32/status/1258586566840238080.

Saffron Tweeter, Hogward Professor. "Dr. Peter Hammond's Book, 'Slavery, Terrorism and Islam,' Says "Islam Is Not a Religion, nor Is It a Cult. In Its Fullest Form, It Is a Complete, Total, 100% System of Life," "Islam Has Religious, Legal, Political, Economic, Social, and Military Components" #Islamization." Twitter, December 20, 2019. https://twitter.com/ShinBwhoa/status/1265314664352632833.

Saffron Tweeter, Hogward Professor. "'…He Further Says "But Their Birth Rates Dwarf the Birth Rates of Christians, Hindus, Buddhists, Jews, and All Other Believers. Muslims Will Exceed 50% of the World's Population by the End of This Century'" #Islamization #ISupportCAA_NRC 21/21"." Twitter, December 20, 2019. https://twitter.com/search?q=%22...He%20further%20says%20"But%20their%20birth%20rates%20dwarf%20the%20birth%20rates%20of%20Christians%2C%20Hindus%2C%20Buddhists%2C%20Jews%2C%20and%20all%20other%20believers.%20Muslims%20will%20exceed%2050%25%20of%20the%20world's%20population%20by%20the%20end%20of%20this%20century%22%22%C2%A0%20%20%23Islamization%20%20%23ISupportCAA_NRC%20%20%2021%2F21%22&src=typed_query.

Saffron Tweeter, Hogward Professor. "'Open, Free, Democratic Societies Are Particularly Vulnerable. He Says "When Politically Correct, Tolerant, and Culturally Diverse Societies Agree to Muslim

Demands for Their Religious Privileges, Some of the Other Components Tend to Creep in as Well'". #Islamization 5/n"." Twitter, December 20, 2019. https://twitter.com/jrconse/statuses/1256207275850633216.

Saffron Tweeter, Hogward Professor. "Profile." Twitter, July 25, 2020. https://twitter.com/Saffron_Tweeter.

Sahgal, Gita. 2020. "Hindutva Past and Present: From Secular Democracy to Hindu Rashtra." *Feminist Dissent*, no. 5: 19–49. https://doi.org/10.31273/fd.n5.2020.757.

Said, Edward W. 1979. *Orientalism*. New York, NY: Vintage Books.

Schumacher, Elizabeth. 2018. "German President Visits 'no-Go' Duisburg Neighborhood." *DW*, March 18, 2018, sec. Germany. https://www.dw.com/en/german-president-visits-no-go-duisburg-neighborhood/a-42960955.

Secret Strangers Wife. "Profile." Twitter, 2019. https://twitter.com/secretnstrange9.

Sen, Somdeep. 2022. "Hindu Nationalists Now Pose a Global Problem." *Al Jazeera*, September 26, 2022. https://www.aljazeera.com/opinions/2022/9/26/violent-hindu-extremism-is-now-a-global-problem.

Shahid, Abdulla. 2022. "Africa Day 2022." Presented at the 76th session of the United Nations General Assembly, New York, May 25. https://www.un.org/pga/76/2022/05/25/africa-day-2022/.

Shahin, Saif. 2020. "User-Generated Nationalism: Interactions with Religion, Race, and Partisanship in Everyday Talk Online." *Information, Communication & Society*, 1–16. https://doi.org/10.1080/1369118X.2020.1748088.

Sikka, Sonia. 2022. "Indian Islamophobia as Racism." *The Political Quarterly* 93 (3): 469–77. https://doi.org/10.1111/1467-923X.13152.

Singh, Rishika. 2022. "The History and Debates about 'Socialist' and 'Secular' in the Preamble of the Constitution." *Indian Express*, September 4, 2022. https://indianexpress.com/article/explained/indian-constitution-preamble-socialist-secular-8129656/.

Smith, Jeff M. "Profile." Twitter, 2011. https://twitter.com/Cold_Peace_.

Squires, Catherine R. 2002. "Rethinking the Black Public Sphere: An Alternative Vocabulary for Multiple Public Spheres." *Communication Theory* 12 (4): 446–68. https://doi.org/10.1111/j.1468-2885.2002.tb00278.x.

Staudenmaier, Rebecca. 2017. "'Forgotten' Duisburg Voters Turn to AfD." *DW*, September 25, 2017. https://www.dw.com/en/forgotten-duisburg-voters-turn-to-germanys-far-right-afd/a-40679900.

Staudenmaier, Rebecca. 2018. "Seehofer: 'Islam Does Not Belong to Germany.'" *DW*, March 16, 2018. https://www.dw.com/en/german-interior-minister-horst-seehofer-islam-doesnt-belong-to-germany/a-42999726.

Suk, Jiyoun, Aman Abhishek, Yini Zhang, So Yun Ahn, Teresa Correa, Christine Garlough, and Dhavan V. Shah. 2021. "#MeToo, Networked Acknowledgment, and Connective Action: How 'Empowerment Through Empathy' Launched a Social Movement." *Social Science Computer Review* 39 (2): 276–94. https://doi.org/10.1177/0894439319864882.

Sullivan, Shannon. 2006. *Revealing Whiteness The Unconscious Habits of Racial Privilege*. Bloomington and Indianapolis, IN: Indiana University Press.

Sutherland, Claire. 2011. "Cosmopolitanism and the Study of German Politics." *German Politics and Society* 29 (3): 1–19. https://doi.org/10.3167/gps.2011.290301.

Sznaider, Natan. 2015. "Hannah Arendt: Jew and Cosmopolitan." *Socio. La Nouvelle Revue Des Sciences Sociales*, no. 4 (April): 197–221. https://doi.org/10.4000/socio.1359.

Tufekci, Zeynep. 2017. *Twitter and Tear Gas: The Power and Fragility of Networked Protest*. New Haven, CT: Yale University Press.

Twitter. 2022. "About Twitter | Our Company and Priorities." Twitter. 2022. https://about.twitter.com/.

Warner, Michael. 2002. "Publics and Counterpublics." *Public Culture* 14 (1): 49–90.

Weisenfeld, Judith. *New World A-Coming Black Religion and Racial Identity during the Great Migration.* New York: NYU Press, 2017. https://nyupress.org/9781479888801/new-world-a-coming.

Wüllenweber, Walter. 2018. "In Deutschland gibt es No-Go-Areas, behaupten Populisten. Ein Ortsbesuch." *Stern*, October 8, 2018. https://www.stern.de/politik/deutschland/deutschland–no-go-areas–ortsbesuch-in-duisburg-marxloh-und-neukoelln-8206968.html.

Yao, Deborah. 2022. "SXSW 2022: Meta CEO Mark Zuckerberg Says Metaverse Is the Internet's next Chapter." *AI Business*, March 15, 2022. https://aibusiness.com/verticals/sxsw-2022-meta-ceo-mark-zuckerberg-says-metaverse-is-the-internet-s-next-chapter.

Zannettou, Savvas, Tristan Caulfield, Emiliano De Cristofaro, Nicolas Kourtelris, Ilias Leontiadis, Michael Sirivianos, Gianluca Stringhini, and Jeremy Blackburn. 2017. "The Web Centipede: Understanding How Web Communities Influence Each Other through the Lens of Mainstream and Alternative News Sources." In *Proceedings of the 2017 Internet Measurement Conference*, 405–17. IMC '17. New York, NY, USA: Association for Computing Machinery. https://doi.org/10.1145/3131365.3131390.

Chapter IV
Exporting Home-Grown American Islamophobia

Introduction

Content drives platforms. While Twitter continues to struggle to monetize its content and turn a profit in the tradition of legacy media companies and its present day competitors (Isaac and Satariano 2022), its user-base continues to grow and the site's functionality has evolved in its utility beyond news circulation or limited conversations since its founding in 2006, instead becoming a public digital "means of social dissemination" (Rosenstiel et al. 2015). And it is the content on Twitter; viral posts, stories, and memes that has received scholarly, journalistic, and public attention and focus. While it is difficult to define the specific conditions whereupon content goes viral (Cheung et al. 2016), extreme content that invokes and produces affect is more likely to resonate with users and achieve peak circulation (Brady, Gantman, and Van Bavel 2020). Equally as important as content, however, are the mechanics of transmission, or the means of social dissemination.

What remains after viral content is long forgotten are the infrastructural linkages forged over time between users that constitute the networks of transmission. Media theorist Marshall McLuhan once declared "the medium is the message" (McLuhan 1964), and while it is imperative to study the rhetorical and ideological messaging strategies of far-right communities, analyzing the medium of Twitter, identifying its structure that allows these groups to communicate, grow, and evolve reveals a new dimension of our understanding of far-right networked politics. To shift from looking at content to networked structures requires though a change of perspective, only available through the technique of data visualization.

Visualizing discursive networks on Twitter by transforming data scrapings into network graphs is one way to illustrate and then examine the material contours of far-right communities and identify how content is spread. Rising above a sea of text, what this technique reveals is further evidence of the dominance of Indian and Indian American actors is producing and circulating Islamophobic hate-speech on Twitter. But visualizing these Islamophobic networked structures also uncovers emerging connections between a specific set of Nigerian activists, those identified with the secessionist Biafran cause, and figures in the former Trump administration—including former President Donald Trump himself—in a strategy designed to instrumentalize home-grown American Islamophobia to raise awareness for Biafran political causes.

https://doi.org/10.1515/9783111032887-004

Thus, this chapter is devoted to understanding the contours of networks that support the circulation of Islamophobic content, examining how network actors are connected, analyzing the way in which American Islamophobic far-right digital publics are structured transnationally, and identifying how information moves within and across these communities. Employing techniques of data visualization and the quantitative affordances of data analytic tools reveals both sub-communities within larger networks and the measurable influence of individual actors within networks, shedding light on the structural dynamics of far-right communication that may not be immediately visible when we scroll through Twitter confronted with discrete forms of hate-speech on our feeds.

By engaging in data visualization alongside traditional forms of feminist and thematic textual analysis, it is possible to see the data in a different way, eschewing a myopic focus on either big or small data, instead "thickening" the trace data left behind on platforms like Twitter by combining methodological techniques; close reading, thematic analysis, and data visualization together (Latzko-Toth, Bonneau, and Millette 2017). While Donna Haraway critiqued the dangers of the technologically and totalitarian mediated gaze that modern, normative data visualizations invoke as part of their historic descendance from colonialist, Western, scientific objectivist knowledge paradigms (Haraway 1988; Friendly 2006), through re-inventive applications, new forms of seeing are possible. However, we must also caution that even seemingly benign methods of visualization are merely descriptive of digitally mediated realities and lack an embedded critical analytical lens (Shahin and Dai 2019, 20). To mitigate this is to value data big and small equally, to reappropriate conventional data analytic tools and methods, thereby centralizing feminist ethics to tell situated stories (Leurs 2017, 136). Producing visualizations as the beginning of analysis to identify the discursive connections that bind actors together rather than situating visualizations as the culmination of the data scraping process centers both actors and narratives as we trace processes of transmission.

Thus, it is imperative to "view tweets as part of a larger tweet 'context'" (Murthy 2017, 564), in this case, the networked structure. A key principle of feminist data science is to consider context within and outside technologically mediated environments (D'Ignazio and Klein 2020), and visualizing the larger communicative context users exist within by transforming scrapes and traces of data using open-source visualization softwares like Gephi helps provide this context (Bastian, Heymann, and Jacomy 2009). Most critically, though, through visualizing these networks and uncovering methods of information transmission, it is possible to consider potential strategies to stem the flow of hate-speech or identify where and why existing processes of content moderation break down.

Increasingly, it is the responsibility of researchers studying digital environments to articulate or at least consider "concrete action for intervening in the increasingly unsafe spaces of social media" (Shepherd et al. 2015, 8). Identifying singular Tweets which contain violent Islamophobic hate-speech or banning individual network actors, is not a sustainable strategy to address the deluge of far-right content on Twitter—which immediately increased as the sale of Twitter was finalized to Elon Musk (Harper 2022). Identifying methods of transmission and network structures provides evidence of far-right ideological supply-chains that can then be disrupted through the implementation of platform-level or legal policies that take aim not at users but at structures.

The recent acquisition of Twitter by Elon Musk, billionaire "tech-bro" and Tesla CEO presents emerging challenges for company implemented content moderation with his avowed belief in a total "free-speech" model of platform governance (Alter 2022; Davis 2021). If in the next chapter we examine possibilities of actionable strategies to disrupt far-right informational infrastructures through harnessing the power of national and international legal structures in Germany and the European Union (EU), here we see global dimensions of these ideological supply chains that underscore the difficulties of stemming the spread of viral hate-speech that stretches across oceans and continents, in some cases fostered not just through individual bad actors, but via powerful institutionalized bodies, such as the former Trump administration. The long-protracted case of former President Trump's Twitter posting activity that violated Twitter's terms of service but only eventually culminated in a ban during the January 6th Insurrection demonstrates not only how Twitter has failed to adopt a strategy to police individual high-profile users inciting violence (Ghaffary 2021), but also how the company has struggled to articulate a concentrated and robust policy to address structural dissemination of hate-speech and (mis)information.

What is apparent from these data visualizations which illustrate far-right communicative practices is the emergence of Global North-South connections not only between white American and Indian networks, but also between MAGA American and Nigerian Biafran Twitter activists and politicians. We see again how Indian Twitter users act as information brokers, hailing Trump supporters on Twitter through tagging and inviting them to engage (Edwards and Stephens 2023), who return the call eagerly circulating content to their own networks. Conversely, Biafran Twitter activists increasingly forge strategic connections to Trump administration officials online as they enact digital campaigns against the Nigerian national government led by then President Muhammadu Buhari (Ochab 2018). Islamophobic networks are not only transnational but multi-scalar, linking institutionalized, everyday users, and activists, thus making them more difficult to disrupt. These two cases explored in this chapter, of the networked influence of Indian accounts within the larger far-right Twitter ecosystem and of the global activist strategy of Biafran actors, serves as a means to visualize the scale of far-right informational infrastructures on Twitter and illustrate the pathways forged by far-right users.

A Digital Cartographer's Tools

Visualizing far-right networks involves the implementation of social network analysis, producing Name Network graphs which illustrate how users are connected to one another in digital space, through the powerful mechanism of the "@" (Zheng and Shahin 2020). This type of network visualization represents who is connected to whom in the network—something not immediately visible through a close-reading of Tweets. Identifying who is connected to whom through graphical visualization illustrates "how actors are connected over the whole network, and thus what paths and obstacles there are for contact, information, and resource flow" (Gruzd and Haythornthwaite 2013). Here, the flow being Islamophobic hate-speech traded across producers and amplifiers.

These visualizations, reflecting periods of monthly conversational peaks, effectively reveal "previously elusive social processes at play" (Palmer 2016). And while normative data visualizations in their traditional formulation purport a "quality of objectivity" (Kennedy et al. 2016, 716), embracing feminist data visualization principles of considering context, embracing pluralism, and examining power and aspiring to empowerment addresses these limitations (D'Ignazio 2017). Connecting content by identifying the viral stories that circulate through networks, examining networks across a plurality of geographic contexts, and considering mechanisms for disrupting far-right supply-chains centralizes feminist ethics in the data visualization process. Ultimately, we can read these visualizations as a form of argument that reveal the knowledge production processes of far-right communities (Klein 2014).

Each visualization is produced according to similar specifications designed to increase the legibility of each data scrape. Graphical manipulations help reveal different dimensions of meaning to the data similar to how the application of a theoretical lens to a written text reveals new themes and connections. While the text or data itself has not changed, looking through different lenses helps different parts of the text or data become visible to the researcher. Employing different statistical measures, algorithmic lay-outs, sizing nodes, and identifying sub-communities by color to increase the legibility of the visualization tells one part of the story of far-right networked communities.

All data visualizations are produced using the open-source data visualization software Gephi which facilitates a series of manipulations (Bastian, Heymann, and Jacomy 2009). Each graph is created using the Yifan-Hu Proportional lay-out, a force-directed graph suited to small to medium networks (Cherven 2015). This algorithmic lay-out calculates the positions of nodes, or in this case network actors, simulating both an attractive and repulsive force between them and has been used in other studies of digital communities (Palmer 2016; Wu 2015). Force-directed graphs help us understand and identify more clearly the connections between nodes in the network with actors who are less connected pushed apart; therefore, nodes that are visualized as close together in the graph have a higher degree of connection and engagement. Edges are lines which represent how individual nodes are connected.

Other measures deployed include adjusting the sizes of the nodes, or Twitter users, based on degree. The larger the degree of a node the more connections it has with other users, as such, larger nodes are more connected than smaller nodes. Measuring nodes by degree measures the influence of users within the network. Identifying the in-degree and out-degree of network actors also reveals connection metrics, in-degree measures how much a node is connected to; the higher a node's in-degree measure the more popular or prestigious this network actor is. Conversely, out-degree measures how much a node connects to other actors, an actor with a high out-degree suggests that the user has a great awareness of other users and is a large promoter or disseminator of information within the network (Gruzd, Paulin, and Haythornthwaite 2016). As such, tracking the in-degree and out-degree measurements of particular nodes reveals which network actors are most influential or prolific in far-right communities.

Within each visualization nodes are partitioned according to their modularity class, which involves splitting the nodes into various subcommunities based on their connectivities, made identifiable by color (Gruzd, Mai, and Kampen 2017). Employing a statistical measure of the network's modularity also gives critical insight into how these publics are organized around information brokers; the higher the modularity of a graph, closer to 1, means more division between subcommunities, and a lower value means a network more tightly clustered around key actors. Identifying the modularity class within a network can be particularity important as it illustrates how single network, or hashtag public, is in fact composed of multiple smaller publics or subcommunities. Tracking #Islamization then becomes a point of entry into a variety of other diverse far-right subcommunities. These digital publics come in and out of being, and while they are not always stable and enduring (Florini 2019), these publics sediment their ideologies over time, pushing for policies, engaging in off-platform activism, and sometimes committing violence.

In addition to the measure of modularity, we can track the density of the network, or how close actors are to one another within the network (Gruzd, Mai, and Kampen 2017, 524). Graphs with a density closer to 1 are considered denser. Therefore, if a graph has a lower density, it is likely because most network actors are only connecting within their subcommunities, not across the entire graph structure, suggesting intra-community siloing. By employing particular algorithmic and statistical measures to scraped data and visualizing these actors into a cohesive network, we can trace the pathways of how hate-speech and (mis)information is circulated by users.

While such techniques reveal the transnationalization of Islamophobic subcommunities across a variety of national contexts, the US, India, and Nigeria, individual actors remain ensconced within nationalist language even as they forge connections across national boundaries based on constructed "civilizational differences (notably religious traditions and their secular legacies)" (Brubaker 2017, 1211), which is to say differences between Christianity, Hinduism, and Islam. This partitioning and crossing becomes particularly apparent in the following cases.

Islamophobia From Global North to South

So, what do far-right digital publics reveal when we visualize them in networked structures? They illustrate a series of transnational global connections featuring users from Nigeria and India, as well as linkages between white American and Indian American MAGA supporters. While the connectivities between MAGA Republicans in the US and Hindu nationalist factions in India are increasingly well documented (Chaudhury 2018), conversely, the linkages between Biafran Nigerians and American MAGA supporters have received less attention. The Biafran independence movement in Nigeria has found common cause with the former Trump administration. Trump specifically has been viewed as championing Christian communities globally in a context where many Biafrans, who are predominately Christian and members of the Igbo ethnic group, viewed the domestic Buhari administration as dismissive of increasingly violent ethnic conflicts between Igbo communities and the predominately Muslim Fulani ethnic group (Akinwotu 2020). These connections demonstrate how home-grown American Islamophobia is recognized as an actionable rhetorical strategy in digital spaces and re-purposed by Biafran digital activists.

Beginning with the first two graphs, of a miniature network Graph A, and a more established Graph B, we start to see the transnational dimensions of Islamophobic publics on Twitter. Graph A depicts a scrape from the American corpus of data from March 25th, 2020, illustrating a small network of three network actors with a density of 0.333. Upon initial visualization examination the graph is unremarkable, a statistically insignificant trace of user connection. However, in recontextualizing these traces to identify the ideological and semantic context (Crosset,

Tanner, and Campana 2018, 941), we see these connections forged based on a shared ideological value of Hindu nationalism that seeks to take aim at the very basis of India's secular democratic constitution which one user Tweeting: "@Singh4Sindhuja @aakashgupta146 India needs Hinduised dictatorship very badly or we may lose this nation. Democracy and Secularism are fertilizers for #Islamization and annihilation of peaceful nation" (VYuvati 2020b).

The #Islamization hashtag is used to suture together a nationalist political conversation suggesting that the liberal, secular democratic state model somehow aids in the imagined processes of Islamization. Democracy is not merely in crisis in the US, but rather is increasingly beleaguered across the globe (Abramowitz and Repucci 2018), under attack by far-right actors who seek to reestablish ethno-racial and religious nationalist states. This rejection of a secular, democratic Indian state is particularly significant against the historic emphasis by Indian nationalist leaders such as Jawaharlal Nehru that the Indian state would remain secular (Ghouse 1978). Graph A sets the standard for future visualizations of networks as illustrating a strong global and transnational dimension of Islamophobic political discourse on Twitter. We see that Islamophobic far-right discourse may be traded amongst users who are engaged in more inwardly focused conversations, with far-right Hindu nationalist Indian users connected via the hashtag, however, far-right Hindu nationalist groups do not remain detached from larger networks for long. And even seemingly closed publics are part of the larger platformed conversation. The dominance of Indian Hindu nationalists on the #Islamization hashtag is further illustrated in Graph B that shows how these networks grow and complexify.

Graph B comes from April 7th, 2020 and features a robust and a centralized network alongside peripheral clusters. The largest and most connective nodes, @AjitsinhJagirda, @sinhapurna13, and @BHARATMACHINE99, are all Indian and Indian American accounts (BHARATMACHINE99 2020; Jagirdar 2013; Ms. Purna/ Otun 2014). The largest in-degree measure is 13 for @sinhapurna13, who stands at the communicative center of graph. There are a total of six communities within this graph with a modularity of 0.383, which suggests a more overall connected network structure, and a density of 0.026 indicting that the graph is more fragmented and dispersed. The peripheral placing of some communities visualizes a form of communicative fragmentation—these users are only making connections within their subcommunities even as one subcommunity dominates the conversation.

The central node of one of these peripheral communities is @NetizenParo with an out-degree of 12, a user discussed in detail in Chapter II as a prolific producer of far-right Islamophobic hate-speech. Here we can physically trace connections connection between Hindu nationalist users to other white far-right American users. For example, we see that @NetizenParo is connected to the user

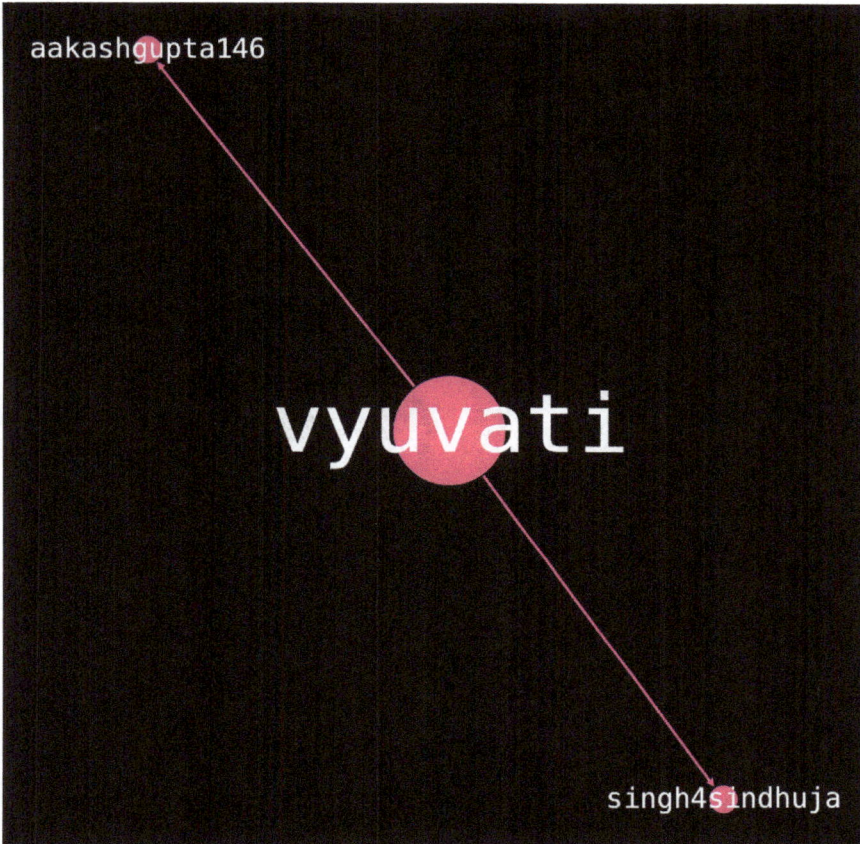

Graph A: USA March 25, 2020.

@DeploraH, a play on the word "deplorable" which Hillary Clinton used to refer to Trump supporters that Trump supporters have since embraced (Reilly 2016). @DeploraH, in her biography describes herself as a "Jewish Conservative & Patriot for Liberty and Freedom...#ScrewIslam #ScrewCommunism #MAGA" (LibertyAndFreedomWillPrevail 2019), showcasing here an emerging form of connectivity between Hindu nationalist Indian Americans and a contingency of Jewish Republicans, who despite Trump's embrace of antisemitic rhetoric at home continue to support his pro-Zionist policies abroad (Field 2017)

Indian users, however, predominate here and engage with the hashtag #Islamization as a means to racialize and Other the presence of Muslim communities in India, with Indian Americans such as @NetizenParo serving as informational influencers in producing Islamophobic discourse among fellow far-right American

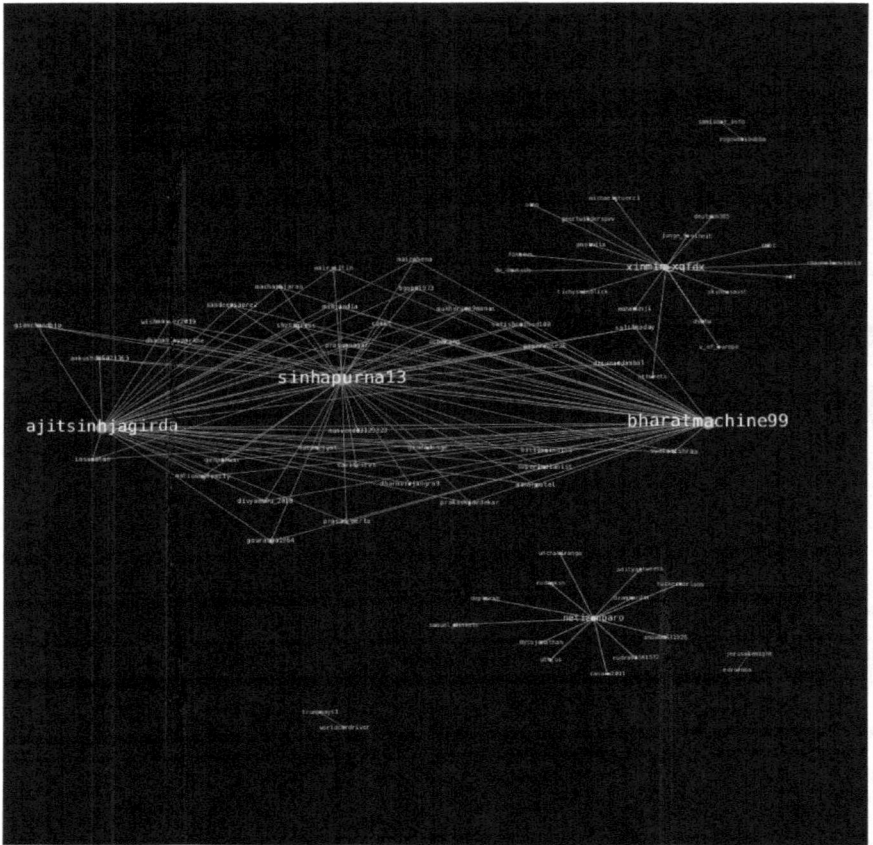

Graph B: USA April 7, 2020.

users. While scholars have documented the emergence of European-American Is-lamophobic far-right movements and digital communities (Caian and Kröll 2015; Froio and Ganesh 2018; Heft et al. 2020b; 2020a), Indian American far-right connec-tions are not only evolving (Leidig 2019, 79), but signal a new frontier of far-right coalition building. We also see the marginality of traditional media sources, such as @FoxNews, apparent in the green graph, itself a peripheral actor within this context compared to social media micro-influencers. On Twitter, these Indian and Indian American micro-influencers are the locus of conversation and content production, rather than traditional media outlets.

Peeling back the layers of this visualization we also see in the periphery, @Trumpgays1. While this community is tangential to the more established com-munities within the network centered around @NetizenParo and @sinhapurna13 for example, its appearance illustrates further complexities of far-right digital communities that exist outside straightforward taxonomical classifications of users. The appearance of @Trumpgays1, an account conceivably of gay Trump-supporters, represents a comparative US development of queer far-right support that has been seen in Europe, whereby LGBTQIA+ rhetoric is instrumentalized by activists who emphasize opposition to Islam and support for the far-right which "ostensibly [supports] liberal defense of gender equality, gay rights, and freedom of speech" (Brubaker 2017, 1193; Tobin 2017).

Caterina Froio and Bharath Ganesh have noted this trend among European far-right political parties who strategically support liberal values, positioning themselves as "as the only, 'authentic', defender of the nation's reputation of tolerance" (2018, 528). The appearance of the handle @Trumpgays1 represents how American far-right discourse is evolving to emphasizes its supposed protection of modern, liberal Western society against an allegedly regressive Muslim community. Far-right discourse, while supporting reactionary gender roles, anti-feminist, anti-gender-equality, and anti-queer sentiments (Fangen and Skjelsbæk 2020, 411), is fundamentally mutable and strategically can be deployed to superficially support women and queer communities. To be contradictory is to allow for the incorporation of a variety of groups—from neighborhood moms and dads to white supremacists to the queer community—under a shared banner of Islamophobic discourse. If far-right communities in digital spaces are able to articulate a "big tent" approach to their coalition building, then this strategy may carry over to offline political mobilizations.

In the next set of visualizations, we start to witness this "big tent" approach in the extreme, seeing further transnationalization of Islamophobia and its instrumentalization in Biafran digital activist campaigns. Here, American Islamophobia as a form of foreign policy during the Trump administration collides with localized, historically specific ethnic and religious conflicts in Nigeria (Kumar 2021). We see in Graph C from May 8th 2020 six communities with a modularity of 0.581 and a density of 0.054, suggesting a more integrated community network, although one where its subcommunities do not feature a great deal of cross-over as demonstrated by the low modularity measure. While we continue to see in the periphery Indian accounts, such as @IndiaFactsOrg, a recurrent user-account producing a large amount of Islamophobic (mis)information shared under the guise of "facts" (IndiaFacts 2013), the significant green subcommunity of network actors is led by a cluster of Nigerian accounts which reappear in the following visualizations.

Instances of Nigerian Twitter activism descend from a rich history of contemporary digital protest such as the #BringBackOurGirls campaign as a response to the militant organization Boko Haram's kidnapping of over two hundred Chibok

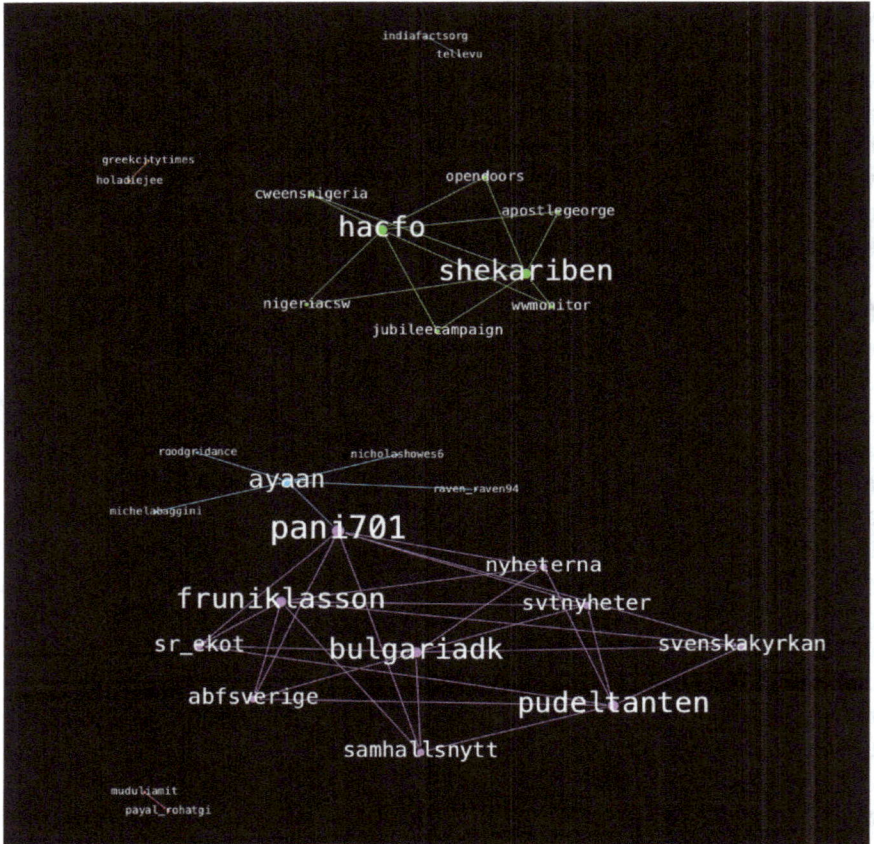

Graph C: USA May 8, 2020.

school girls in 2014 and more recently the #EndSARS movement designed to draw attention to police brutality and the violent actions of the Special Anti-Robbery Squad (SARS) in 2020 (Abimbade, Olayoku, and Herro 2022; Atela et al. 2021; Faniyi 2023). Both hashtag campaigns are instances of Nigerian feminist digital protest (Faniyi 2023). The digital activities of anti-Muslim Biafran activists are thus imbricated within these broader traditions of Nigerian digital activism, but also must be read against Nigeria's colonial history and indigenous ethnic and religious conflicts.

The sudden appearance of Biafran Twitter users as a central cluster using the hashtag #Islamization may seem on the surface surprising. It might appear that in Nigeria, a nation with the fifth largest Muslim population in the world and a roughly equal breakdown of Christians and Muslims (Diamant 2019), that Islamophobia would not appear as a potent ideological force. However, Nigeria's colonial period and subsequent Biafran War (1967–1970) between Nigeria and the secessionist Republic of Biafra laid the groundwork for contemporary conflicts between Nigerian Biafrans, predominately Christian and members of the Igbo ethnic group, and members of the Fulani ethnic group who are predominately Muslim (Pierri and Barkindo 2016).

Between 1884 and 1960, Nigeria was subject to British colonization. However, as an occupying power, the British implemented a strategy of in-direct rule informed by what has been characterized as Hausa-Fulani "sub-colonialism" (Harnischfeger 2006, 42; Ochonu 2008). After the independence movement, the Biafran War (1967–1970) later broke out and was primarily led by the ethnic Igbo group to realize an independent republic of Biafra in South-Eastern Nigeria (Morrison 2005; Johnson and Olaniyan 2017). After the extreme violence of the Biafran War (1967–1970) and a period of military rule post-war, in 1999 Nigeria shifted to a form of imperfect democracy (Harnischfeger 2006, 44). Samuel Désiré Johnson, in nuancing the ethnic and religious tension in the state, notes that historically speaking, "Islam was...associated with the dominant ethnic group" of the Fulani (2017, 264). For Christian Igbo Nigerians who identify more saliently as Biafrans, this group has since experienced political marginalization in the post-war reunified Nigerian state (Johnson and Olaniyan 2017). For many Biafrans, notions of supposed "Fulanization" of society and the concept of Islamization are imagined as one and the same and indelibly linked back to historic political conflicts such as the Biafran War (1967–1970) (S. D. Johnson 2017, 265)

As such, Biafran usage of the hashtag #Islamization, while locally and regionally specific, also strategically invokes American rhetorics of Islamophobia. As Samuel F. C. Daly notes regarding historic Biafra media strategies, "Biafran propaganda intended for the outside world [has] argued that the war was a battle between Biafran Christians and Nigerian Muslims—a gross simplification, but one that was effective in mobilizing sentiment nonetheless" (2017). The same process is at work on Twitter today with Biafran activists seeking to position contemporary clashes between sedentary Christian farmers and nomadic Fulani Muslim herdsmen in the Middle Belt region as fundamentally a conflict between Christians and Muslims to win sympathy from conservative and far-right American constituencies. And there is no better place to build these affective coalitions than on Twitter.

The deployment of the hashtag #Islamization among Biafran Twitter in Graph D alongside the tagging of American political officials demonstrates how Biafran digital activists are actively producing a mediated narrative of contemporary conflict, critiquing the national Nigerian government and Buhari administration as not merely marginalizing Igbo constituencies but implementing a structural political and Islamic religious take-over of the state that resonates with American far-right domestic narratives of Christian imperilment (Green 2016).

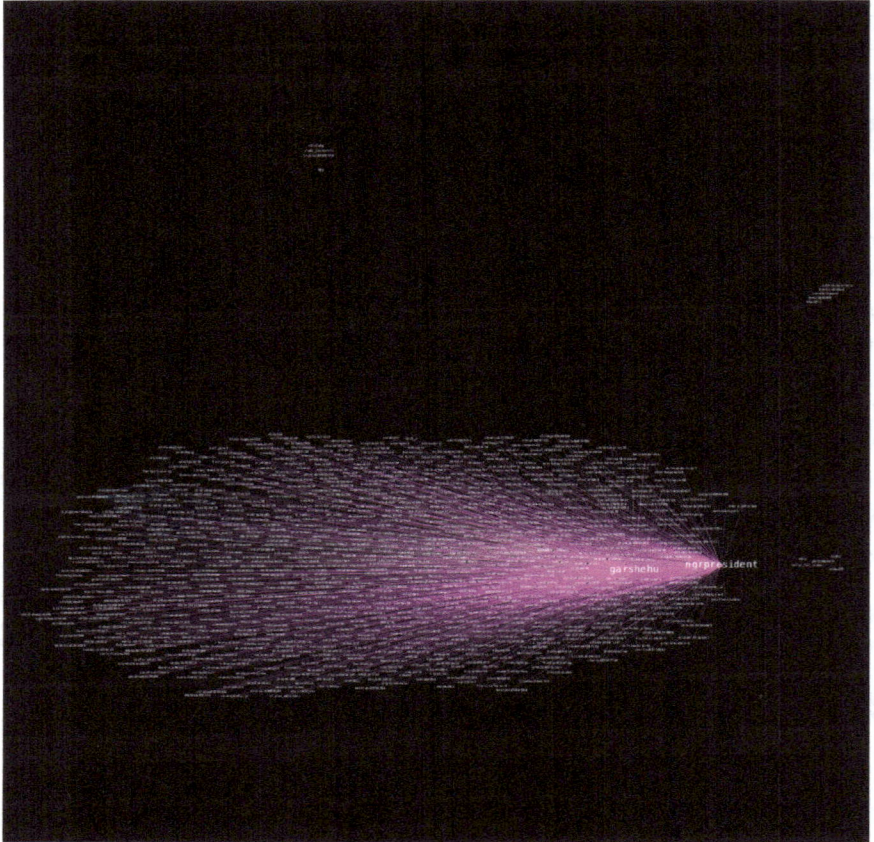

Graph D: USA June 17, 2020.

Graph D from June 17th, 2020, while very fragmented with a density of 0.003, illustrates a structure where most nodes connect back to two network actors, @NGRPresident and @GarShehu, which are the Twitter accounts for former Nigerian President Muhammadu Buhari and Garbu Shehu, the then Official Spokesperson to the President of Nigeria (Buhari 2014; Shehu 2015), both with in-degree measures of 855. While there are some peripheral communities on the side, with the graph featuring a modularity of 0.127 with a total of 6 communities, the key actors are these two central accounts. Biafran activists deploy the #Islamization hashtag to connect user accounts and conversation back to President Buhari and his spokesman Garbu Shehu to place political pressure on both these figures.

Examining the CSV file of this particular data scrape, @AloyEjimakor, appears as a central actor and discursive architect in this networked structure. Aloy Ejimakor serves as the Special Counsel for the Indigenous People of Biafra (IPOB) leader and activist, Mazi Nnamdi Kan, who has been controversially extradited to Nigeria from Kenya and imprisoned for allegedly inciting violence (Udeajah 2022). Aloy Ejimakor reappropriates the #Islamization tag to viral affect, forwarding a narrative of Christian imperilment and tapping into existing political dynamics: "Let it be known to @GarShehu who accused #IPOB of LYING on #Christian persecution in #Nigeria that PERSECUTION is: When the @NGRPresident proclaimed #97versus5 When Danjuma, OBJ, PANDEF, CAN, others decried #Islamization &; When Christians are killed in the North with impunity" (Ejimakor 2020).

Both President Muhammadu Buhari and his People's Democratic Party (PDP) in Nigeria have been critical of Biafran separatist leaders and the broader secessionist movement (Amamkpa and Mbakwe 2015, 16; Sahara Reporters 2022), with Twitter suspending a Tweet from Buhari in 2021 that threatened violence against the Eastern Security Network (ESN), an armed group affiliated with the leading Biafran secessionist organization IPOB (Akinwotu 2021). IPOB has an active physical political and digital presence and is located predominately in the Igbo-dominated South-Eastern area of Nigeria (Nwofe 2019, 26). The organization has been remarkably adapt with digital campaigns, but its activism has also taken a darker turn with recruitment of social media micro-influencers who have increasingly called for armed violence on social media platforms, which have been situated as a "new frontline" in the Biafran fight (Disinformation Team 2022).

We see here, however, that Biafran activists are not merely stoking intraregional tensions or communicating with the larger Biafran diaspora on social media platforms (Disinformation Team 2022), but on Twitter these activists are dynamically working to connect to sympathetic international coalitions—like American MAGA Republicans—even as these connections will become more explicit in the next graph. Specifically, Graph E makes visible a myriad of on-going tensions between IPOB, Buhari, and Biafran supporters against the backdrop of a Biafran secessionist revival, protracted violence from Islamic terrorist groups such as Boko Haram, and instances of police brutality accompanied by physical and digital protests with the #EndSARS movement.

With these parallel political processes on-going, Biafran supporters took advantage of the #Islamization hashtag to spread their message of persecution at the hands of the Buhari-led government, calling on an interview Garba Shehu gave discussing alleged targeting killings of Christian farmers where he suggested IPOB had been manufacturing a paid media campaign to highlight the killings for

Western aid and attention (Premium Times 2020). Shehu is quoted as stating that IPOB and Christian NGOs in the country were "using the cover of Christianity and calling for a U.S. Special Envoy to be appointed to stop the 'genocide' of Christians in Nigeria. But the real purpose is to drive a wedge between the Nigerian government and its U.S. and UK/European allies" (Terhemba Daka 2020).

These statements by Garba Shehu provoked @AloyEjmakor to re-affirm not merely the supposed #Islamization of the Nigerian state but to draw attention to the targeted murders of Christian Nigerians in the Northern region where a majority of Muslim Hausa and Fulani groups are located. Bundling these accounts together and strategically using the #Islamization, while certainly speaking to an indigenous audience of Biafran supporters familiar with local politics, demonstrates a utilitarian form of religious reductionist framing to reach a larger audience. This strategy of highlighting supposedly fundamental tensions between Muslims and Christians to Western digital audiences unfamiliar with Nigerian history and ethnic politics, such as American conservatives and far-right groups, serves to forward a narrative of totalitarian Muslim violence, thus helping the Biafran cause gain international visibility and support.

Considering these ethnic and religious tensions then, the appearance of Biafran activists and Twitter users within this corpus of data is not surprising, especially given increasing contemporary digital engagement by Biafran activists and IPOB supporters on Twitter and other social media platforms (Nwofe 2019; Nwofe and Goodall 2019). Contemporary usages of social media to draw international support and visibility to the Biafran cause also relate to historic media campaigns led by Biafran groups during the Biafran War (1967–1970) via radio and print means to attract support and resources from external Western states (Doron 2014, 227). The religious conflict rhetoric on display in digital communications on Twitter shares an ideological connection to war-time messaging deployed by Biafrans which was strategically designed to appeal to "foreign Christian sympathizers" (Omenka 2010, 369). Today, Biafran activists repurpose this reductionist religious rhetoric even while historians have noted that the "Christian Igbo vs. Muslim Hausa/Fulani stereotype...collapses under scrutiny" (Omenka 2010, 368). Biafran activists return to this rhetoric because it is effective in drumming up Western Christian support while also speaking to local groups within the same Tweet.

@AloyEjimakor uses the #Islamization hashtag alongside nationally specific hashtags like #97versus5, referring to an infamous comment from Buhari, to hail Biafran supporters familiar with this national context. In a 2015 speech, Buhari disregarded a commitment to represent a plurality of constituents outside his own supporters, suggesting that communities in areas that gave him 97% of the vote will not be treated the same as constituent in areas that gave him 5%

of the vote (Nwangwu 2018). This comment has been pointed to by Biafran support-ers as evidence of a pattern of disregard of minority voices by the Buhari admin-istration. In the Tweet @AloyEjimakor also suggests that Buhari has supposedly dismissed charges of Islamization from Nigerian political figures and organizations including Danjuma, OBJ, PANDEF, and CAN, a collection of political figures and or-ganizations.

Danjuma refers to the Nigerian General Theophilus Yakubu Danjuma, a phi-lanthropist and former Minister of Defense for the former Christian President Olu-segun Matthew Okikiola Aremu Obasanjo, known as OBJ (Daniel 2019; Ty Danjuma Foundation 2020). PANDEF refers to the Pan Niger Delta Forum, an NGO (Akpan-Nsoh 2018), and CAN refers to the Christian Association of Nigeria, a Christian ecu-menical body (CAN, n.d.). And while not explicitly apparent in this Tweet, the issue of supposed targeted attacks on Christians looms in the background of the text and has become not merely a national Nigerian issue of concern from non-profits and local figures but has gained an international resonance particularly among white Christian American Republicans.

During Buhari's visit to the US in 2018, then President Trump brought up the issue of killings of Christian farmers in the Middle Belt region leading to a boost in media coverage of the issue (BBC News 2018). Biafran secessionists have supported Trump's rhetoric of supposed global Christian persecution as validating their expe-riences under a Buhari-led government (Akpan-Nsoh 2018). So, even after former President Trump's enactment of a travel-ban targeting Nigeria and his own infa-mous comment calling African nations including Nigeria "shithole countries" (D. Smith 2018), he has remained a supported figure in the South-Eastern Igbo region of Nigeria by Biafrans supporters who view Trump as an ally to the cause (D. J. Smith 2022).

Within right-wing American digital media circles as well, the killings of Chris-tian farmers by Fulani herdsman has featured heavily in reports from far-right publications such as *Breitbart* which frequently covers the topic alongside other sensationalist stories of Christian murder and persecution at the hands of Boko Haram in the state (Reyes 2021; Williams 2018). The publicization of the murders in the international media has been remarkably effective, with one of the largest American Catholic digital newspapers reporting that Nigeria was "'becoming world's biggest killing ground of Christians'" (Crux Staff 2020).

But what appears in both the headlines of traditional stories and the narra-tives circulated on Twitter by Biafran activists is a simplified message of religious persecution that elides other dimensions of the conflict, such as a competition over land resources in the Middle Belt between nomadic herdsmen and farming agri-culturalists and the larger ecological context of increased desertification due to cli-mate change (Lenshie and Jacob 2020; Nugent 2018). On Twitter, the structure of succinct posts further allows Biafran activists to reduce the complexities of very real forms of indigenous conflict into a religious civilationalist clash between Muslims and Christians that invites both attention and support from external states and actors, particularly the Trump administration.

Trump's support of white Christian groups at home dovetails with his racialized critique of American Muslims and the larger global Muslim community. This rhetoric has been particularly apparent on Twitter, his favored medium of both political communication and policy making until he was banned (Kreis 2017). Trump has frequently disseminated racist, conspiratorial anti-Muslim discourse, from falsely suggesting Muslim Americans cheered as the Twin Towers fell on 9/11 to intimating that the immigration of Muslim refugees to Europe would increase terrorism (Khan et al. 2021). Trump's racialized critiques against Muslims and Islam on Twitter has been theorized as a "strategy to build kinship with the Americans who harbor similar sentiments" (Khan et al. 2021, 11). In this case, the sharing of Islamophobic content by a range of users across geographical contexts serves as a means to build kinship globally through the sharing of anti-Muslim sentiments.

And in the next graph, Graph E, we also see how Biafran activists move beyond deploying general religious civilationalist rhetoric to begin actively connecting to Trump and the then Trump-led State Department in a means to again international visibility and American political support for supposed Christian persecutions in Nigeria. At this time, the State Department was led by Mike Pompeo who has extensive ties to far-right, anti-Muslim organizations (Bridge Initiative Team 2017). Graph E, below, illustrates these strategic deployments by Biafran activists to the American MAGA movement as well as regional nations, including Kenya.

Graph E is from July 4th, 2020, Independence Day in the US. This network features a density of 0.048 and a modularity of 0.102 with a total of 9 communities, but it is immediately apparent that Nigerian Twitter accounts dominant the structure with the largest subcommunity visible in pink. Major nodes within the graph include @StateDepart, which is the handle of the US State Department, former President Trump's Twitter account @RealDonaldTrump, and @StateHouseKenya, which is the account associated with the President of Kenya. Other accounts include @EmekaGift, a Biafran activist (Gift 2011), @MaziNnamdiKanu, the current IPOB leader (Kanu 2018), @UrugwiroVillage, which is the Twitter account of the President of Rwanda Paul Kagame (Presidency | Rwanda 2011), @PaulKagame, the personal account of Rwandan President Paul Kagame (Kagame 2009), and @ntvkenya, a national Kenyan television station NTV Kenya (NTV Kenya 2009), with each of these users featuring an in-degree measure of 82. But this potpourri of users are linked together through the strategy of hashtagging by self-identified Biafran activist @ChinasaNworu (Nworu 2015).

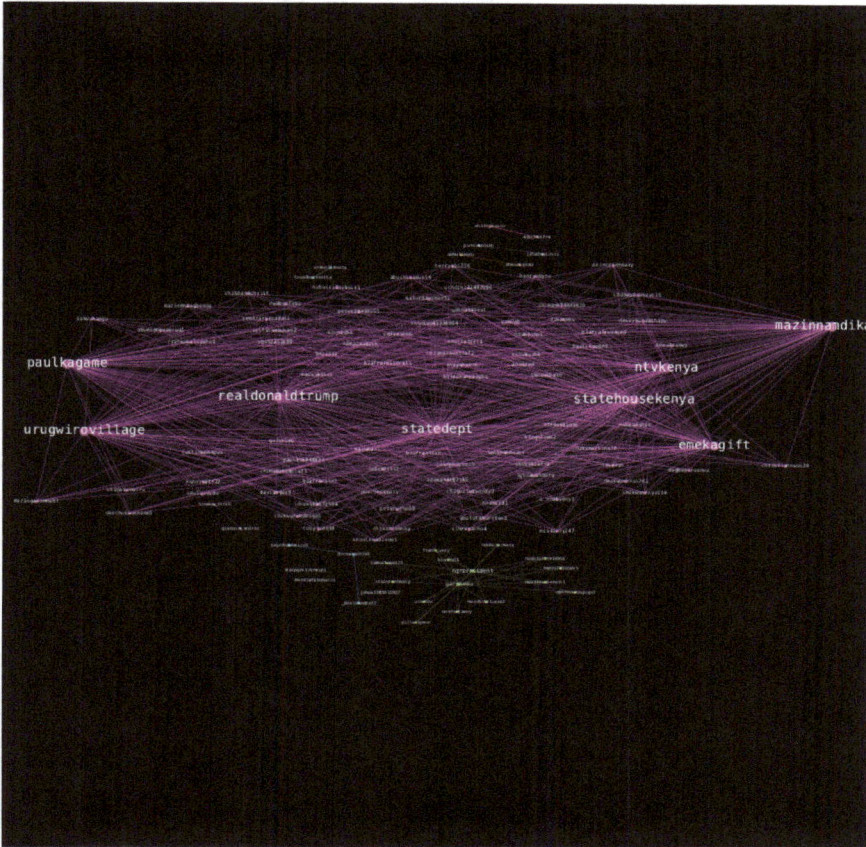

Graph E: USA July 4, 2020.

@ChinasaNworu Tweets "#IPOB calls for #Christians to stand up against #Islami-
zation of #Nigeria @realDonaldTrump @EmekaGift @StateDept @MaziNnamdiKa-
nu @StateHouseKenya @UrugwiroVillage @PaulKagame @ntvkenya https://t.co/
GwpQ7ocG5q." As is clear with the Tweet and Graph F, the accounts named by
@ChinasaNworu appear as major nodes within the visualization, with the link out-
sourcing to a press release from IPOB:

> We are calling on Judeo-Christians in Nigeria to stand up against the upcoming jihadists sol-
> diers scattered all over Nigeria to Islamize the country. The country is clearly coming to an
> end; Christians must not allow Islam to humiliate them again in Nigeria. All politicians in Bia-
> fra-land must come out and defend their land because Fulani has taken over (IPOB PRESS
> RELEASE 2020)

Biafran activists like @ChinasaNworu, with over 75,000 followers, again deploy this theme of Christian persecution to globalize the Biafran cause in line with historic forms of Biafran propagandizing. What is different, and particularly dangerous, today, though is that these contemporary Christian connectivities being forged are part of a larger far-right ecosystem, not merely to governmental entities, non-profits, or religious organizations as we saw in the 1960s. Furthermore, we see the similarities in apocalyptic language here used by IPOB and Biafran activists that also defines far-right American and European political communication and ideology (Michelsen and de Orellana 2020, 128). If one's country, and society, is indeed coming to an end, then taking extraordinary, violent political measures to stem this collapse becomes not only thinkable but legitimized in this worldview.

IPOB also uses specific rhetoric such as the terms Islamization and jihad that perform a parallel function of connecting to local audiences in the South-East already familiar with historic conflicts and the activities of Boko Haram which has been classified as a jihadist terrorist group (Azumah 2015; Pérouse de Montclos 2016), that also speaks to far-right American audiences familiar with this language in the context of the War on Terror and Trumpist oratory. So, while the context here is deeply nuanced and historically specific, the structure of Twitter that facilitates the creation of multiple discursive publics alongside content disembedding enables activists like @ChinasaNworu to "open up" a Biafran enclave and also call forth the attention of the American far-right public by situating Nigerian Muslims as agents of terror (Florini 2019)

The connection to American accounts such as Trump and the State Department signals that Biafran activists seek to strategically play upon an American Republican belief of domestic and international Christian imperilment at the hand of Muslims. The case of endangered Christian farmers in Nigeria becomes in the far-right American imagination unimpeachable evidence of global Christian imperilment, with white nationalist narratives of white racial imperilment not ideologically far way (Azani et al. 2020, 5). And this is even as contemporarily and historically Christian privileges, ideologies, and values have been embedded alongside white supremacy in American culture and law (Joshi 2020). While the context in Nigeria is nationally distinct, this shared grammar of Islamophobic rhetoric demonstrates a strong connection between the digital Biafran community and white far-right American networks and political figures.

And while these various accounts were linked together with @ChinasaNworu's Tweet, we see different users clustered in slightly different spatial areas, with Trump and the US State Department at the center, and the Kenyan accounts clustered together in a similar fashion as the Rwandan accounts. This partitioning of communities visualizes that even as the overall network structure is transnational, within the digital landscape of Twitter national communities still re-emerge and are re-constituted discursively within virtual spaces, such as is the case in the following graph.

Graph F: USA August 24, 2020.

In this next graph, Graph F from August 24th, 2020 we see that while Twitter allows for competing and parallel publics to emerge and make connections, in other instances discursive communities on mainstream digital platforms can remain nationally partitioned. Graph F illustrates remnants of previous trends, such as the dominance of Indian accounts and Nigerian activists. This graph features a low density of 0.017 and a modularity of 0.815. With 10 communities, as is visible, the graph is highly fragmented, but we can focus on two relevant groups with the highest in-degree measures: the Indian and Nigerian communities within the network structure.

The first community of note is the connected by a user with the top in-degree measure of 13, @ByRakeshSimha which is connected to the Hindu nationalist account @IndiaFactsOrg with an in and out-degree of 1, an account that purports to publish objective, professional information but is a far-right, Hindu nationalist publication (IndiaFacts 2013). @IndiaFactsOrg Tweets an article written by @ByRakeshSimha, stating: "[t]he takeaway for India is that a rapidly growing Muslim minority should never be taken lightly, writes Rakesh Simha. @ByRakeshSimha #Islamization #Muslims #Riots #IndianDemographics #Lebanon #Muslims #Jihadis https://t.co/rAcVrbILVv" (IndiaFacts 2020). Linking here supposed instances of political instability in Muslim-majority nations and fear-mongering about a demographic increase in Muslim citizens in the Indian state as a supposed security issue—the hashtags of #Islamization #Muslims #Jihadis #Riots making this connection explicit.

This preoccupation with demography has become a particularly explicit part of racialized Islamophobic discourse among German and European digital communities and demonstrates how for Indian Hindu nationalists, religious difference is increasingly racialized, whereby "Hindutva emphasizes difference through the racialization of Muslims to reinstate Hindu and Muslim as irreconcilably separate selves" which increasingly "emerges in transnational dialogue and relations," here, in dialogue with white Western nationalists (Cháirez-Garza et al. 2022, 206; Natrajan 2022).

The last community of note in this visualization is in the upper right-hand corner and features several accounts from previously displayed Nigerian networks structures including Donald Trump, the Kenyan State House, etc., clustering around another Biafran activist, @PillarSpace with an out-degree of 8 (Pillar's SpAcE 2019), which included a post re-Tweeting the earlier Tweet and the IPOB press release. While these partitioned, fragmented communities may capture ephemeral moments in time on Twitter, forgotten in the following days, weeks, and months of posting, it is through such repeated interaction that users form ideological bonds, connections, and coalitions via Twitter's structural affordances.

Conclusion

Islamophobia, while articulated in nationally and historically specific contexts, is increasingly becoming a strategic form of political rhetoric in online spaces that achieves an affective global resonance. As this chapter has demonstrated, Islamophobia is both a form of foreign policy and a rhetorical strategy used by Biafran activists (Khan et al. 2021, 11). Islamophobic hashtags are recognized and instrumentalized by international agents, like Biafran digital activists. Islamophobic communities; American, Nigerian, and Indian, while focused on particular nationalistic concerns, situate themselves as aligned using civilationalist language. Bracketing a focus on Islamophobia in national contexts thus limits our understanding of new chains of transmission of hate-speech and conspiratorial discourses, from India to the US and the US to Nigeria.

We also see that Indian Twitter users are prolific in terms of producing Islamophobic content and that this content resonates with American users. Conversely, Islamophobic hashtags and rhetoric are being deployed by Biafran activists as a means by which to conduct digital campaigns to connect to former President Trump and the US State Department and other far-right actors and institutions. Biafran activists are capitalizing on American Christian conservativism and narratives of Christian civilationalist imperilment to achieve their own regional goals in South-East Nigeria. The hashtags might come and go, but digital rhetoric increasingly accompanies off-platform policy shifts and instances of political violence. In India we have seen the passage of anti-Muslim legislation such as the CAA-NRC by the BJP-led government, which signals the transformation of digital political rhetoric into concrete policies that have accompanied increasing cases of anti-Muslim violence (Ramachandran 2020).

The consequences of increasing usages of Islamophobic language by Biafran activists online are still developing but are a topic of concern. While Biafran groups and IPOB remain marginalized by the Nigerian state, the Nigerian government has been progressively destabilized by escalating, everyday violence including clashes in the Middle Belt and religiously targeted killings (Obadare 2022b; 2022a). The inflammatory rhetoric circulated on Twitter by Biafran activists has the opportunity to inflame and inform real on-the-ground armed constituencies (Ojo 2020), a dangerous prospect given the past history of what historians have defined as an Igbo genocide during the 1967–1970 War (Korieh 2013).

Islamophobic content is increasingly becoming transmitted across more global networks via an eclectic group of micro-influencers and digital activists, and the transnationalized nature of these networks presents particular challenges for content moderation, especially given Musk's disinterested approach to the topic. If content moderation does not eminent from the platform itself, might national governments or supranational organizations such as the European Union (EU) be the only institutional actors to actualize change? The next chapter will show possibilities of nationally based content moderation and approaches pioneered by civil collectives.

References

Abimbade, Oluwadara, Philip Olayoku, and Danielle Herro. 2022. "Millennial Activism within Nigerian Twitterscape: From Mobilization to Social Action of #ENDSARS Protest." *Social Sciences & Humanities Open* 6 (1): 100222. https://doi.org/10.1016/j.ssaho.2021.100222.

Abramowitz, Michael J., and Sarah Repucci. 2018. "Democracy Beleaguered." *Journal of Democracy* 29 (2): 128–42. https://doi.org/10.1353/jod.2018.0032.

Akinwotu, Emmanuel. 2020. "'He Just Says It as It Is': Why Many Nigerians Support Donald Trump." *The Guardian*, October 31, 2020, sec. World news. https://www.theguardian.com/world/2020/oct/31/he-just-says-it-as-it-is-why-many-nigerians-support-donald-trump.

Akinwotu, Emmanuel. 2021. "Twitter Deletes Nigerian President's 'Abusive' Biafra Tweet." *The Guardian*, June 2, 2021, sec. World news. https://www.theguardian.com/world/2021/jun/02/twitter-deletes-nigerian-presidents-abusive-biafra-tweet.

Akpan-Nsoh, Inemesit. 2018. "PANDEF Seeks Adherence to Pacts of Nation's Founding Fathers." *The Guardian Nigeria*, April 10, 2018, sec. National. https://guardian.ng/news/pandef-seeks-adherence-to-pacts-of-nations-founding-fathers/.

Alter, Charlotte. 2022. "Elon Musk and the Tech Bro Obsession With 'Free Speech.'" *Time*, April 29, 2022. https://time.com/6171183/elon-musk-free-speech-tech-bro/.

Amamkpa, Anthony Williams, and Paul Uche Mbakwe. 2015. "Conflict Early Warning Signs and Nigerian Government Response Dilemma: The Case Of Increasing Agitations for Statehood by Indigenous People of Biafra (IPOB) and Movement for the Actualization of Sovereign State of Biafra (MASOB)." *African Journal of History and Archaeology* 1 (8): 10–20.

Atela, Martin, Ayobami Ojebode, Racheal Makokha, Marion Otieno, and Tade Aina. 2021. "Women Organising in Fragility and Conflict: Lessons from the #BringBackOurGirls Movement, Nigeria." *Gender & Development* 29 (2–3): 313–34. https://doi.org/10.1080/13552074.2021.1979323.

Azani, Eitan, Liram Koblenz-Stenzler, Lorena Atiyas-Lvovsky, Dan Ganor, Arie Ben-Am, and Delilah Meshulam. 2020. "The Far Right – Ideology, Modus Operandi and Development Trends." Herzliya, Israel: International Institute for Counter-Terrorism.

Azumah, John. 2015. "Boko Haram in Retrospect." *Islam and Christian–Muslim Relations* 26 (1): 33–52. https://doi.org/10.1080/09596410.2014.967930.

Bastian, Mathieu, Sebastien Heymann, and Mathieu Jacomy. 2009. "Gephi: An Open Source Software for Exploring and Manipulating Networks." In *Proceedings of the Third International ICWSM Conference (2009)*, 361–62. Denmark: Aalborg University Denmark. https://vbn.aau.dk/ws/files/328840013/154_3225_1_PB.pdf.

BBC News. 2018. "How Trump Stirred Controversy in Nigeria." *BBC News*, May 1, 2018, sec. Africa. https://www.bbc.com/news/world-africa-43964932.

BHARATMACHINE99. "Profile." Twitter, March 31, 2020. https://twitter.com/search?q=BHARATMACHINE99&src=typed_query&f=user.

Brady, William J., Ana P. Gantman, and Jay J. Van Bavel. 2020. "Attentional Capture Helps Explain Why Moral and Emotional Content Go Viral." *Journal of Experimental Psychology: General* 149: 746–56. https://doi.org/10.1037/xge0000673.

Bridge Initiative Team. 2017. "Mike Pompeo | Factsheet: Islam, Muslims, Islamophobia | The Bridge Initiative." *Bridge Initiative* (blog). 2017. https://bridge.georgetown.edu/research/factsheet-mike-pompeo/.

Brubaker, Rogers. 2017. "Between Nationalism and Civilizationism: The European Populist Moment in Comparative Perspective." *Ethnic and Racial Studies* 40 (8): 1191–1226. https://doi.org/10.1080/01419870.2017.1294700.

Buhari, Muhammadu. 2014. "Profile." Twitter. 2014. https://twitter.com/MBuhari.

Caian, Manuela, and Patricia Kröll. 2015. "The Transnationalization of the Extreme Right and the Use of the Internet." *International Journal of Comparative and Applied Criminal Justice* 39 (4): 331–51. https://doi.org/10.1080/01924036.2014.973050.

CAN. n.d. "About CAN." *Christian Association of Nigeria* (blog). https://cann.org/about-can.

Cháirez-Garza, Jesús F., Mabel Denzin Gergan, Malini Ranganathan, and Pavithra Vasudevan. 2022. "Introduction to the Special Issue: Rethinking Difference in India through Racialization." *Ethnic and Racial Studies* 45 (2): 193–215. https://doi.org/10.1080/01419870.2021.1977368.

Chaudhury, Aadita. 2018. "Why White Supremacists and Hindu Nationalists Are so Alike." *Al Jazeera*, December 13, 2018.

Cherven, Ken. 2015. *Mastering Gephi Network Visualization*. Birmingham, UK: Packt Publishing. http://gephi.michalnovak.eu/Mastering%20Gephi%20Network%20Visualization.pdf.

Cheung, Ming, James She, Alvin Junus, and Lei Cao. 2016. "Prediction of Virality Timing Using Cascades in Social Media." *ACM Transactions on Multimedia Computing, Communications, and Applications* 13 (1): 2:1–2:23. https://doi.org/10.1145/2978771.

Crosset, Valentine, Samuel Tanner, and Aurélie Campana. 2018. "Researching Far Right Groups on Twitter: Methodological Challenges 2.0." *New Media & Society* 21 (4): 939–61.

Crux Staff. 2020. "Nigeria Is Becoming World's 'Biggest Killing Ground of Christians.'" *Crux*, August 1, 2020. https://cruxnow.com/church-in-africa/2020/08/nigeria-is-becoming-worlds-biggest-killing-ground-of-christians.

Daly, Samuel F. C. 2017. "Biafra's Crisis of Faith." *The Republic* (blog). November 2, 2017. https://republic.com.ng/octobernovember-2017/biafra-crisis-of-faith/.

Daniel, Eniola. 2019. "Obasanjo's Story, Aremu Set to Hit the Stage." *The Guardian*, October 13, 2019, sec. Arts. https://guardian.ng/art/obasanjos-story-aremu-set-to-hit-the-stage/.

Davis, Terrance. 2021. "Elon Musk and Tech-Bro Futurism." *The Signal* (blog). October 26, 2021. https://georgiastatesignal.com/elon-musk-and-tech-bro-futurism/.

Diamant, Jeff. 2019. "The Countries with the 10 Largest Christian Populations and the 10 Largest Muslim Populations." *Pew Research Center*, April 1, 2019. https://www.pewresearch.org/fact-tank/2019/04/01/the-countries-with-the-10-largest-christian-populations-and-the-10-largest-muslim-populations/.

D'Ignazio, Catherine. 2017. "Feminist Data Visualization." Medium. January 22, 2017. https://medium.com/@kanarinka/what-would-feminist-data-visualization-look-like-aa3f8fc7f96c.

D'Ignazio, Catherine, and Laura F. Klein. 2020. *Data Feminism*. Cambridge: MIT Press.

Disinformation Team. 2022. "Ipob: Nigerian 'media Warriors' Call for Killings on Social Media over Biafra." *BBC News*, May 11, 2022, sec. Africa. https://www.bbc.com/news/world-africa-61354014.

Doron, Roy. 2014. "Marketing Genocide: Biafran Propaganda Strategies during the Nigerian Civil…" *Journal of Genocide Research* 16 (2–3): 227–46. http://dx.doi.org/10.1080/14623528.2014.936702.

Edwards, Emily Lynell, and David F Stephens Jr. 2023. "(Hash)Tagging Intersection(Ality): Black and Palestinian Experiences on Twitter." *Communication, Culture and Critique*, April, 1–8. https://doi.org/10.1093/ccc/tcad013.

Ejimakor, Aloy. 2020. "Let It Be Known to @GarShehu Who Accused #IPOB of LYING on #Christian Persecution in #Nigeria That PERSECUTION Is: When the @NGRPresident Proclaimed #97versus5 When Danjuma, OBJ, PANDEF, CAN, Others Decried #Islamization & When Christians Are Killed in the North with Impunity." Twitter. June 9, 2020. https://twitter.com/AloyEjimakor/status/1270296793721470984.

Fangen, Katrine, and Inger Skjelsbæk. 2020. "Editorial: Special Issue on Gender and the Far Right." *Politics, Religion & Ideology* 21 (4): 411 – 15. https://doi.org/10.1080/21567689.2020.1851866.

Faniyi, Ololade. 2023. "A Herstory of #EndSars: Nuances of Intersectionality in Nigeria's Movement against Police Brutality." Master of Arts, Bowling Green, OH: Bowling Green State University.

Field, Les. 2017. "Anti-Semitism and Pro-Israel Politics in the Trump Era: Historical Antecedents and Contexts." *Middle East Report*, no. 284/285: 52 – 54.

Florini, Sarah. 2019. *Beyond Hashtags: Racial Politics and Black Digital Networks.* New York: New York University Press.

Friendly, Michael. 2006. "A Brief History of Data Visualization." In *Handbook of Computational Statistics: Data Visualization*, edited by Chun-houh Chen, Wolfgang Karl Härdle, and Antony Unwin, 1 – 43. Heidelberg, GR: Springer-Verlag.

Froio, Caterina, and Bharath Ganesh. 2018. "The Transnationalisation of Far Right Discourse on Twitter Issues and Actors That Cross Borders in Western European Democracies." *European Societies* 21 (4): 513 – 39.

Ghaffary, Shirin. 2021. "Why Twitter Finally Banned Trump." *Vox*, January 8, 2021. https://www.vox.com/recode/22221543/twitter-suspended-trump-account-permanent-ban.

Ghouse, Mohammad. 1978. "Nehru and Secularism." *Journal of the Indian Law Institute* 20 (1): 103 – 16.

Gift, Emeka. "Profile." Twitter, 2011. https://twitter.com/EmekaGift.

Green, Emma. 2016. "Most American Christians Believe They're Being Persecuted." *The Atlantic*, June 30, 2016. https://www.theatlantic.com/politics/archive/2016/06/the-christians-who-believe-theyre-being-persecuted-in-america/488468/.

Gruzd, Anatoliy, and Caroline Haythornthwaite. 2013. "Enabling Community Through Social Media." *JOURNAL OF MEDICAL INTERNET RESEARCH* 15 (10).

Gruzd, Anatoliy, Phillip Mai, and Andrea Kampen. 2017. "A How to for Using Netlytic to Collect and Analyze Social Media Data: A Case Study of the Use of Twitter During the 2014 Euromaiden Revolution in Ukraine." In *The SAGE Handbook for Social Media Research Methods*, edited by Luke Sloan and Anabel Quan-Haase, 513 – 29. Los Angeles, CA: SAGE Publications.

Gruzd, Anatoliy, Drew Paulin, and Caroline Haythornthwaite. 2016. "Analyzing Social Media and Learning Through Content and Social Network Analysis: A Faceted Methodological Approach." *Journal of Learning Analytics* 3 (3): 46 – 71.

Haraway, Donna. 1988. "Situated Knowledges: The Science Question in Feminism and the Privilege of Partial Perspective." *Feminist Studies* 14 (3): 575 – 99.

Harnischfeger, Johannes. 2006. "Islamisation and Ethnic Conversion in Nigeria." *Anthropos* 101 (1): 37 – 53.

Harper, Shaun. 2022. "Hate Speech Rises On Twitter After Elon Musk Takes Over, Researchers Find." *Forbes*, October 31, 2022, sec. Diversity, Equity, and Inclusion. https://www.forbes.com/sites/shaunharper/2022/10/31/elon-musk-twitter-takeover-leads-to-n-word-and-hate-speech-increase-lebron-james-calls-for-action/?sh=59780f12dd99.

Heft, Annette, Eva Mayerhöffer, Susanne Reinhardt, and Curd Knüpfer. 2020a. "Organization Beyond Breitbart: Comparing Right-Wing Digital News Infrastructures in Six Western Democracies." *Policy and Internet* 12 (1): 20 – 45.

Heft, Annette, Eva Mayerhöffer, Susanne Reinhardt, and Curd Knüpfer. 2020b. "Toward a Transnational Information Ecology on the Right? Hyperlink Networking among Right-Wing Digital News Sites in Europe and the United States." *The International Journal of Press/Politics.* https://doi.org/10.1177/1940161220963670.

IndiaFacts. 2013. "Profile." Twitter. 2013. https://twitter.com/IndiaFactsOrg.

IndiaFacts. 2020. "The Takeaway for India Is That a Rapidly Growing Muslim Minority Should Never Be Taken Lightly, Writes Rakesh Simha. @ByRakeshSimha #Islamization #Muslims #Riots #IndianDemographics #Lebanon #Muslims #Jihadis Https://T.Co/RAcVrbILVv." Twitter. August 17, 2020. https://twitter.com/IndiaFactsOrg/status/1295331047299674112.

IPOB PRESS RELEASE. 2020. "Nigerians Christians Should Stand up against the Islamization of the Country – IPOB." *Obong Express*, March 7, 2020. https://www.obongexpress.com/2020/07/nigerians-christians-should-stand-up.html.

Isaac, Mike, and Adam Satariano. 2022. "Twitter Reports Growth in Revenue and Users as Elon Musk Prepares to Take Over." *The New York Times*, April 28, 2022, sec. Business. https://www.nytimes.com/2022/04/28/technology/twitter-first-quarter-earnings-elon-musk.html.

Jagirdar, ajitsinh. "Profile." Twitter, 2013. https://twitter.com/AjitsinhJagirda.

Johnson, Idowu, and Azeez Olaniyan. 2017. "The Politics of Renewed Quest for a Biafra Republic in Nigeria." *Defense & Security Analysis* 33 (4): 320 – 32. https://doi.org/10.1080/14751798.2017.1382029.

Johnson, Samuel Désiré. 2017. "The Second Religious Globalization in Africa: Changes in the Religious Landscape and the Consequences for Social Peace: The Case of Cameroon." *International Review of Mission* 106 (2): 261 – 67.

Joshi, Khyati Y. 2020. *White Christian Privilege The Illusion of Religious Equality in America*. New York: NYU Press. https://nyupress.org/9781479840236/white-christian-privilege.

Kagame, Paul. "Profile." Twitter, 2009. https://twitter.com/PaulKagame.

Kanu, Mazi Nnamdi. "Profile." Twitter, 2018. https://twitter.com/MaziNnamdiKanu.

Kennedy, Helen, Rosemary Lucy Hill, Giorgia Aiello, and William Allen. "The Work That Visualisation Conventions Do." *Information, Communication & Society* 19, no. 6 (2016): 715–35. https://doi.org/10.1080/1369118X.2016.1153126.

Khan, Mohsin Hassan, Farwa Qazalbash, Hamedi Mohd Adnan, Lalu Nurul Yaqin, and Rashid Ali Khuhro. 2021. "Trump and Muslims: A Critical Discourse Analysis of Islamophobic Rhetoric in Donald Trump's Selected Tweets." *SAGE Open* 11 (1): 1 – 16. https://doi.org/10.1177/21582440211004172.

Klein, Lauren F. "Visualization as Argument." Presented at the Genres of Scholarly Knowledge Production Conference, Umea University, Sweden, December 16, 2014. http://lklein.com/american-studies/visualization-as-argument/.

Korieh, Chima J. 2013. "Biafra and the Discourse on the Igbo Genocide." *Journal of Asian and African Studies* 48 (6): 727 – 40. https://doi.org/10.1177/0021909613506455.

Kreis, Ramona. 2017. "The 'Tweet Politics' of President Trump." *Journal of Language and Politics* 16 (4): 607 – 18. https://doi.org/10.1075/jlp.17032.kre.

Kumar, Deepa. 2021. "Rightwing and Liberal Islamophobia: The Change of Imperial Guard from Trump to Biden." *South Asian Review* 42 (4): 408 – 12. https://doi.org/10.1080/02759527.2021.1899517.

Latzko-Toth, Guillaume, Claudine Bonneau, and Melanie Millette. 2017. "Small Data, Thick Data: Thickening Strategies for Trace-Based Social Media Research." In *The SAGE Handbook of Social Media Research Methods*, edited by Luke Sloan and Quan-Haase, 199 – 214. Los Angeles, CA: SAGE Publications.

Leidig, Eviane Cheng. 2019. "Immigrant, Nationalist and Proud: A Twitter Analysis of Indian Diaspora Supporters for Brexit and Trump." *Media and Communication* 7 (1): 77 – 89. https://doi.org/10.17645/mac.v7i1.1629.

Lenshie, Nsemba Edward, and Patience Kondu Jacob. 2020. "Nomadic Migration and Rural Violence in Nigeria: Interrogating the Conflicts between Fulani Herdsmen and Farmers in Taraba State." *Ethnic Studies Review* 43 (1): 64–95. https://doi.org/10.1525/esr.2020.43.1.64.

Leurs, Koen. 2017. "Feminist Data Studies: Using Digital Methods for Ethical, Reflexive and Situated Socio-Cultural Research." *Feminist Review* 115: 130–54.

LibertyAndFreedomWillPrevail. "Profile." Twitter, 2019. https://twitter.com/DeploraH.

McLuhan, Marshall. 1964. *Understanding Media The Extensions Of Man.* New York, NY: Penguin Group.

Michelsen, Nicholas, and Pablo de Orellana. 2020. "Pessimism and the Alt-Right: Knowledge, Power, Race and Time." In *Pessimism in International Relations Provocations, Possibilities, Politics*, edited by Tim Stevens and Nicholas Michelsen, 119–36. Cham: Springer International Publishing.

Morrison, Jago. 2005. "Imagined Biafras: Fabricating Nation in Nigerian Civil War Writing." *ARIEL* 36 (1–2): 5–26.

Ms. Purna/Otun. "Profile." Twitter, 2014. https://twitter.com/sinhapurna13.

Murthy, Dhiraj. 2017. "The Ontology of Tweets: Mixed Methods Approaches to the Study of Twitter." In *The SAGE Handbook of Social Media Research Methods*, edited by Luke Sloan and Anabel Quan-Haase, 559–72. London, UK: SAGE Publications.

Natrajan, Balmurli. 2022. "Racialization and Ethnicization: Hindutva Hegemony and Caste." *Ethnic and Racial Studies* 45 (2): 298–318. https://doi.org/10.1080/01419870.2021.1951318.

NTV Kenya. "Profile." Twitter, 2009. https://twitter.com/ntvkenya.

Nugent, Ciara. 2018. "Land Conflict Has Long Been a Problem in Nigeria. Here's How Climate Change Is Making It Worse." *Time*, June 28, 2018. https://time.com/5324712/climate-change-nigeria/.

Nwangwu, Chikodiri. 2018. "Ako-Na-Uche versus Nzogbu-Nzogbu: Interrogating the Rupture between Igbo Elite and Their Lumpen in Igbo Nationalism." African Heritage Foundation. https://media.africaportal.org/documents/Ako-na-Uche-versus-Nzogbu-nzogbu.pdf.

Nworu, Chinasa. "Profile." Twitter, June 2015. https://twitter.com/ChinasaNworu.

Nwofe, Emmanuel S. 2019. "The Internet and Activists' Digital Media Practices: A Case of the Indigenous People of Biafra Movement in Nigeria." *IAFOR Journal of Media, Communication & Film* 6 (1). https://doi.org/10.22492/ijmcf.6.1.02.

Nwofe, Emmanuel S., and Mark Goodall. 2019. "The Web as an Alternative Communication Resource for Pro-Biafra Independent Movements in Nigeria: The Case of Indigenous People of Biafra." *The Athens Journal of Mass Media and Communications* 5 (1): 51–72.

Obadare, Ebenezer. 2022a. "Gruesome 'Blasphemy' Killing Brings Nigeria's Long-Running Ethno-Religious Divide Into Sharp Focus." *Council on Foreign Relations* (blog). May 16, 2022. https://www.cfr.org/blog/gruesome-blasphemy-killing-brings-nigerias-long-running-ethno-religious-divide-sharp-focus.

Obadare, Ebenezer. 2022b. "Escalating Violence Is Putting Nigeria's Future on the Line." Brief. Council on Foreign Relations. https://www.cfr.org/in-brief/escalating-violence-putting-nigerias-future-line.

Ochab, Ewelina U. 2018. "Trump May Not Be Wrong On the Fulani Herdsmen Crisis In Nigeria." *Forbes*, May 4, 2018, sec. World Affairs. https://www.forbes.com/sites/ewelinaochab/2018/05/04/trump-may-not-be-wrong-on-the-fulani-herdsmen-crisis-in-nigeria/.

Ochonu, Moses. 2008. "Colonialism within Colonialism: The Hausa-Caliphate Imaginary and the British Colonial Administration of the Nigerian Middle Belt." *African Studies Quarterly* 10 (2 & 3): 33.

Ojo, John Sunday. 2020. "Governing 'Ungoverned Spaces' in the Foliage of Conspiracy: Toward (Re) Ordering Terrorism, from Boko Haram Insurgency, Fulani Militancy to Banditry in Northern Nigeria." *African Security* 13 (1): 77–110. https://doi.org/10.1080/19392206.2020.1731109.

Omenka, Nicholas Ibeawuchi. 2010. "BLAMING THE GODS: CHRISTIAN RELIGIOUS PROPAGANDA IN THE NIGERIA–BIAFRA WAR*." *The Journal of African History* 51 (3): 367–89. https://doi.org/10.1017/S0021853710000460.

Palmer, Stuart. 2016. "Birds of a Feather: The Geographic Interconnection of Australian Universities on Twitter." *Journal of Applied Research in Higher Education* 8 (1): 88–100. https://doi.org/10.1108/JARHE-01-2015-0002.

Pérouse de Montclos, Marc-Antoine. 2016. "A Sectarian Jihad in Nigeria: The Case of Boko Haram." *Small Wars & Insurgencies* 27 (5): 878–95. https://doi.org/10.1080/09592318.2016.1208286.

Pierri, Zacharias, and Atta Barkindo. 2016. "Muslims in Northern Nigeria: Between Challenge and Opportunity." In *Muslim Minority-State Relations: Violence, Integration, and Policy*, edited by Robert Mason, 133–53. The Modern Muslim World. New York: Palgrave Macmillan US. https://doi.org/10.1007/978-1-137-52605-2_6.

Pillar's SpAcE. 2019. "Profile." Twitter. 2019. https://twitter.com/PillarSpace.

Premium Times. "IPOB Spending $85,000 Monthly to Discredit Nigeria Internationally – Presidency." *Premium Times*, June 7, 2020. https://www.premiumtimesng.com/news/headlines/396584-ipob-spending-85000-monthly-to-discredit-nigeria-internationally-presidency.html.

Presidency | Rwanda. "Profile." Twitter, 2011. https://twitter.com/UrugwiroVillage.

Ramachandran, Sudha. 2020. "Hindutva Violence in India: Trends and Implications." *Counter Terrorist Trends and Analyses* 12 (4): 15–20.

Reilly, Katie. "Read Hillary Clinton's 'Basket of Deplorables' Remarks About Donald Trump Supporters." *Time*, September 10, 2016. https://time.com/4486502/hillary-clinton-basket-of-deplorables-transcript/.

Reyes, Gabrielle. 2021. "Nigeria: Fulani Jihadists Kill 45 Christian Farmers in 'Barbaric' Attack." *Breitbart*, December 22, 2021, sec. Africa. https://www.breitbart.com/africa/2021/12/22/nigeria-fulani-jihadists-kill-45-christian-farmers-in-barbaric-attack/.

Rosenstiel, Tom, Jeff Sonderman, Kevin Loker, Maria Ivancin, and Nina Kjarval. 2015. "How People Use Twitter in General." American Press Institute. https://www.americanpressinstitute.org/publications/reports/survey-research/how-people-use-twitter-in-general/.

Sahara Reporters. 2022. "How Governor Uzodinma, Other Political Leaders Are Deliberately Working Against Release Of Nnamdi Kanu – IPOB | Sahara Reporters." *Sahara Reporters*, November 1, 2022, sec. News. https://saharareporters.com/2022/11/01/how-governor-uzodinma-other-political-leaders-are-deliberately-working-against-release.

Shehu, Garba. 2015. "Profile." Twitter. 2015. https://twitter.com/GarShehu.

Shepherd, Tamara, Aubrey E. Harvey, Tim Jordan, Sam Srauy, and Kate M. Miltner. 2015. "Histories of Hating." *Social Media + Society*, 1–10. https://doi.org/10.1177/2056305115603997.

Smith, Daniel Jordan. 2022. "Why Is Donald Trump So Popular in Southeastern Nigeria and What Can We Learn from It?: Undermining Truth and Enabling Corruption." In *Corruption and Illiberal Politics in the Trump Era*, edited by Donna M. Goldstein and Kristen Drybread. Routledge.

Smith, David. 2018. "After 'shithole Countries' Row, Trump Tries Flattery with Nigerian President." *The Guardian*, April 30, 2018, sec. US news. https://www.theguardian.com/us-news/2018/apr/30/donald-trump-nigerian-president-visit-muhammadu-buhari.

Squires, Catherine R. 2002. "Rethinking the Black Public Sphere: An Alternative Vocabulary for Multiple Public Spheres." *Communication Theory* 12 (4): 446 – 68. https://doi.org/10.1111/j.1468-2885.2002.tb00278.x.

Terhemba Daka, Abuja. "IPOB Using Christianity to Ignite War in Nigeria, Presidency Alleges." *The Guardian Nigeria*, June 8, 2020, sec. National. https://guardian.ng/news/ipob-using-christianity-to-ignite-war-in-nigeria-presidency-alleges/.

Tobin, Robert Deam. 2017. "Gays for Trump? Homonationalism Has Deep Roots." *The Gay & Lesbian Review Worldwide* 24 (3): 5 – 8.

Ty Danjuma Foundation. 2020. "Lt. Gen. Theophilus Yakubu Danjuma GCON (Rtd)." Ty Danjuma Foundation. 2020. https://tydanjumafoundation.org/board-of-trustees/lt-gen-theophilus-yakubu-danjuma-gcon/.

Udeajah, Gordi. 2022. "UK Court Grants Kanu Permission for Judicial Review." *The Guardian Nigeria News – Nigeria and World News*, October 11, 2022. https://guardian.ng/features/law/uk-court-grants-kanu-permission-for-judicial-review/.

VYuvati. "Profile." *Twitter* (blog), March 17, 2020. https://twitter.com/VYuvati.

Williams, Thomas D. 2018. "Muslim Militants Burn Alive Christian Pastor and His Family in Nigeria." *Breitbart*, August 30, 2018, sec. National Security. https://www.breitbart.com/national-security/2018/08/30/muslim-burn-christian-pastor-family-nigeria/.

Wu, Shirely. 2015. "Understanding the Force." Medium. July 10, 2015. https://medium.com/@sxywu/understanding-the-force-ef1237017d5.

Zheng, Pei, and Saif Shahin. 2020. "Live Tweeting Live Debates: How Twitter Reflects and Refracts the US Political Climate in a Campaign Season." *Information, Communication & Society* 23 (3): 337 – 57. https://doi.org/10.1080/1369118X.2018.1503697.

Chapter V
Visualizing Networks, (Mis)Information, & Islamophobia In German Networks

Introduction

Hate-speech and violent far-right political content on our feeds often feels like a flash flood, appearing without warning in a sudden deluge before receding to a steady, yet ever present drip. Mainstream social media platforms like Twitter serve as a stage for the (re)presentation of far-right content that originates from external extremist websites such as the imageboard site 4chan, message-board platform 8kun, the growing plethora of alt-tech platforms such as Parler, Gab, and Truth Social (Johnson et al. 2022), or fringe digital news sites. While much of this far-right content including text, image, and video and the conspiracy theories embedded therein, are not directly sourced from Twitter, on the platform they reach a much broader audience and become mainstreamed as part of our digital cultural vernacular (Papasavva et al. 2020, 885; Voué, De Smedt, and De Pauw 2020). As such, Twitter is a critical platform where far-right political networks manifest and circulate their political ideologies to larger audiences. In extending a focus to far-right German networks on Twitter, this chapter continues to examine far-right network structures by shifting its emphasis to look at a larger ecology of the German far-right, recontextualizing traces to identify where far-right content is sourced from, and crucially, considering strategies and challenges to limit the flow of this content.

Content moderation teams and policies have been increasingly gutted in the wake of Musk's acquisition of the platform, but even in a more normalized corporate environment, these groups and processes may only address the symptoms of far-right political movements rather than the underlying ideological pathology of far-right politics in Germany, the US, and elsewhere. There is a growing movement among policymakers and politicians, particularly in the European Union (EU), and in Germany in particular, to enact policy solutions to address both the spread of hate-speech and (mis)information on platforms (Vernick 2022). Non-profit organizations (NGOs), civil society actors, and activists are also increasingly pressuring Twitter to more effectively protect users from violent harassment and hate-speech, such as through American-led initiatives like #WeCounterHate from the organization Life After Hate and the German NGO HateAid which fights against digital violence (Aziz 2019; HateAid 2021).

https://doi.org/10.1515/9783111032887-005

Twitter, as a US company, was founded and operates in the context of a definitively American permissive, libertarian-inspired free speech ethos which emphasizes the tech sphere as a "'marketplace of ideas,'" even of possibly objectionable content, provided there are buyers (Hong 2022, 79), whereas the EU and Germany stand in stark contrast. Germany has recently passed the German Network Enforcement Act (NetzDG), a harbinger of the impending implementation of the EU Digital Services Act (DSA) (Noyan 2021). Both the EU and Germany have taken the approach of regulating technology companies based on existing national and supranational speech norms. For example, Germany's post-war stringent speech laws outlaw publicly denying the Holocaust and the presentation of Nazi symbols and propaganda (*German Criminal Code (Strafgesetzbuch – StGB)* 1998), and this has carried over into contemporary technology-specific laws such as NetzDG which requires platforms with over two million users to immediately remove manifestly "illegal" speech within 24-hours with fines of up to €50 million for noncompliance (Lomas 2020).

Despite critics suggesting that this policy may lead to "over-blocking" of content, "there is no empirical proof of over-removal or other harmful effects on online speech due to it[s]" implementation (Heldt 2020). As such, when considering how to address hate-speech, (mis)information, and violence on social media platforms, the German NetzDG Act has been situated as either a model to follow to curb hate-speech or a possible template to be abused by authoritarian regimes interested in implementing policies of digital censorship (Heldt 2020; Zurth 2020). However, as we will see, NetzDG's model of requiring the deletion of individual content instances does not address the structural ways in which social media platforms such as Twitter encourage the articulation of hate-speech—nor can it fully address the growth of a symbiotic far-right external platform ecosystem that originates the extremist content shared on Twitter (Griffin 2022).

It would be difficult to posit Twitter's future approach to content moderation even in a more regularized corporate climate, much less given the tensions between Musk and now former and remaining Twitter management as a result of his belief in "free speech absolutism" (Alter 2022). In reality, Musk's approach has resulted in less of a free speech haven and more in the haphazard banning of journalists, parody accounts, and other critics as hate-speech soars unchecked. Musk's thin-skinned reaction to satire accounts and comparative advertiser concerns about how to maintain a presence on a platform increasingly bedeviled by damaging content underscores the complexity of addressing hate-speech on the site given these competing commercial interests and personality clashes (Mac et al. 2022). And, regardless of Musk's management style and predilections, Twitter is obligated to follow EU laws and American Federal Trade Commission

(FTC) consent orders governing how companies manage the privacy of consumer data (Heath 2022), issues which have already become corporate flashpoints.

Furthermore, Musk's mass-firings of Twitter employees and the parallel departure of numerous critical staff and teams underscores how Musk's chaotic, "hardcore" leadership style is presenting challenges not only for enacting content moderation (Mac, Isaac, and McCabe 2022), but for the operationalization of basic company functionalities such as processing payroll. However, we can look to the recent history of how the platform has engaged in content moderation and dealt with hate-speech and (mis)information to consider its possible path forward. Twitter and its competitors such as Meta, Snapchat, Reddit, and now Tik Tok, have all struggled to moderate extremist speech and (mis)information (Tarasov 2021), when they have been so inclined as to enforce their policies at all. Fundamentally, the central issue with content moderation has been that these "new public fora" or public squares (Hong 2022, 85), exist also as commercial platforms, whereby the most engaging and affective content that entices users is often of the extremist variety (Brady, Gantman, and Van Bavel 2020; Papacharissi 2015), therefore giving platforms a vested interest in encouraging this type of content production.

When mainstream platforms have engaged in systemic content moderation it is often in a reactive fashion after extreme cases of violence, abuse, or political crisis. Examples include the gruesome trend of live-streaming murders and mass-shootings on Twitch or the coordinated attempt of Russian-produced bots to seed (mis)information during the 2016 American presidential election on Facebook (Gunia 2019; Hartmann 2018). Twitter has gone through a range of strategies to engage in content moderation, its latest being the introduction of Community Notes, formerly Bird Watch, where users themselves could provide additional context on Tweets that were potentially misleading (Coleman 2021), this strategy coming after the platform's memeable "this claim is disputed" warning label was introduced to be placed on potentially non-factual Tweets (Haysom 2020). However, as this chapter will demonstrate, the issue of content moderation goes far beyond a discrete group of bad actors on platforms.

Exploring and visualizing far-right German networks inadvertently reveals the way in which far-right Islamophobic content on Twitter and other extremist rhetoric and narratives merely surface on the platform, rather, they are cultivated and sourced from a series of external sites. As such, any discussion of content moderation must take into account the larger platformed ecosystem rather than focus myopically on a singular social media site. Ultimately, the solutions to the steady stream of far-right extremist content on Twitter cannot be solely implemented by platforms themselves but rather require national and international legal regulation, such as through the passage of NetzDG and strategic campaigns from NGOs that force platforms to make tangible changes.

Ultimately, what makes the issue of content moderation so difficult is that while Twitter and other platforms may enact stricter polices, enacting a significant change to their existing complacent protocols, far-right extremist content frequently originates from a diverse platformed ecosystem populated by news sites and alt-tech far-right platforms that market themselves as venues void of content moderation and thus become shelters for a variety of violent, racist, far-right extremist content which then flows back to Twitter. Critically, these sites often do not meet the NetzDG's threshold of two million users, and thus slip through the cracks, because they are smaller and less trafficked.

And even when mainstream platforms on the "Clearnet," or searchable web, have actively sought to scrub objectionable content, such as the video of the Christchurch, New Zealand mosque shooting, this genre of content continues to circulate on the "Darknet," or ecosystem of platforms not accessible through a simple search engine search (Solon 2019). It is essentially impossible to stem the flow of all extremist content solely through enacting content moderation because fringe external sites continue to operate. As Mohit Agarwal notes, "taking down [content] will only hide it from view" (2021, 3). As long as there are individuals and groups who ascribe to a set of far-right ideologies, there will be far-right content in our digital ecosystem. The question is thus twofold—how to address the surfacing of far-right content on mainstream platforms and how to address the underlying pathology of far-right politics in societies more broadly.

To delve into puzzle, we can look at far-right German Twitter networks to consider practically these dynamics of content moderation, off-platform ecologies, and possibilities of legal addressment of extremist speech. Examining a series of data visualizations which illustrate conversational peaks and influential network actors serves as a point of departure to consider tangible strategies. In any approach to content moderation or the legal banning of certain forms of speech, the first step is to identify precisely what type of speech is in certain contexts objectionable and to then identify its modes of transmission.

Circulating Hate-Speech: Fake News in the German Media Ecosystem

The following section visualizes a series of network graphs all produced using the data visualization software Gephi, employing the algorithmic Yifan-Hu layout, partitioned according to modularity class with communities and actors identifiable via color, sized by degree, and examined in terms of in/out-degree as a metric of network influence and connectivity. Read together in a series, these German graphs tell a story of a heavily nationalized "German Twittersphere" (Münch et al. 2019), where traditionally influential and institutional accounts move the conversation forward and where explicit news content in the form of news stories, of varying quality and accuracy, is the major driver of (mis)information and Islamophobic hate-speech. While in the German Twittersphere it may appear that content moderation is a simple proposition because of the prevalence of a discrete collection of bad actors, in fact, looking under the hood of these graphs illustrates a dynamic and diverse external platform ecosystem of fringe news sites and alternative platforms not even on the Darknet, but accessible via the Clearnet, that spew extremist content.

Graph G: Germany March 27, 2020.

This dynamic is immediately apparent in the first data visualization from March 27th, 2020, a graph which demonstrates a high degree of modularity and 15 distinct subnetworks within the structure. Looking at the lay-out of the graph, despite the fact that we see multiple sub-clusters, there is one large community centered around the biggest node: @jouwatch, with the top in-degree measurement of 33. @jouwatch is the formerly suspended handle for the far-right, German news outlet *Journalistenwatch*, or Journalist Watch (Journalistenwatch 2012). Comparatively, the user with the next highest in-degree, of 4, is the account @Tagesspiegel, the handle for the German mainstream legacy news publication *Daily Mirror* based in Berlin (Tagesspiegel 1945). While Twitter may provide the possibility for individual accounts to produce news content, either from journalists or now (micro)influencers, within German circles, formal news institutions still remain primarily influential, even if they are dubious outlets. Twitter facilitates both multi-mediated public conversation and another outlet for journalists and news outlets to share their stories, dissolving the boundary between public conversation and journalism. Natalie Fenton notes in discussing the effects of digital technology upon journalistic production practices that platforms like Twitter which are "spaces for online discussion," ultimately "blur into the wider provision of news" (2010, 563). This becomes particularly problematic when it comes to the circulation of seemingly factual yet false and racialized, Islamophobic, conspiratorial content on the site.

Far-right digital news outlets like the German *Journalistenwatch* and *Anon-News*, as well as their American counterparts like *Breitbart*, are unique new media outlets defined by their production of niche, salacious, and frequently unvetted coverage speaking to a fragmented far-right audience (Edwards 2020, 2), that increasingly spurs greater public conversation on Twitter. Fringe news sites like @jouwatch are critical network actors within German far-right digitally networked communities, producing not only Islamophobic, racialized coverage, but also circulating homophobic and misogynist content that galvanizes other parts of the far-right German coalition. Ultimately, within the context of the German Twittersphere, the origin source and most influential user accounts are not grassroots far-right influencers or unaffiliated individuals, but rather institutionalized accounts, thus evidencing the complexity of the larger far-right "information ecosystem" Twitter exists within (Zannettou et al. 2017).

@jouwatch is at the center of Graph H but also re-appears as a key network actor in other visualizations, so a more detailed examination of the news outlet is necessary. *Journalistenwatch*, founded in 2011, is financially connected to an American Islamophobic conservative think-tank, the Middle East Forum, which has been described as a "right-wing anti-Islam think tank that spreads misinformation, creates 'watchlists' targeting academics, and advocates hawkish foreign policy" (Bridge Initiative Team 2018). As recently as 2016, the Middle East Forum listed *Journalistenwatch* as one of its supported projects (Schmidt 2017). The Middle East Forum is founded by conservative historian Daniel Pipes who has published a plethora of highly critical pieces about Islam and Muslim communities since the 1990s (D. Pipes 1995; D. Pipes 2001).

From a financial perspective, the connection between *Journalistenwatch* and the Middle East Forum demonstrates the articulation of a growing Transatlantic ideological symbiosis between Islamophobic far-right networks in Germany and the US that extend beyond digital coalition building on Twitter towards material political linkages. Nico Schmidt, a reporter for the mainstream German newspaper *Die Zeit*, in an investigative report on *Journalistenwatch* discussing these financial connections emphasized the emergence of a transnational German-American *Neue Recht* or New Right (2017). This harkens back to the formulation of the French New Right or *Nouvelle Droite* in the 1960s, which was strongly influenced intellectually by neo-reactionary Alain de Benois, who has simultaneously sought to promote a shared, homogenous French identity while positioning Islam and immigration as anathema to French cultural values (Shurts 2022). These dynamics are incredibly familiar in today's political contexts in the US and Germany.

In categorizing *Journalistenwatch's* coverage, Schmidt notes that the *"Gewöhnlich schwankt der Tenor der Texte zwischen Islamkritik und kuscheligem AfD-Rechtspopulismus"* (2017), or that the "tenor of texts varies between criticism of Islam and cozy, AfD right-wing populism." Social media sites such as Twitter essentially provide a transnational public platform for fringe news outlets such as *Journalistenwatch* to reach new American audiences and strengthen ties with existing readers. Studies examining the circulation of far-right "fake news" content on Twitter have noted that the outlet not only reaches a German national audience, but increasingly has developed an American readership as well (Heft et al. 2020b; 2020a). While *Journalistenwatch* is not the most connected or prestigious outlet, it stands out for its prolific production of Tweets and its centralized position within far-right Twitter networks (Heft et al. 2020b; 2020a).

In this type of scenario, where a singular account has an outsized influence and is a constant poster, we may ask, why would the enforcement of a stricter content moderation policy on Twitter not be enough? Why not de-platform? Or, might the implementation of Community Notes on *Journalistenwatch's* posts provide additional factual context to the spurious stories they share? In the case of providing added context to Tweets or labels indicating the presence of non-factual information, these interventions have not proven to be successful (Papakyriakopoulos and Goodman 2022, 2548), and, in American contexts there is evidence that conservative or right-leaning users in particular uniquely disregard these labels and continue to engage with content when it is clearly marked as disputed or untrue (Lees, McCarter, and Sarno 2022). As such, this attempt at "soft moderation" as it is termed (Papakyriakopoulos and Goodman 2022, 2541), is ineffectual. Users continue to share, and produce, their own "fake news" on Twitter because of "partisan polarization," or, in the parlance of political science, "out-group hatred" (Osmund-sen et al. 2020). However, this form of hatred is not merely semantic or termino-logical in so far as the phrase "out-group" sanitizes it, but increasingly this hatred is targeted towards certain marginalized groups—Muslim communities—as well as women, queer communities, and the Jewish community.

Simply banning these accounts is not an effective strategy of "hard modera-tion" either (Zannettou 2021). While banning or de-platforming certain high-profile offenders can decrease the toxicity of discourse on sites to some extent (Jhaver et al. 2021), this type of moderation only addresses singular sites rather than the larg-er digital platform ecosystem where far-right actors and ideas continue to migrate, circulate, and proliferate. This is precisely the issue with @jouwatch, which re-mains an active news site and maintains today a presence on Gettr, an alternative social media site founded by former Trump spokesman and advisor Jason Miller, known for his hardline anti-immigration views and affinity with white nationalist literature and writing (Rogers and DeParle 2019).

Similar in structure to Twitter, Gettr is part of a genre of platforms defined as alternatives to mainstream social media platforms such as Twitter, Facebook, or Instagram, which both far-right and mainstream conservatives allege to have lib-eral biases (Clayton 2020). These alternative platforms are situated as bastions of free speech but are rife with technical challenges, have minor user bases in com-parison to mainstream platforms, and have struggled to implement content mod-eration policies of their own (Hart 2021; Lee 2021; Teh 2022). Gettr, for example, has failed to address instances of child sex abuse imagery and terroristic content including videos of beheadings (B. Gilbert 2021; Scott and Nguyen 2021).

@jouwatch, in making the switch to Gettr after its own de-platforming is mere-ly part of a larger trend of far-right actors and outlets in either shifting to an al-ternative site or paralleling one's presence on Twitter with participation on Gettr or another alt-tech platform. Despite the growing pains alt-tech platforms face (Johnson et al. 2022), they continue to proliferate and offer a subterranean network between mainstream social media sites, more extreme platforms like 4chan, and the Darknet. As concerning as the growth of these alt-tech platforms may be, with Gettr boasting a growing user-base in the US after podcast-influencer Joe Rogan's creation of an account and its emerging popularity in Brazil (Lahut 2022; Lima 2021), what has also emerged as a new challenge is the symbiosis be-tween far-right accounts on mainstream platforms and a completely different dig-ital medium—private messaging apps.

@jouwatch, in addition to maintaining a presence on Gettr also boasts its own Telegram channel, representing a larger trend of increased usage by far-right ac-tors of messaging platforms such as Telegram or Signal to communicate directly and privately with audiences. Users on messaging applications like Telegram can create channels and share multi-media information, images, text, videos, and files. Telegram, an encrypted platform initially used by journalists and activists living under authoritarian governments seeking to communicate (Schwirtz 2021), has since become incredibly popular with far-right actors in the US and in Germany (Dockery 2022). @jouwatch, for example, has over 12,800 subscribers to its Telegram channel. This is to say that the implementation of hard content moderation on Twitter does not fully disrupt the supply chain of far-right content in the larger digital media ecosystem. Twitter serves as both a staging ground for mainstream socially conversative users to become radicalized, who then journey to alt-tech platforms, and a stage where extremist content produced on these external platforms is (re)presented to a more mainstream or what far-right actors would call "normie" audience (Chapelan 2021, 285). These external sites that feed content to Twitter thus act as "tastemakers" of the larger Internet (Hine et al. 2017, 1), making content moderation on Twitter an exercise in plugging a dam with duct tape.

Regardless of the off platform connectivities of far-right accounts, another critical problem is presented by Twitter's built-in functionality of hashtagging and quote Tweeting, where users re-Tweet a post but frame it with their own comment. This allows users to re-frame content with their own rhetorical and ideological messages despite the intended message or meaning of the origin post. While hashtags are not unique to Twitter, they serve a particular function on the platform and have taxonomical and archival properties, grouping messages and content together so they become more legible to certain audiences on the platform (Losh 2019, 52). Hashtags can be understood as "framing" tools that advance particular political narratives and messages for activists (Bennett and Segerberg 2015), and they are deployed by users and activists of all political persuasions on Twitter (Edwards et al. 2021, 16).

Far-right users make liberal use of hashtags within the German Twittersphere taking content such as a story from mainstream sources like @Tagesspiegel, visible in the graph, about how a supposed majority of police officers in the German state of Hesse are concerned that the country may be "Islamized" (*Der Tagesspiegel* 2020), repurposing the story using a series of hashtags including #Islamisierung, #IslamicTerrorism, and #Extremismus. In re-framing the article with this series of hashtags users on Twitter are able to draw upon the authority of the @Tagesspiegel as a respected news source but completely elide the more complex context presented in the story—that Hesse police officers have been under investigation for far-right extremism including sharing images of Hitler and racist epitaphs in private chat groups (*Der Tagesspiegel Online* 2018; Salmen 2019). Hashtagging alongside content including images, texts, videos, and links works to generate "affective intensities" which then produce publics (Gajjala et al. 2023, 8), hashtags thus are both effective *and* affective tools at the disposal of users on Twitter (Edwards et al. 2021, 8). Using quote Tweeting and tagging, far-right German users on Twitter are able to re-frame and create new content to be circulated on the platform regardless of where the source originates from.

As such, this singular visualization illustrates the informational infrastructure that makes up far-right German networked publics on Twitter. Far-right actors on Twitter utilize built-in platform affordances such as hashtagging and quote-Tweeting to disseminate their messages more effectively and affectively to reach sympathetic audiences on the platform. Conversely, we can see through the de-platforming of certain bad actors the larger, vibrant media ecosystem underneath and adjacent to Twitter which is composed of alt-tech platforms and messaging applications. This presents fundamental challenges for the implementation of either platform specific policies of hard moderation or the enactment of legal policies such as NetzDG which may fail to capture the influence of smaller niche sites or private communication channels.

The following graph illustrates a repetition of these same trends, here from April 7th, 2020. Graph H has a very low density of 0.007, which suggests that the larger network itself is diffuse and fragmented and visibly we can see each community is siloed into their own conversational clusters. There are 24 communities in total within this network with a modularity of 0.911. The top in-degree measures feature users including @welt, a mainstream German news organization with an in-degree of 20 (WELT 2007) and a German far-right activist supportive of Trump and Q Anon, @LenaMoser6, with an in-degree of 12 (LenaMoser6 2020).

What gained significant traction in this graph was users re-Tweeting @Reimund_Ruhe's Tweet mentioning @LenaMoser6: "*@LenaMoser6 Leider, Leider, – wie lange noch ? Mit jedem Tag mehr #Merkel-Regime wird Deutschland weiter beschädigt [swearing face] #Massenmigration #Umvolkung #Islamisierung #Deindustrialisierung Abschaffung der #Demokratie und #Meinungsfreiheit ! #MerkelMussWeg wird tägl. WICHTIGER #Steinmeier auch!*" (Reimund_Ruhe 2021), which translates to "Sadly, sadly – how much longer? With every day more of the Merkel regime, Germany will be damaged. Mass migration, population, Islamization, deindustrialization, abolition of democracy and freedom of opinion. Merkel's gotta go is more important with every day! Steinmeir also!"

Here, Steinmeir refers to German Federal President Frank-Walter Steinmeier (Der Bundespräsident 2021), and the poster references Merkel's previous policy decisions to allow the entrance of asylum seekers into Germany. Among far-right German micro-influencers and everyday users we see an association made between immigration, deindustrialization, and supposed democratic and demographic decline, themes that are constitutive in American far-right media discourse that link together immigration with a supposed loss of American manufacturing jobs and larger processes of globalization (Edwards 2020), also signaling the generic-

Graph H: Germany April 7, 2020.

ness of far-right populist ideology among German and American digital communities. Duisburg and Detroit become interchangeable, and so to do Turkish and Syrian Muslim immigrant communities in the transnational far-right imagination. Islam, however, becomes a critical floating signifier in German and American far-right circles to be constructed as Othered and racialized, and in constructing this Other, the racial, ethnic, and religiously homogenous white national German and American community becomes visible.

Alongside these users, another institutional voice becomes legible: @Polizei-Berlin_E, which is the official Twitter account for the German Berlin Police Department with an in-degree of 7 (Polizei Berlin Einsatz 2014). Looking at these accounts in tandem; an institutional news organization, a far-right conspiracy theorist, and a governmental agency, reveals the beginnings of a far-right preoccupation with conspiracy theories and mosques against the backdrop of the COVID-19 pandemic but also illustrates again the power of hashtagging in advancing conspiratorial and extreme rhetorical framings of news and information on Twitter.

@welt appears in this graph related to a story titled *"Wenn der Muezzin "Bleibt zu Hause!" ruft"* or "When the Muezzin calls out 'Stay home!'" (WELT 2020). The story focuses on the threat of COVID-19 spread through religious gatherings of all types and discusses how a ban on congregating for religious purposes has strained German communal life. @welt appeared as such an influential network actor because of this story, with users were connecting back to @welt as it was the origin source of the news article. Far-right users then picked up the story and re-circulated it, falsely suggesting that Muslim communities in particular contributed to the spread of COVID-19 because of practices of communal prayer at Friday services or due to holidays such as Ramadan, a trend also visible in the traditional British press media but here was spearheaded by individual German Twitter users (Poole and Williamson 2021).

Connecting directly to this story within the same data scrape, @PolizeiBerlin_E Tweeted, *"Bei Gebetsrufen versammelten sich heute vor einer Moschee in #Neukölln ca. 300 Personen. Dem Imam, dem OA @BerlinNkl & unseren Kolleg. gelang es nur zum Teil, die Anwesenden zum Abstandhalten zu bewegen. Das Gebet wurde im Einvernehmen mit dem Imam vorzeitig beendet. #covid19,"* which translates to "[t]oday about 300 people gathered in before the New Cologne Mosque. The Imam, the OA @BerlinNkl, and our colleagues only partially were able to get those present to keep their distance. An agreement with the Imam was reached to end the prayer early #covid19" (Polizei Berlin Einsatz 2020).

The spread of COVID-19 in Germany and supposed Muslim gatherings became a key topic of conversation among far-right German circles early in the pandemic. What these top three in-degree users illustrate here is that perfectly legitimate news stories and events—the topic of religious communities during the pandemic and a potential mass gathering in New Cologne—becomes fodder for far-right users to advance racist, Islamophobic messaging using the #Islamisierung and other hashtags. We can also see that transnationalized users like @LenaMoser6 command attention and influence with the network structure, suggesting an ideological symbiosis between far-right German political beliefs, the MAGA coalition, and the Q Anon movement.

Islamophobic hate-speech in Germany is diffuse and fragmented among a variety of different communities on Twitter rather than focused on key network actors as the graphs visualize. The scattered nature of this digitally networked community demonstrates both the ubiquity of Islamophobic hate-speech among German users and illustrates the challenges of content moderation. If (mis)information and hate-speech are centered around certain high-profile network actors, then account suspension may address the problem in a limited sense.

When Islamophobic hate-speech is organic and diffuse on platforms such as Twitter *and* produced off platform on Telegram, Gettr, or even hosted on formalized yet fringe digital publications like *Journalistenwatch,* it becomes almost impossible to prevent, particularly in a corporate climate that is hostile to hard moderation strategies. Musk, for example, recently decreed that the company will no long enforce its COVID-19 (mis)information policy (Lomas 2022). With platforms disinclined to rigorously enforce hard content moderation policies, or, in the case of Twitter, are led by a Chief Executive Officer who has flirted with violent far-right conspiracy theories and supported the re-platforming of influential white nationalists, neo-Nazis, and far-right politicians (D. Gilbert 2022), far-right actors on and off platform are entering an increasingly conducive environment to spread propaganda and radicalize new adherents.

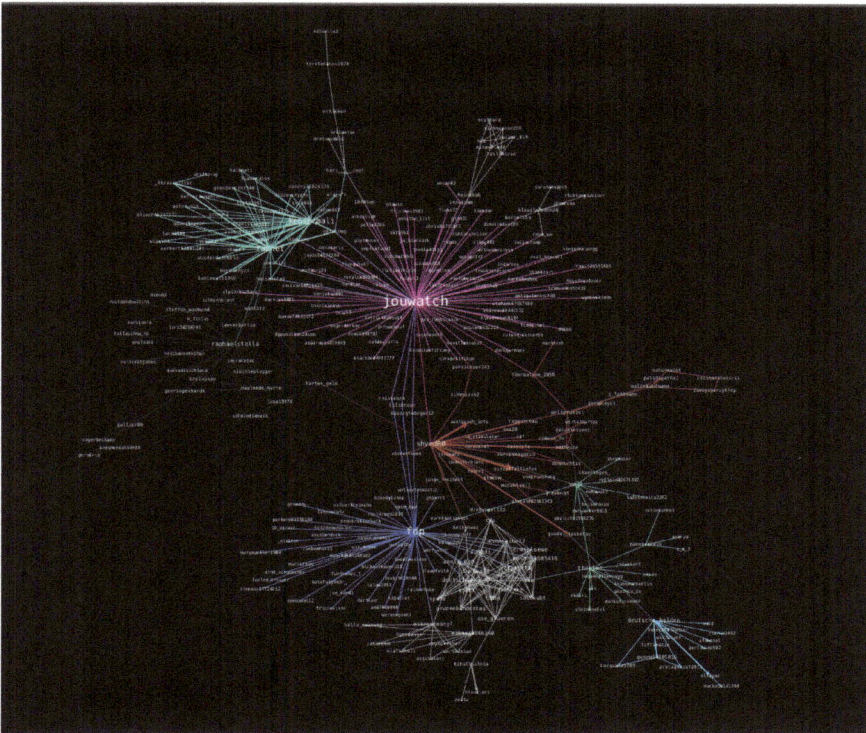

Graph I: Germany May 1, 2020.

These users are often connected back to external sites, such as fringe news outlets like *Journalistenwatch,* or users who maintain parallel presences on other platforms which play a critical role in looping back Islamophobic hate-speech and conspiracy theories to Twitter. In the extremely fragmented Graph I from May 1ˢᵗ, 2020, with a density of 0.004 and a modularity of 0.817, while the 29 communities appear siloed, @jouwatch continues to dominate the structure, even when we filter out the peripheral communities who comprised less than 5% of the network and utilize the Yifan Hu lay-out instead of the Yifan-Hu Proportional lay-out to produce a more legible visualization. @jouwatch boasts a commanding 90 degree measurement, illustrating its prestige and influence in the community. The power of its gravitational pull is evident in the graph. The content that garnered such attention was a news interview with a principal of a Mainz school who wore a t-shirt with the Arabic script that read هداية or "Hidayah," which means guidance (Jouwatch 2020). @jouwatch posted about this as evidence of "Islamization" of German public schools. And again, while @jouwatch has since been suspended on Twitter, it continues to produce news stories on its website with an entire section devote to the topic of "Islam" and its supposed dangers.

Conversely, in the next graph from June 5ᵗʰ, 2020 featuring 20 communities, a low density of 0.01, and a modularity of 0.831, far-right micro-influencers like the suspended account @Impronaut1 dominate the conversation, however, we also see the persistence of institutionalized actors like @drdavidberger and @Uwe_Junge_MdL, an anti-Merkel publicist and an AfD politician and former military official (Berger 2010; Junge 2016), as major network actors within the German far-right Twittersphere. These publics may include a diverse typography of German users, and audiences coalesce around accounts from far-right micro-influencers, news outlets, both fringe and mainstream, as well as governmental or institutional actors. And while in far-right German Twitter publics the origin source of conservations frequently may come from news stories or institutional accounts, it is everyday users who amplify and re-frame the content for their own aims, acting as critical messengers.

Frequently network actors with the highest out-degree metric have been suspended, such as @Impronaut1, @LenaMoser6, or @jouwatch. Seemingly this might suggest that Twitter's content moderation policies function effectively to target (mis)information spreaders. However, the barrier to attaining a high out-degree number is extremely low. One must only connect heavily with other users; simply being very active on Twitter allows one to achieve a high-out degree. Achieving a high in-degree requires some level of influence, trust, and popularity among the community. In other words, with every suspended high out-degree user another account can quickly usurp this position and continue to amplify (mis)information.

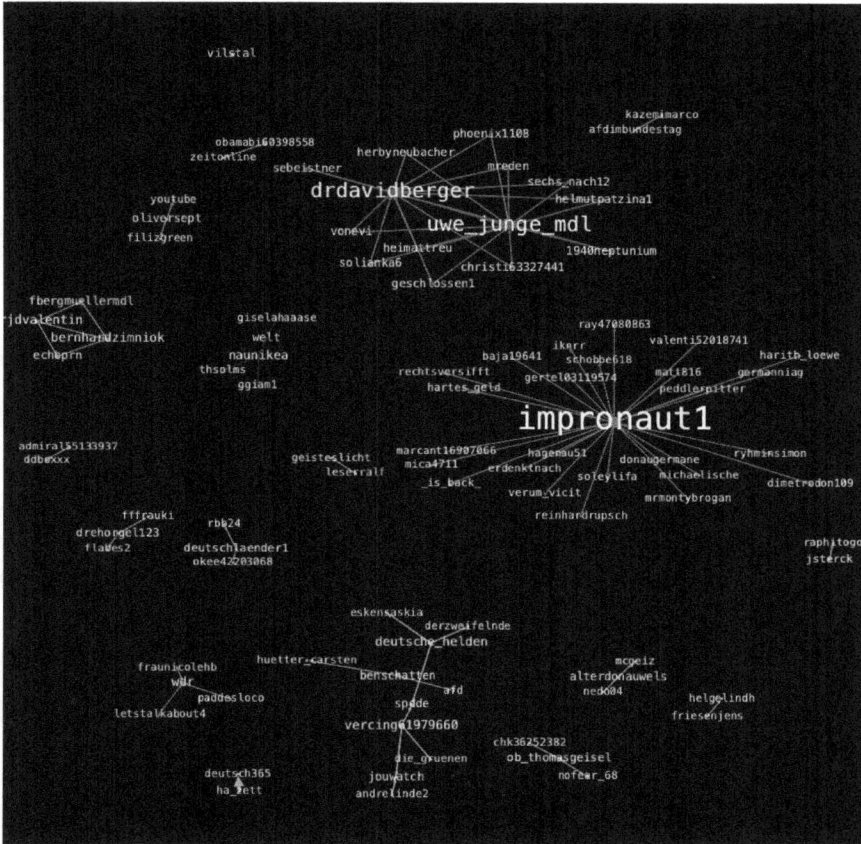

Graph J: Germany June 5, 2020.

Twitter invites users to engage in public conversation through posting and hashtagging, which the company situates as a means to allow "people to easily follow topics they are interested in" and to "categorize those Tweets" (Twitter n.d.). The ability of far-right users, or any users, to hashtag and re-categorize content on the platform allows posters to essentially re-create an alternative archive of information, here one that forwards a conspiratorial, extreme, Islamophobic narrative. Tweets, images, text, and links within the digitally mediated environment of Twitter are polysemous in meaning (Keller 2002, 8), and thus practices of hashtagging serve to taxonomize, categorize, and even transform that content to be consumed and traded among members of far-right publics.

The last two graphs, from July 27th, 2020 and August 8th, 2020 solidify these trends of user appropriation of content and re-affirm the dominance of news out-

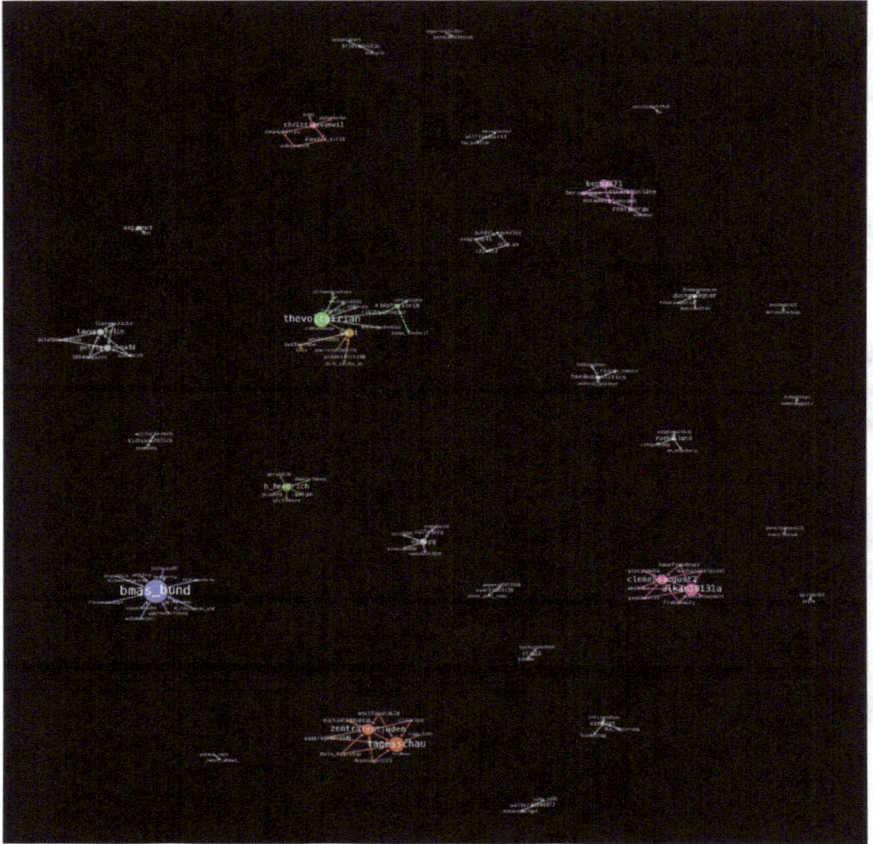

Graph K: Germany July 27, 2020.

lets within the German far-right Twittersphere. While Graph K from July 27th, 2020 is very dispersed with a density of 0.007 and a modularity 0.929, including 29 separate communities, the user with the second highest in-degree measure is @tagesschau, a mainstream national and international German news agency (tagesschau 2007). Here users connected to @tagesschau because of its publication of a news story concerning the President of the Central Council of Jews, Josef Schuster, discussing the resurgence of antisemitism in Germany (tagesschau 2020). While the article ostensibly focused on the issue of antisemitism, far-right German users were connecting to @tagesschau to comment on Schuster's remarks, instead suggesting that Schuster had no right to draw attention to antisemitism in Germany because of his support of immigration, circuitously arguing that Muslims, not native Germans, are the true originators of antisemitism in the country.

A Tweet from @Westfalen1670 with an out-degree of 2 makes this claim explicit: "*@tagesschau Wer den Import von Antisemiten befördert und aufkommenden #Antisemitismus dazu benutzt den politischen Gegner der #Bundesregierung zu diskreditieren, der ist eine Marionette und keine Vertretung seiner Gemeinde @ZentralratJuden #Islamisierung*" (Westfalen1670 2020a), which translates to "[a]nyone who supports the importation of antisemitism and uses emerging antisemitism to discredit the government is a puppet and not representative of his community." @Westfalen1670's comments about Schuster being a "puppet" minimizes actual record high instances of antisemitic violence in Germany as the alleged fault of the Jewish community because of their support for immigrants, predominately Muslim asylum seekers. This illustrates how far-right reactionary ideologies overlap in their targeting of marginalized communities (DW 2021), both Jews and Muslims. In a singular Tweet, @Westfalen1670 accomplishes a huge ideological leap—that Muslim immigrants, not Germans, are the source of antisemitic violence in Germany and that German Jews are in league with Muslim immigrants to discredit the German state. Antisemitism is imbricated alongside Islamophobia in the context of far-right conspiracy theories.

The final German graph from August 8th, 2020, which like the final American graph, summarizes larger patterns evident in this far-right ecosystem. This graph has a density of 0.01 and a modularity of 0.772 with 17 communities and features recurrent bad actors such as @Deutschlaender1 and @R1chtungswieser, as well as far-right news websites like @anonynews. Repeating key trends, the top in-degree user for this graph is @welt with an in-degree measure of 27. The Tweet that causes the major linkages from @welt focuses similarly on issues of Muslim demographics, here in Lebanon. The Tweet states: "*[a];s der #Libanon noch eine christliche Mehrheit hatte, war er die "Schweiz des Nahen Ostens", seit die Islamisten dominieren geht es bergab, jetzt droht der Staatsbankrott. #Islamisierung...*" (Ebner 2020).

The Tweet states, "[w]hen Lebanon had a Christian majority, it was the 'Switzerland of the Near East,' since Islamic dominance things have gone downhill with bankruptcy. Islamization." The Tweet then links to an article about the then recent explosion in the Lebanese port of Beirut published in *Welt* (Stocker 2020). The article discusses the explosion and makes an argument that since the Muslim population of Lebanon has risen the state has become increasingly destabilized; a specious argument that flattens and ignores the state's unique challenges related to civil war, globalization, and refugee movements into the country (Faour 2007). This type of argument about demography appears across multiple contexts—American, Indian, and German—illustrating similar rhetorical strategies of far-right emphasis on racial demographics across these different national contexts.

The graph also boasts a large subcommunity centered around @cducsubt, which is the Twitter handle of the CDU-CSU faction in the German Bundestag, in-

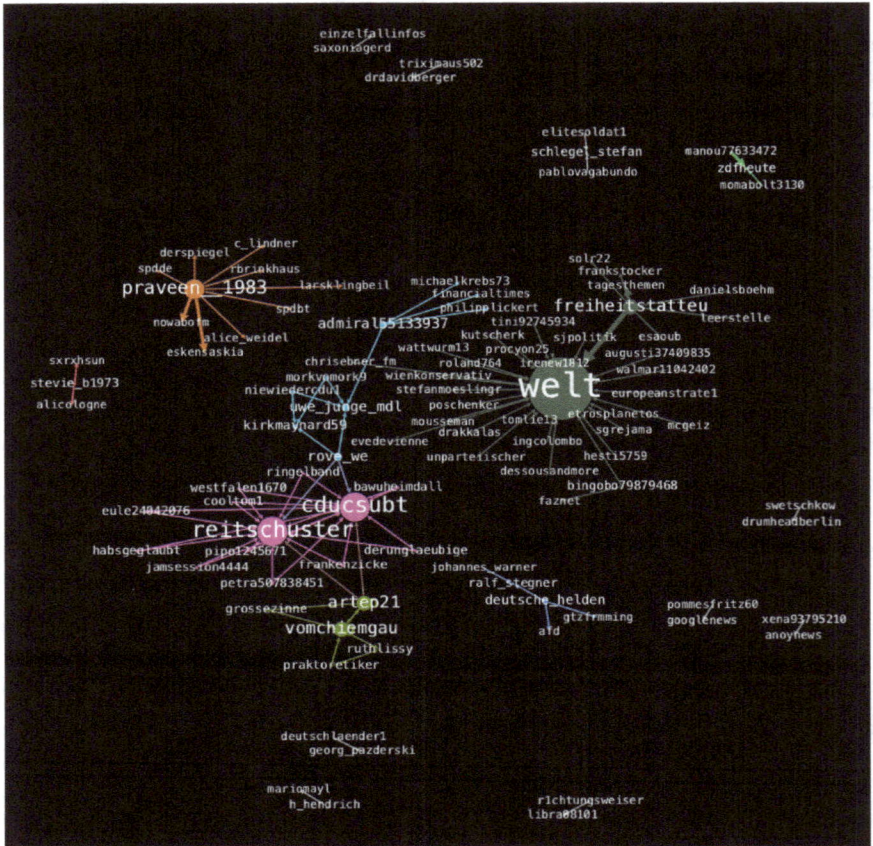

Graph L: Germany August 8, 2020.

cluding the CDU and its partner party in the state of Bavaria, the Die Christlich-Soziale Union (CSU) (CDU/CSU 2009)

The focus on @cducsubt also includes a discussion of Lebanon. The Tweet that spurs focus on @cducsubt as well as @reitschuster in the same community with an in-degree of 13, originates from the user @Westfalen1670 again, stating: *"Eine Teil des Textes aus einem Artikel von Boris @reitschuster über #Beirut. In 30 Jahren braucht der Leser nur noch 'Libanon' streichen und 'Deutschland' einfügen. Dank #SPD #Merkel & der @cducsubt"* (Westfalen1670 2020b). @Westfalen1670, as a user with 1494 followers essentially amplifies the accounts of @cducsubt and @reitschuster, when he Tweets: "[a] piece of the text of the article from Boris @reitschuster about Beirut. In thirty years, the user will just have to delete Lebanon and replace Germany. Thanks #SPD, #Merkel, and the @cducsubt." @Westfalen1670 appears in the pink community, but is a smaller node compared to the @cducsubt and @reitschuster in terms of degree size with an out-degree of 2. However, it is the commentary and connections @Westfalen1670 makes that are absolutely critical as they spur discussion and conversation amongst the larger network structure community.

In the case of this graph series, we see that far-right German Islamophobic digital publics are complex, fragmented communities that cluster around real-world events whether that is political policies or news events related to the COVID-19 pandemic. Dubious journalism from fringe outlets such as @jouwtach or @anonynews as well as authentic mainstream news stories from reputable outlets such as @welt are all equally picked up by far-right users who provide their own racialized, Islamophobic, inaccurate framings of headlines and stories. The stories that resonate with users based upon contextual analysis of Tweet content from the graphs focuses primarily on visible and aural displays of Muslim religiosity in Germany. And in the context of the COVID-19 public health crisis, issues of religious worship are racialized and utilized by far-right actors to advance conspiratorial narratives.

But if this is the state of the German ecosystem on Twitter, how might it be possible to materially address the torrent of hate-speech and (mis)information on the platform? Looking at different strategies Twitter has deployed over the course of company's history offers some insight into what could be done, and what types of policies, if any, are likely to be articulated in the current context of a highly fractious corporate take-over by Musk. There is also an increasing appetite for technology regulation from both entities like the European Union (EU) and even the American Republican Party. This final section engages with recent histories of Twitter's content moderation policy and its failures to address (mis)information and hate-speech while considering alternative strategies whether that be legislation or citizen advocacy.

Content Moderation Failures and Opportunities

Content moderation has been a perennial and vexing problem for social media platforms like Twitter which operate on user-generated content, with Zizi Papacharissi classifying contemporary social medias as "content farms" rather than platforms (Papacharissi 2022). Unlike traditional medias which produce their own content following internal corporate policies, industry guidelines, and federal laws, new media platforms have had to contend with moderating and managing user-generated content that ranges from the distasteful to the illegal. Content moderation is a commercial strategy employed by new media companies where corporations make and enforce rules about what content can and cannot be shared or produced on their site (Gerrard 2020, 748), with much of the actual implementation of identifying and removing flagged content often carried out by precariously employed contract workers (S. T. Roberts 2021). Increasingly platforms have sought to develop algorithms to automate these processes with varied success (Gorwa, Binns, and Katzenbach 2020).

As per Section 230 of the Communications Decency Act of 1996 in the US, not only are platforms not liable for the user-generated content posted on their sites, but they retain the power to articulate their own community standards, deciding what content is acceptable or unacceptable on the platform (Congress 1996). Despite this latitude, most mainstream platforms have developed and enact content moderation policies, even if they unevenly or capriciously enforce such policies (Wilson and Land 2021, 1046–1047). Unlike obvious examples of objectionable and illegal content, such as child sex abuse imagery or live-streamed videos of mass shootings, hate-speech has long presented a problem for platforms because of the slipperiness of the label and the persistent influence of the "libertarian roots of the early web, the belief that all speech, no matter how vile or offensive, is not only protected, but an essential part of what makes the Internet what it is" (Shepherd et al. 2015, 4).

Twitter, since its founding in 2006, has gone through many iterations of content moderation strategies updating both its definitions of hate-speech or hateful conduct and zigzagging between various initiatives and strategies of soft and hard content moderation, and the company ambled along until the 2010s. 2011 was a watershed moment for Twitter as activists in Tunisia took to the physical streets to oust President Zine El Abidine Ben Ali and demand democratic reforms and began using the digital streets of Twitter to spread their message to a global audience (Poell and Darmoni 2012). These pro-democracy protests in Tunisia are recognized as the start of the Arab Spring where citizens and activists in Libya, Egypt, Yemen, Syria, and Bahrain began similar campaigns protesting for democratization and other social reforms.

Critically, these activists made strategic use of social media, particularly Twitter, to both communicate to coalitions inside the country and to attract attention and support from a global allies (Howard and Hussain 2013). The Arab Spring has been alternatively been discussed or derided as a "Twitter Revolution" (Gladwell 2010; Jenkins 2013; Tufekci 2011). However, regardless of its categorization as a success or failure, the Arab Spring undeniably presented Twitter's first major content moderation challenge as activists took to the platform to post both excoriating anti-governmental Tweets and graphic images and videos of police, military, and security forces enacting brutal violence upon citizens, which ostensibly violated its policies.

Allowing these images to continue circulating because of their political significance positioned the company tangentially as supporting not merely a generic
freedom of expression, but enhanced Twitter's legitimacy as a platform for serious
political discourse and activism (Common 2020, 140), an authentic digital public
square thus raising the stakes of content moderation. However, in proceeding
years, Twitter, like other technology companies, has at times sided with authoritarian interests and acquiesced to removing content deemed objectionable by states
such as Turkey (Silverman 2015). The "country-withheld Tweet policy" continues
to be implemented, effectively censoring user-produced content to comply with individual state laws (Deep 2022).

And, until this 2014, the largest content moderation challenges social media
companies faced were primarily related to political activism of pro-democracy
movements, until far-right content became more visible and extreme. 2014 precipi-
tated the American rightward swing and inaugurated a new media ecology dominated by far-right extremist culture and the influence of fringe communities and
platforms which we can trace back to #GamerGate. There are numerous assess-
ments and summaries of the complex incident (Aghazadeh et al. 2018), but in
short, #GamerGate was a misogynistic harassment campaign initially targeting
feminist game designer Zoë Quinn, alleging they had an unethical romantic relationship with game reporter Nathan Grayson that influenced positive coverage of
Quinn's work, with right-wing trolls rallying around a superficial cry of "ethics in
games journalism" to engage in digital harassment (Dewey 2014).

The #GamerGate movement brought together a collection of extreme misogynistic and far-right actors originating from 4chan but quickly spread to Twitter, with
the hashtag #GamerGate and the seemingly anodyne phrase calling for "ethics in
games journalism" becoming rhetorical coverage for a vitriolic and violent reaction to the perceived increased representation of women, people of color, and
queer communities in the video game industry (Todd 2015). #GamerGate expanded
to target academics as well, with supporters suggesting scholarly discussion of feminism and video games was evidence of a coordinated conspiracy between the
"elite" interests of journalists and researchers to "destroy" the games industry
(Chess and Shaw 2015).

While the campaign began on 4chan, #GamerGate became visible and tangible
on Twitter, and involved doxxing, violent threats, and harassment of Quinn as well
as other prominent female game designers and critics such as Brianna Wu and
Anita Sarkeesian. #GamerGate in terms of its multi-platform character, reliance
on hashtags, and ideological miasma of extreme misogyny, homophobia, transpho-
bia, and racism was a critical precursor to the resurgence of digitally driven far-
right populist politics in the US (Bezio 2018). Other similar violent harassment campaigns targeting women of color followed on Twitter including attacks against

Black comedian Leslie Jones and Vietnamese-American actress Kelly Marie Tran who starred in the female-led *Ghostbusters* reboot and *Star Wars* franchise respectively (Blodgett and Salter 2018; Karlis 2017). While far-right digital discourse and politicking may originate in peripheral corners of the Internet, it becomes materially meaningful when it spreads to mainstream platforms like Twitter.

Following #GamerGate, Donald Trump won the 2016 American presidential election, and while it is reductive to suggest his capture of the White House was powered by a digital army of clever "shitposters" (Phillips, Beyer, and Coleman 2017), the far-right digital cultural shift was evident through the influence of new fringe digital outlets like *Breitbart* and the spread of election (mis)information on social media circulated by both Americans and Russian bots (Jamieson 2020; J. Roberts and Wahl-Jorgensen 2022). Following these high-profile instances of extreme misogynistic digital harassment of public figures and the troubling spread of (mis)information, Twitter, following in the steps of its competitors, attempted to enact more substantive content moderation standards with more detailed definitions of hate-speech (Jeong 2016)

Despite this, while still under the leadership of Jack Dorsey, Twitter struggled to adapt to a new era of digital culture dominated increasingly by far-right extremists (Ganesh 2018, 31), encapsulated by former President Trump's prolific usage of Twitter to articulate not only administrative policies and communicate official information but to serve as a megaphone amplifying white supremacist, misogynistic, Islamophobic, anti-immigrant positions, conspiracy theories, and at times incomprehensible speech (Gounari 2018). Twitter's application of the public official or public interest exception to its rules allowed Trump to continue broadcasting his views until finally his account was banned for continuing to incite anti-state violence during the January 6 Insurrection (Conger, Isaac, and Frenkel 2021). Although since Musk's acquisition of the company and a simple Twitter poll asking if the former President should have his account re-instated, Trump has been allowed back on the platform but has not yet posted (Primack and King 2022), preferring to remain on his own platform Truth Social.

As such, even during periods of more stable corporate leadership, Twitter had not developed a comprehensive and successful content moderation policy. And now, the long-term implications of Musk's leadership at the company are still unclear. However, in addition to mass lay-offs including contractors at the company tasked with implementing content moderation policies (Ortutay and O'Brien 2022), researchers have identified an "unprecedented" uptick in violent, racist hate-speech and the re-platforming of multiple accounts of white supremacists and other far-right figures (Frenkel and Conger 2022). There will be tensions between Musk's position as a "free speech" absolutist with a penchant for Tweeting white nationalist and antisemitic memes and the legal realities of ensuring the company is in compliance with the EU's Digital Services Act (DSA) which include much stricter rules related to content moderation and features financial penalties of 6 % of a company's global annual turnover should a corporation fail to meet its standards.

Twitter has thus gone through a range of content moderation strategies, none of which could be identified as broadly successful; however, Musk's takeover has inaugurated a new era of chaotic management which presents not only challenges in terms of enacting content moderation through a skeletal workforce but for civil and governmental actors attempting to push the company to comply with certain regulations or societal norms. Even in the most ideal situation, content moderation is incredibly difficult as hate-speech is contextual (Wilson and Land 2021, 1029). This is to say, language and rhetoric can have different meanings in different community contexts, not to mention platforms such as Twitter fail to engage in moderation in local, indigenous languages allowing problematic content to slip past (Mathur et al. 2018).

So, if effective moderation will not come voluntarily from Twitter, what *are* the possible strategies of disrupting the supply-chain of Islamophobic hate-speech on the platform? As this chapter has explored, even enacting forms of hard moderation; de-platforming particular accounts is not an airtight solution because of the larger networked platform ecosystem far-right actors can continue to operate within and around. Even before the tumultuous Musk acquisition, Twitter's Hateful Conduct Policy provided strategic gaps that allowed the company to avoid dealing with nuanced, contextual instances of hate-speech, harassment, and (mis)information:

> You may not promote violence against or directly attack or threaten other people on the basis of race, ethnicity, national origin, caste, sexual orientation, gender, gender identity, religious affiliation, age, disability, or serious disease…You may not use hateful images or symbols in your profile image or profile header. You also may not use your username, display name, or profile bio to engage in abusive behavior, such as targeted harassment or expressing hate towards a person, group, or protected category (Twitter 2021)

In their policy, Twitter goes on to emphasize that it aims to prevent abuse of groups that have been "historically marginalized," however, Twitter only acts upon hate-speech if it contains a specific "violent threat" towards a particular group or individual such as references to mass murder or violence targeting a specific group, incitement of violence against specific groups, or *repeated* racialized slurs, suggesting a singular use of slurs or hateful imagery is acceptable (Twitter 2021), or that indirect threats and attacks may in fact not violate policies. While far-right communities on Twitter are incredibly strategic in toeing the line of content moderation policies, as we have seen with their strategic re-framing of existing or external content on the platform, since Musk's take-over there has been an explosion of explicit, violent content on the platform (Spangler 2022). And in the specific case of Islamophobic content, platform moderation policies appear explicitly designed to elide dealing with these contextual forms of hate-speech.

At the current juncture there appear to be two avenues to address the crisis of hate-speech on the platform. One possible strategy is through applying pressure via EU policy and nationally specific legislation, such as in Germany. The Digital Services Act (DSA) and NetzDG both stand to impose financial penalties for technology companies which fail to comply with standards including content moderation, user-protection of data, (mis)information elimination, and protection of freedom of speech. In 2023, EU Digital Chief Thierry Breton has articulated a plan to "stress test" Twitter to ensure compliance with the DSA (Fung 2022), and more importantly, has raised the prospect of a $500 million fine or even temporary suspension of the service in the EU should Musk fail to comply with the DSA (Milmo and Rankin 2022).

The EU represents a major market for Twitter and the bloc's insistence on compliance with the DSA could represent the most painful political pressure point that could be applied to Twitter to ensure some basic level of content moderation on the platform. However, this would only ensure Twitter returns to a normative level of compliance. But as we have seen through the numerous examples of hate-speech, (mis)information, and conspiracy theories festering on the platform, that is not enough. Twitter has not only failed to address this type of content and the prospects for addressing it only grow more grim as the company limps along with Musk at the helm after his elimination of rank and file trust and safety contractors and the firing of General Counsel and the Head of Legal, Policy, and Trust at the company, Vijaya Gadde (Conger, Mac, and Isaac 2022; Ortutay et al. 2022)

Conversely, both before and after Musk's acquisition of the platform some of the most active and promising possibilities for addressing hate-speech on the platform have come from civil society actors and organizations—through coordinated campaigns. In Germany in particular there have been instances of NGOs effectively legally petitioning platforms to take greater action in removing hate-speech. HateAid, a nonprofit that offers support to victims of digital violence and fights against hate-speech on social media platforms successfully partnered with a German journalist who was subject to sexist harassment on Twitter, suing the platform for failing to delete the illegal content, winning the case including a €6,000 fine (HateAid 2021). This instance, while financially irrelevant to a platform like Twitter, represented a key moment in terms of citizen and NGO legal advocacy where a social media company was fined in the German court system for allowing the spread of hate-speech (HateAid 2021). These cases provide a template with which other individual German, and EU citizens, in conjunction with NGOs, may utilize existing legal avenues to pressure technology platforms to moderate their content.

In the context of the US, in the wake of the Musk takeover of the platform a series of NGOs and activists including Media Matters for America, Accountable Tech, and the National Association for the Advancement of Colored People (NAACP), have banded together under the #StopToxicTwitter campaign hashtag, penning a letter to major advertisers including Amazon, HBO, and Apple asking them to pause their advertising on Twitter, which draws 90% of its revenue from digital advertising, or leave the platform entirely (Dang 2022; Tangalakis-Lippert 2022). 51 of the 100 named brands in the letter have paused advertising resulting in a major drop in revenue, with Musk lashing out at activists as allegedly attempting to "destroy free speech" (Tabahriti 2022). Whether such campaigns are sustainable and able to realize structural change of the larger platformed digital media ecosystem is less clear.

However, these coordinated pressure campaigns by civil actors, NGOs, activists, and private citizens may be effective mechanisms of forcing Twitter either to comply with content regulation standards enshrined in law or to pressure the platform to act to address sudden trends of hate-speech, both on a case-by-case basis. These forms of protest and legal penalty are individuated solutions to structural problems of how our platformed digital ecosystem is organized. Critically, these campaigns are only successful when they are backed either by risk of major financial penalty or banning from certain markets. However compelling financial penalties may be, a full ban, for example from the EU bloc, is unlikely. We can look to the US federal government flipflopping on banning ByteDance's massively successful app TikTok due to is possible misuse of American consumer data as a dress rehearsal for how the EU might engage with Twitter (Coldewey 2022); public criticism and a possible financial slap on the wrist.

In the current context, potential elimination of Twitter from the Apple App store, which allows Apple consumers to download applications, presents a greater threat. Apple has removed alt-tech apps from its app store due to lapses in content moderation that allowed for the proliferation of dangerous and illegal content that violated its App Store Review Guidelines (Peters and Lyons 2021). Recently, Musk has sparred with Apple CEO Tim Cook, suggesting that Apple was considering removing Twitter from its App store, but he later walked back these claims (Milmo 2022). Just as Twitter makes up a critical part of a larger digital media ecosystem alongside other social media platforms, these pieces of infrastructure; the Google Play Store and the Apple App Store, where consumers are able to access and download digital platforms or applications also present a space where civil pressure could be asserted through boycotts, campaigns, or new legislation.

While Twitter may not be invested in processes of content moderation, these avenues of legal challenges in the EU and financial penalties created by consumer boycotts and campaigns remain some of the only options for the public to address the crisis of far-right hate-speech in digital spaces at the current moment. It may be impossible to eliminate or de-platform sites where extremists gather entirely, the resurrection of Kiwi Farms and 8kun signals the regenerative quality of the far-right (Hall 2022). However, forcing Twitter to apply to some level content moderation policies even on a case-by-case basis represents a tangible decrease in abuse users suffer. More importantly, the implementation of hard content moderation strategies could starve far-right groups of more mainstream socially conservative audiences to radicalize. Pushing for stricter content moderation policies on Twitter will not address the root causes of a resurgence of racialized, ethnic, and religious nationalist far-right movements, but it will cut off far-right groups from a critical medium through which they spread their messages.

Conclusion

This chapter has explored the German far-right informational ecosystem on and beyond Twitter, identifying patterns of (mis)information transmission and key influential actors, such as mainstream and fringe digital news sites as well as alt-tech platforms which constitute a crucial substratum between mainstream platforms and extremist sites. We have seen the way in which individual users makes use of the affordances of the platform to strategically re-frame content, images, and new stories with Islamophobic, conspiratorial rhetoric through the mechanism of hashtagging and quote-Tweeting.

On mainstream platforms it is not the dominance of far-right actors such as @jouwatch that is most concerning, rather it is average, everyday users who act as grassroots information amplifiers and transmitters of Islamophobic content. Concerningly, the practices of individual users in spreading Islamophobic far-right content does not breach Twitter's Hateful Conduct policy, which itself is strategically articulated to elide dealing with contextual or implicit issues of hate-speech, violence, or (mis)information. And in a new corporate environment led by Elon Musk these extreme actors are emboldened. Ultimately, the most disturbing pattern presented in the German graph series is the ease at which everyday users are able to reappropriate mainstream news stories or information for their own purposes to further disseminate racist, Islamophobic, and conspiratorial far-right discourse on the platform.

Content moderation policies such as Twitter's Hateful Conduct policy are not operationalized to address the racialized, conspiratorial, Islamophobic conversations users engage in and around hashtags such as #Islamisierung. Through the simple act of adding the hashtag #Islamisierung to a Tweet and "@"ing accounts, far-right German users are able to create new narratives, networks, and realties. While Twitter has gone through a variety of content moderation strategies over the past several years, at times trying to address instances of targeted harassment and (mis)information, Musk's acquisition of the platform and his affection for far-right positions under the guise of "free speech absolutism" has created an environment not only where there is a material inability of Twitter to engage in content moderation practices because of mass lay-offs, but a shift in company policy towards an embrace of increasingly extreme speech.

The path forward to address the growing crisis of far-right extremist rhetoric on the platform will rely upon legal and civil advocacy whereby territory specific regulations and laws coupled with threat of severe financial penalty may be the only way forward for governmental and civil actors to force Twitter to enact a basic level of compliance. Despite this, far-right content and actors continue to proliferate on Twitter circulating stories, memes, images, and conspiracies that originate from darker corners of the Internet, some of which Musk himself has amplified. In this next chapter, we look at conspiracy networks and how viral conspiracies emerge on the platform Twitter targeting Muslim communities and other marginalized groups. Looking specifically at the way in which (mis)information circulates on Twitter reveals not only how conspiracies are repurposed historically and contemporarily but illustrates how Islamophobia serves as the core of a transnationalized form of far-right ideology.

References

Agarwal, Mohit. 2021. "Freedom, Decentralisation and the Regulation of Content on Social Media." https://mohit.uk/work/written-files/socialmedia2021.pdf.

Aghazadeh, Sarah A., Alison Burns, Jun Chu, Hazel Feigenblatt, Elizabeth Laribee, Lucy Maynard, Amy L. M. Meyers, Jessica L. O'Brien, and Leah Rufus. 2018. "GamerGate: A Case Study in Online Harassment." In *Online Harassment*, edited by Jennifer Golbeck, 179–207. Human–Computer Interaction Series. Cham: Springer International Publishing. https://doi.org/10.1007/978-3-319-78583-7_8.

Alter, Charlotte. 2022. "Elon Musk and the Tech Bro Obsession With 'Free Speech.'" *Time*, April 29, 2022. https://time.com/6171183/elon-musk-free-speech-tech-bro/.

Aziz, Afdhel. 2019. "The Power Of Purpose: How We Counter Hate Used Artificial Intelligence To Battle Hate Speech Online." *Forbes*, December 25, 2019. https://www.forbes.com/sites/afdhelaziz/2019/12/25/the-power-of-purpose-how-we-counter-hate-used-artificial-intelligence-to-battle-hate-speech-online/.

Bennett, W. Lance, and Alexandra Segerberg. 2015. "Communication in Movements." In *The Oxford Handbook of Social Movements*, edited by Donatella Della Porta and Mario Diani, 367–82. Oxford, UK: Oxford University Press.

Berger, David. "Profile." Twitter, 2010.

Bezio, Kristin MS. 2018. "Ctrl-Alt-Del: GamerGate as a Precursor to the Rise of the Alt-Right." *Leadership* 14 (5): 556–66. https://doi.org/10.1177/1742715018793744.

Binder, Matt. 2022. "Suddenly 'Q' of the QAnon Conspiracy Theory Has Returned after a Years-Long Hiatus." *Mashable*, June 25, 2022, sec. Life. https://mashable.com/article/q-qanon-conspiracy-theory-returns-8kun.

Bivens, Rena. 2015. "Under the Hood: The Software in Your Feminist Approach." *Feminist Media Studies* 15 (4): 714–17. https://doi.org/10.1080/14680777.2015.1053717.

Blodgett, Bridget, and Anastasia Salter. 2018. "Ghostbusters Is For Boys: Understanding Geek Masculinity's Role in the Alt-Right." *Communication, Culture and Critique* 11 (1): 133–46.

Bond, Shannon. 2022. "Elon Musk Said Twitter Wouldn't Become a 'hellscape.' It's Already Changing." *NPR*, October 31, 2022, sec. Technology. https://www.npr.org/2022/10/31/1132906782/elon-musk-twitter-pelosi-conspiracy.

Brady, William J., Ana P. Gantman, and Jay J. Van Bavel. 2020. "Attentional Capture Helps Explain Why Moral and Emotional Content Go Viral." *Journal of Experimental Psychology: General* 149: 746–56. https://doi.org/10.1037/xge0000673.

Bridge Initiative Team. 2018. "FACTSHEET: MIDDLE EAST FORUM." Georegetown University. https://bridge.georgetown.edu/research/factsheet-middle-east-forum/.

Caplan, Robyn, Lauren Hanson, and Joan Donovan. 2018. "Dead Reckoning Navigating Content Moderation After "Fake News"." New York: Data & Society Institute.

CDU/CSU. 2009. "Profile." Twitter. 2009. https://twitter.com/cducsubt.

Chapelan, Alexis. 2021. "'Swallowing the Red Pill': The Coronavirus Pandemic and the Political Imaginary of Stigmatized Knowledge in the Discourse of the Far-Right." *Journal of Transatlantic Studies* 19 (3): 282–312. https://doi.org/10.1057/s42738-021-00073-2.

Chess, Shira, and Adrienne Shaw. 2015. "A Conspiracy of Fishes, or, How We Learned to Stop Worrying About #GamerGate and Embrace Hegemonic Masculinity." *Journal of Broadcasting & Electronic Media* 59 (1): 208–20. https://doi.org/10.1080/08838151.2014.999917.

Clayton, James. 2020. "Social Media: Is It Really Biased against US Republicans?" *BBC News*, October 27, 2020, sec. Technology. https://www.bbc.com/news/technology-54698186.

Coldewey, Devin. 2022. "They're Not Going to Ban TikTok (But...)." *TechCrunch*, November 1, 2022, sec. Social. https://techcrunch.com/2022/11/01/theyre-not-going-to-ban-tiktok-but/.

Coleman, Keith. 2021. "Introducing Birdwatch, a Community-Based Approach to Misinformation." *Twitter* (blog). January 25, 2021. https://blog.twitter.com/en_us/topics/product/2021/introducing-birdwatch-a-community-based-approach-to-misinformation.

Common, MacKenzie F. 2020. "Fear the Reaper: How Content Moderation Rules Are Enforced on Social Media." *INTERNATIONAL REVIEW OF LAW, COMPUTERS & TECHNOLOGY* 34 (2): 126–52. https://doi.org/10.1080/13600869.2020.1733762.

Conger, Kate, Mike Isaac, and Sheera Frenkel. 2021. "Twitter and Facebook Lock Trump's Accounts After Violence on Capitol Hill." *The New York Times*, January 6, 2021, sec. Technology. https://www.nytimes.com/2021/01/06/technology/capitol-twitter-facebook-trump.html.

Conger, Kate, Ryan Mac, and Mike Isaac. 2022. "Elon Musk Fires Twitter Employees Who Criticized Him." *The New York Times*, November 15, 2022, sec. Technology. https://www.nytimes.com/2022/11/15/technology/elon-musk-twitter-fired-criticism.html.

Congress. 1996. *Communications Decency Act (CDA). 47 U.S. Code § 230 – Protection for Private Blocking and Screening of Offensive Material.* Vol. 230. https://www.law.cornell.edu/uscode/text/47/230.

Dang, Sheila. 2022. "'Toxic Twitter' Activists Ramp up Pressure on Brands after Trump Account Reinstated." *Reuters*, November 22, 2022, sec. Technology. https://www.reuters.com/technology/toxic-twitter-activists-ramp-up-pressure-brands-after-trump-account-reinstated-2022-11-21/.

Deep, Aroon. 2022. "Exclusive: Twitter Closes Major Loophole for Government-Censored Tweets." *Entrackr*, August 24, 2022. https://entrackr.com/2022/08/exclusive-twitter-closes-major-loophole-for-government-censored-tweets/.

Der Bundespräsident. "Federal President Frank-Walter Steinmeier." *Bundespräsidialamt* (blog), 2021. https://www.bundespraesident.de/EN/Federal-President/federal-president-node.html.

Der Tagesspiegel. 2020. "Umfrage unter 17.000 Beamten: Mehr als jeder vierte Polizist in Hessen fürchtet Islamisierung Deutschlands," February 3, 2020. https://www.tagesspiegel.de/politik/mehr-als-jeder-vierte-polizist-in-hessen-furchtet-islamisierung-deutschlands-4140829.html.

Der Tagesspiegel Online. 2018. "Rechtsextremes Netzwerk: Weitere Suspendierung wegen rechtsextremer Chatgruppe," December 19, 2018. https://www.tagesspiegel.de/politik/weitere-suspendierung-wegen-rechtsextremer-chatgruppe-3072145.html.

Dewey, Caitlin. 2014. "The Only Guide to Gamergate You Will Ever Need to Read." *The Washington Post*, 2014, sec. Internet Culture. https://www.washingtonpost.com/news/the-intersect/wp/2014/10/14/the-only-guide-to-gamergate-you-will-ever-need-to-read/.

Dockery, Wesley. 2022. "Germany Cracks down on Far-Right Telegram Users – DW – 02/09/2022." *DW*, February 9, 2022, sec. Politics. https://www.dw.com/en/germany-cracks-down-on-far-right-telegram-users/a-60715438.

DW. 2021. "Germany Sees Spike in Antisemitic Crimes – Reports." *DW*, February 11, 2021. https://www.dw.com/en/germany-sees-spike-in-antisemitic-crimes-reports/a-56537178.

Ebner, Christian. 2020. ""Als Der #Libanon Noch Eine Christliche Mehrheit Hatte, War Er Die "Schweiz Des Nahen Ostens", Seit Die Islamisten Dominieren Geht Es Bergab, Jetzt Droht Der Staatsbankrott. #Islamisierung Https://Welt.de/Wirtschaft/Article212450215/Libanon-Die-Schweiz-Des-Nahen-Ostens-Will-Sich-an-China-Verkaufen.Html... via @welt." Twitter. July 31, 2020. https://twitter.com/ChrisEbner_FM/status/1289082117180334080.

Edwards, Emily. 2020. "24-Hours in the Alt-Right Media Ecosystem: Analyzing Race, Space, and Labor in Breitbart's Coverage of the Mollie Tibbetts Murder." *Critical Studies in Media Communication* 38 (1): 32–45. https://doi.org/10.1080/15295036.2020.1851735.

Edwards, Emily, Sarah Ford, Radhika Gajjala, Padmini Ray Murray, and Kiran Vinod Bhatia. 2021. "Shaheen Bagh: Making Sense of (Re)Emerging 'Subaltern' Feminist Political Subjectivities in Hashtag Publics through Critical, Feminist Interventions." *New Media & Society.* https://doi.org/10.1177/14614448211059121.

Faour, Muhammad A. 2007. "Religion, Demography, and Politics in Lebanon." *Middle Eastern Studies* 43 (6): 909–21. https://doi.org/10.1080/00263200701568279.

Fenton, Natalie. 2010. "News in the Digital Age." In *The Routledge Companion to News and Journalism*, edited by Stuart Allen, 557–67. London New York: Routledge.

Frenkel, Sheera, and Kate Conger. 2022. "Hate Speech's Rise on Twitter Is Unprecedented, Researchers Find." *The New York Times*, December 2, 2022, sec. Technology. https://www.nytimes.com/2022/12/02/technology/twitter-hate-speech.html.

Fung, Brian. 2022. "Twitter Must Comply with Europe's Platform Rules, EU Digital Chief Warns Musk in Virtual Meeting | CNN Business." *CNN*, November 30, 2022. https://www.cnn.com/2022/11/30/tech/twitter-eu-compliance-warning/index.html.

Gajjala, Radhika, Emily Lynell Edwards, Debipreeta Rahut, Ololade Margaret Faniyi, Bedadyuti Jha, Jhalak Jain, Aiman Khan, and Saadia Farooq. 2023. "Transnationalising Dadis as Feminist Political/Activist Subjects." *Feminist Encounters: A Journal of Critical Studies in Culture and Politics* 7 (1): 08. https://doi.org/10.20897/femenc/12886.

Ganesh, Bharath. 2018. "The Ungovernability of Digital Hate Culture." *Journal of International Affairs* 71 (2): 30 – 49.

German Criminal Code (Strafgesetzbuch – StGB). 1998. *German Criminal Code (Strafgesetzbuch – StGB)*. https://www.gesetze-im-internet.de/englisch_stgb/englisch_stgb.html.

Gerrard, Ysabel. 2020. "Social Media Content Moderation: Six Opportunities for Feminist Intervention." *Feminist Media Studies* 20 (5): 748 – 51. https://doi.org/10.1080/14680777.2020.1783807.

Gilbert, Ben. 2021. "A Pro-Trump Social Media Service Built on 'freedom of Speech' Isn't Moderating Some Child Pornography." *Business Insider*, August 16, 2021. https://www.businessinsider.com/pro-trump-social-media-service-not-moderating-some-child-pornography-2021-8.

Gilbert, David. 2022. "Elon Musk Is Turning Twitter Into a Haven for Nazis." *Vice*, November 29, 2022. https://www.vice.com/en/article/n7zm9q/elon-musk-twitter-nazis-white-supremacy.

Gladwell, Malcolm. 2010. "Small Change." *The New Yorker*, September 27, 2010. https://www.newyorker.com/magazine/2010/10/04/small-change-malcolm-gladwell.

Gorwa, Robert, Reuben Binns, and Christian Katzenbach. 2020. "Algorithmic Content Moderation: Technical and Political Challenges in the Automation of Platform Governance." *Big Data & Society* 7 (1): 2053951719897945. https://doi.org/10.1177/2053951719897945.

Gounari, Panayota. 2018. "Authoritarianism, Discourse and Social Media: Trump as the 'American Agitator.'" In *Critical Theory and Authoritarian Populism*, edited by Jeremiah Morelock. London: University of Westminster Press. https://www.academia.edu/38010773/Authoritarianism_Discourse_and_Social_Media_Trump_as_the_American_Agitator.

Griffin, Rachel. 2022. "New School Speech Regulation as a Regulatory Strategy against Hate Speech on Social Media: The Case of Germany's NetzDG." *Telecommunications Policy* 46 (9): 102411. https://doi.org/10.1016/j.telpol.2022.102411.

Gunia, Amy. 2019. "Facebook Restricts Live-Streaming in Wake of Christchurch." *Time*, May 15, 2019. https://time.com/5589478/facebook-livestream-rules-new-zealand-christchurch-attack/.

Hall, Ellie. 2022. "The Notorious Kiwi Farms Is Back Online." *BuzzFeed News*, October 19, 2022, sec. Tech. https://www.buzzfeednews.com/article/ellievhall/kiwi-farms-back-online-keffals-campaign-null.

Hart, Robert. 2021. "Parler's Popularity Plummets As Data Reveals Little Appetite For Returning 'Free Speech' App Favored By Conservatives." *Forbes*, June 2, 2021. https://www.forbes.com/sites/roberthart/2021/06/02/parlers-popularity-plummets-as-data-reveals-little-appetite-for-returning-free-speech-app-favored-by-conservatives/.

Hartmann, Margaret. 2018. "Facebook Haunted by Its Handling of 2016 Election Meddling." *New York Magazine*, March 18, 2018. https://nymag.com/intelligencer/2018/03/facebook-haunted-by-its-handling-of-2016-election-meddling.html.

HateAid. 2021. "HateAid Sets a Precedent in Germany: Twitter Must Pay 6,000 Euros Financial Compensation for Not Removing Sexist Insults to a User." Berlin: HateAid gGmbH. https://hateaid.org/press-release-twitter-precedent/.

Haysom, Sam. 2020. "'This Claim Is Disputed' Twitter Meme Is Here to Question Your Baseless Statements." *Mashable*, November 17, 2020. https://mashable.com/article/twitter-this-claim-is-disputed-meme.

Heath, Alex. 2022. "Elon Musk Is Putting Twitter at Risk of Billions in Fines, Warns Company Lawyer." *The Verge*, November 10, 2022. https://www.theverge.com/2022/11/10/23451198/twitter-ftc-elon-musk-lawyer-changes-fine-warning.

Heft, Annette, Eva Mayerhöffer, Susanne Reinhardt, and Curd Knüpfer. 2020a. "Organization Beyond Breitbart: Comparing Right-Wing Digital News Infrastructures in Six Western Democracies." *Policy and Internet* 12 (1): 20–45.

Heft. 2020b. "Toward a Transnational Information Ecology on the Right? Hyperlink Networking among Right-Wing Digital News Sites in Europe and the United States." *The International Journal of Press/Politics*. https://doi.org/10.1177/1940161220963670.

Heldt, Amélie. 2020. "Germany Is Amending Its Online Speech Act NetzDG... but Not Only That." *Internet Policy Review*. https://policyreview.info/articles/news/germany-amending-its-online-speech-act-netzdg-not-only/1464.

Hine, Gabriel Emile, Jeremiah Onaolapo, Emiliano De Cristofaro, Nicolas Kourtellis, Ilias Leontiadis, Riginos Samaras, Gianluca Stringhini, and Jeremy Blackburn. 2017. "Kek, Cucks, and God Emperor Trump: A Measurement Study of 4chan's Politically Incorrect Forum and Its Effects on the Web." *ArXiv:1610.03452 [Physics]*, October. http://arxiv.org/abs/1610.03452.

Hong, Mathias. 2022. "Regulating Hate Speech and Disinformation Online While Protecting Freedom o..." *Journal of Media Law* 14 (1): 76–96. https://doi.org/10.1080/17577632.2022.2083679.

Howard, Philip N., and Muzammil M. Hussain. 2013. *Democracy's Fourth Wave?: Digital Media and the Arab Spring*. Oxford Studies in Digital Politics. New York: Oxford University Press.

Jamieson, Kathleen Hall. 2020. *Cyberwar: How Russian Hackers and Trolls Helped Elect a President: What We Don't, Can't, and Do Know*. Oxford: Oxford University Press.

Jenkins, Henry. 2013. "Twitter Revolutions?" In *Spreadable Media Creating Value and Meaning in a Networked Culture*, edited by Henry Jenkins, Sam Ford, and Joshua Green. New York: NYU Press. https://spreadablemedia.org/essays/jenkins/index.html.

Jeong, Sarah. 2016. "The History of Twitter's Rules." *Vice*, January 14, 2016, sec. Technology. https://www.vice.com/en/article/z43xw3/the-history-of-twitters-rules.

Jhaver, Shagun, Christian Boylston, Diyi Yang, and Amy Bruckman. 2021. "Evaluating the Effectiveness of Deplatforming as a Moderation Strategy on Twitter." *Proceedings of the ACM on Human-Computer Interaction* 5 (CSCW2): 381:1–381:30. https://doi.org/10.1145/3479525.

Johnson, Hailey, Karl Volk, Robert Serafin, Cinthya Grajeda, and Ibrahim Baggili. 2022. "Alt-Tech Social Forensics: Forensic Analysis of Alternative Social Networking Applications." *Forensic Science International: Digital Investigation*, Proceedings of the Twenty-Second Annual DFRWS USA, 42 (July): 301406. https://doi.org/10.1016/j.fsidi.2022.301406.

Journalistenwatch. "Profile." Twitter, 2012. https://twitter.com/jouwatch.

Jouwatch. 2020. "Islamisierung an Höchster Stelle: Mainzer Grundschulrektorin Wirbt Im MOMA Für Die Führung Des Korans," April 30, 2020, sec. Frontpage. https://www.journalistenwatch.com/2020/04/30/islamisierung-stelle-mainzer/.

Junge, Uwe. "Profile." Twitter, 2016. https://twitter.com/Uwe_Junge_MdL.

Karlis, Nicole. 2017. "Threats against Kelly Marie Tran Highlight a Fear of Women Who Break Sexist Stereotypes | Salon.Com." *Salon*, December 28, 2017. https://www.salon.com/2017/12/28/threats-against-kelly-marie-tran-highlight-a-fear-of-women-who-break-sexist-stereotypes/.

Keller, Douglas. 2002. "Critical Perspectives on Visual Imagery in Media and Cyberculture." *Journal of Visual Literacy* 22 (1): 81–90.

Lahut, Jake. 2022. "Joe Rogan Joins GETTR, a MAGA Alternative to Twitter, Following Rep. Marjorie Taylor Greene's Ban." *Business Insider*, January 3, 2022. https://www.businessinsider.com/joe-rogan-joins-gettr-a-maga-alternative-to-twitter-after-mtg-ban-2022-1.

Lee, Micah. 2021. "Inside Gab, the Online Safe Space for Far-Right Extremists." *The Intercept*, March 15, 2021. https://theintercept.com/2021/03/15/gab-hack-donald-trump-parler-extremists/.

Lees, Jeffrey, Abigail McCarter, and Dawn M. Sarno. 2022. "Twitter's Disputed Tags May Be Ineffective at Reducing Belief in Fake News and Only Reduce Intentions to Share Fake News Among Democrats and Independents." *Journal of Online Trust and Safety* 1 (3). https://doi.org/10.54501/jots.v1i3.39.

LenaMoser6. "Profile." Twitter, 2020. https://twitter.com/LenaMoser6.

Lima, Cristiano. 2021. "Analysis | Gettr, Parler, Gab Find a Fanbase with Brazil's Far-Right." *Washington Post*, November 9, 2021. https://www.washingtonpost.com/politics/2021/11/09/gettr-parler-gab-find-fanbase-with-brazils-far-right/.

Lomas, Natasha. 2020. "Germany Tightens Online Hate Speech Rules to Make Platforms Send Reports Straight to the Feds." *TechCrunch*, June 19, 2020. https://techcrunch.com/2020/06/19/germany-tightens-online-hate-speech-rules-to-make-platforms-send-reports-straight-to-the-feds/.

Lomas, Natasha. 2022. "Twitter Says It's No Longer Enforcing COVID-19 Misleading Information Policy." *TechCrunch*, November 29, 2022. https://techcrunch.com/2022/11/29/twitter-covid-29-misleading-info-policy-change/.

Losh, Elizabeth. 2019. *Hashtag*. Object Lessons. London, UK: Bloomsbury Publishing.

Mac, Ryan, Mike Isaac, and David McCabe. 2022. "Resignations Roil Twitter as Elon Musk Tries Persuading Some Workers to Stay." *The New York Times*, November 17, 2022, sec. Technology. https://www.nytimes.com/2022/11/17/technology/twitter-elon-musk-ftc.html.

Mac, Ryan, Benjamin Mullin, Kate Conger, and Mike Isaac. 2022. "A Verifiable Mess: Twitter Users Create Havoc by Impersonating Brands." *The New York Times*, November 11, 2022, sec. Technology. https://www.nytimes.com/2022/11/11/technology/twitter-blue-fake-accounts.html.

Mathur, Puneet, Rajiv Shah, Ramit Sawhney, and Debanjan Mahata. 2018. "Detecting Offensive Tweets in Hindi-English Code-Switched Language." In *Proceedings of the Sixth International Workshop on Natural Language Processing for Social Media*, 18–26. Melbourne, Australia: Association for Computational Linguistics. https://doi.org/10.18653/v1/W18-3504.

Milmo, Dan. 2022. "Elon Musk 'Resolves' Apple Row over 'Removal of Twitter from IPhone Store.'" *The Guardian*, December 1, 2022, sec. Technology. https://www.theguardian.com/technology/2022/dec/01/elon-musk-resolves-apple-row-over-removal-of-twitter-from-iphone-store.

Milmo, Dan, and Jennifer Rankin. 2022. "EU Raises Prospect of Big Fine or Ban If Twitter Fails to Follow New Legislation." *The Guardian*, November 30, 2022, sec. Technology. https://www.theguardian.com/technology/2022/nov/30/eu-raises-prospect-of-big-fine-or-ban-if-twitter-fails-to-follow-new-legislation.

Münch, Felix Victor, Ben Thies, Cornelius Puschmann, and Axel Bruns. 2019. "Mining Influencers in the German Twittersphere: Mapping a Language-Based Follow Network (IC2S2 2019) | Snurblog." Presented at the International Conference on Computational Social Science, Amsterdam, July 18. https://snurb.info/node/2590.

Noyan, Oliver. 2021. "Germany's Push for Tighter Tech Regulation." *Euractiv*, July 26, 2021, sec. Internet governance. https://www.euractiv.com/section/internet-governance/news/germanys-push-for-tighter-tech-regulation/.

Ortutay, Barbara, Tom Krisher, Matt O'Brien, and AP. 2022. "Musk Takes over Twitter, Fires Content Moderation Chief and Now Policing Hate Speech Is His Job." *Fortune*, October 29, 2022. https://fortune.com/2022/10/29/musk-twitter-content-moderation-policing-hate-speech/.

Ortutay, Barbara, and Matt O'Brien. 2022. "Twitter Layoffs Slash Content Moderation Staff as New CEO Elon Musk Looks to Outsource." *USA TODAY*, November 15, 2022. https://www.usatoday.com/story/tech/2022/11/15/elon-musk-cuts-twitter-content-moderation-staff/10706732002/.

Osmundsen, Mathias, Alexander Bor, Peter Bjerregaard Vahlstrup, Anja Bechmann, and Michael Bang Petersen. 2020. "Partisan Polarization Is the Primary Psychological Motivation behind Political Fake News Sharing on Twitter." PsyArXiv. https://doi.org/10.31234/osf.io/v45bk.

Papacharissi, Zizi. 2015. "Affective Publics and Structures of Storytelling: Sentiment, Events and Mediality." *Information, Communication & Society* 19 (3): 307–24. https://doi.org/10.1080/1369118X.2015.1109697.

Papacharissi, Zizi. 2022. "Don't Call Them Platforms. Or Town Squares. They Are Not That. They Are Content Farms." Tweet. *Twitter.* https://twitter.com/zizip/status/1524755858357460993.

Papakyriakopoulos, Orestis, and Ellen Goodman. 2022. "The Impact of Twitter Labels on Misinformation Spread and User Engagement: Lessons from Trump's Election Tweets." In *Proceedings of the ACM Web Conference 2022*, 2541–51. Virtual Event, Lyon France: ACM. https://doi.org/10.1145/3485447.3512126.

Papasavva, Antonis, Savvas Zannettou, Emiliano De Cristofaro, Gianluca Stringhini, and Jeremy Blackburn. 2020. "Raiders of the Lost Kek: 3.5 Years of Augmented 4chan Posts from the Politically Incorrect Board." *Proceedings of the International AAAI Conference on Web and Social Media* 14 (May): 885–94.

Peters, Jay, and Kim Lyons. 2021. "Apple Removes Parler from the App Store." *The Verge*, January 10, 2021. https://www.theverge.com/2021/1/9/22221730/apple-removes-suspends-bans-parler-app-store.

Phillips, Whitney, Jessica Beyer, and Gabriella Coleman. 2017. "Trolling Scholars Debunk the Idea That the Alt-Right's Shitposters Have Magic Powers." *Vice*, March 22, 2017. https://www.vice.com/en/article/z4k549/trolling-scholars-debunk-the-idea-that-the-alt-rights-trolls-have-magic-powers.

Pipes, D. 2001. "The Danger Within: Militant Islam in America." *Commentary* 112 (4). https://www.commentary.org/articles/daniel-pipes/the-danger-within-militant-islam-in-america/.

Pipes, Daniel. 1995. "There Are No Moderates: Dealing with Fundamentalist Islam." *The National Interest*, no. 41: 48–57.

Poell, Thomas, and Kaouthar Darmoni. 2012. "Twitter as a Multilingual Space: The Articulation of the Tunisian Revolution Through #Sidibouzid." SSRN Scholarly Paper. Rochester, NY. https://papers.ssrn.com/abstract=2154288.

Polizei Berlin Einsatz. 2014. "Profile." Twitter. 2014. https://twitter.com/PolizeiBerlin_E.

Polizei Berlin Einsatz. "Bei Gebetsrufen Versammelten Sich Heute Vor Einer Moschee in #Neukölln ca. 300 Personen. Dem Imam, Dem OA @BerlinNkl & Unseren Kolleg. Gelang Es Nur Zum Teil, Die Anwesenden Zum Abstandhalten Zu Bewegen. Das Gebet Wurde Im Einvernehmen Mit Dem Imam Vorzeitig Beendet. #covid19." *Twitter* (blog), April 3, 2020. https://twitter.com/PolizeiBerlin_E/status/1246140615936573440.

Poole, Elizabeth, and Milly Williamson. 2021. "How Racist Narratives about Muslims in the British Press Were Reconfigured during the Initial Peak of COVID-19." The London School of Economics and Political Science. *British Politics and Policy at LSE* (blog). September 7, 2021. https://blogs.lse.ac.uk/politicsandpolicy/press-reporting-muslims-covid19/.

Primack, Dan, and Hope King. 2022. "Elon Musk Reinstates Trump's Twitter Account after Poll."
Axios, November 20, 2022. https://www.axios.com/2022/11/20/donald-trump-back-on-twitter-elon-
musk.

Reimund_Ruhe. "@LenaMoser6 Leider, Leider, - Wie Lange Noch? Mit Jedem Tag Mehr #Merkel-
Regime Wird Deutschland Weiter Beschädigt [Swearing Face] #Massenmigration #Umvolkung
#Islamisierung #Deindustrialisierung Abschaffung Der #Demokratie Und #Meinungsfreiheit!
#MerkelMussWeg Wird Tägl. WICHTIGER! #Steinmeier Auch!" Twitter, April 4, 2021. https://
twitter.com/Reimund_Ruhe/statuses/1246372406467403776.

Roberts, Jason, and Karin Wahl-Jorgensen. 2022. "Reporting the News: How Breitbart Derives
Legitimacy from Recontextualised News." *Discourse & Society* 33 (6): 833–46. https://doi.org/
10.1177/09579265221095422.

Roberts, Sarah T. 2021. *Behind the Screen Content Moderation in the Shadows of Social Media.* New
Haven, CT: Yale University Press. https://yalebooks.yale.edu/9780300261479/behind-the-screen.

Rogers, Katie, and Jason DeParle. 2019. "The White Nationalist Websites Cited by Stephen Miller."
The New York Times, November 18, 2019, sec. U.S. https://www.nytimes.com/2019/11/18/us/
politics/stephen-miller-white-nationalism.html.

Salmen, Ingo. 2019. "Rechtsextremismus-Verdacht in Hessen: Polizist soll Daten an Neonazis
weitergegeben haben." *Der Tagesspiegel Online*, January 10, 2019. https://www.tagesspiegel.de/
politik/polizist-soll-daten-an-neonazis-weitergegeben-haben-4998472.html.

Schmidt, Nico. 2017. "Die Amerika-Connection der Neuen Rechten." *Die Zeit*, December 17, 2017, sec.
Kultur. https://www.zeit.de/kultur/2017-12/journalistenwatch-neue-rechte-finanzierung.

Schwirtz, Michael. 2021. "Telegram, Pro-Democracy Tool, Struggles Over New Fans From Far Right."
The New York Times, January 26, 2021, sec. World. https://www.nytimes.com/2021/01/26/world/
europe/telegram-app-far-right.html.

Scott, Mark, and Tina Nguyen. 2021. "Jihadists Flood Pro-Trump Social Network with Propaganda."
POLITICO, August 2, 2021, sec. Technology. https://www.politico.com/news/2021/08/02/trump-
gettr-social-media-isis-502078.

Shepherd, Tamara, Aubrey E. Harvey, Tim Jordan, Sam Srauy, and Kate M. Miltner. 2015. "Histories of
Hating." *Social Media + Society*, 1–10. https://doi.org/10.1177/2056305115603997.

Shurts, Sarah. 2022. "Identity, Immigration, and Islam: Neo-Reactionary and New-Right Perceptions
and Prescriptions." *Journal of the History of Ideas* 83 (3): 477–99. https://doi.org/10.1353/
jhi.2022.0023.

Silverman, Jacob. 2015. "Why Is Twitter Aiding Turkish Censorship?" *The Baffler*, April 8, 2015. https://
thebaffler.com/latest/twitter-turkey.

Solon, Olivia. 2019. "Six Months after Christchurch Shootings, Videos of Attack Are Still on
Facebook." *NBC News*, September 20, 2019. https://www.nbcnews.com/tech/tech-news/six-
months-after-christchurch-shootings-videos-attack-are-still-facebook-n1056691.

Spangler, Todd. 2022. "Twitter Blames Flood of N-Words, Other Racist Slurs Following Musk's
Takeover on an Organized 'Trolling Campaign.'" *Variety*, October 30, 2022. https://variety.com/
2022/digital/news/twitter-n-word-racist-slurs-musk-trolling-campaign-1235417866/.

Stocker, Frank. 2020. "Jetzt Steht Die "Schweiz Des Nahen Ostens" Vor Dem Zusammenbruch." *Welt*,
July 31, 2020, sec. LIBANON. https://www.welt.de/wirtschaft/plus212450215/Libanon-Jetzt-steht-
die-Schweiz-des-Nahen-Ostens-vor-dem-Zusammenbruch.html.

Tabahriti, Sam. 2022. "Elon Musk Says Activist Pressure on Twitter Advertisers Is an Attempt to
'Destroy Free Speech in America.'" *Business Insider*, November 4, 2022, sec. Tech. https://

www.businessinsider.com/elon-musk-says-twitter-activist-groups-trying-destroy-free-speech-2022-11.

tagesschau. 2007. "Profile." Twitter. 2007. https://twitter.com/tagesschau.

tagesschau. 2020. "Antisemitismus in Deutschland 'Einfach Mal Die Rote Karte Zeigen.'" *Tagesschau*, July 22, 2020. https://www.tagesschau.de/inland/schuster-halle-101.html.

Tagesspiegel. 1945. "Profile." Twitter. September 22, 1945. https://twitter.com/Tagesspiegel.

Tangalakis-Lippert, Katherine. 2022. "The #StopToxicTwitter Coalition Urging Brands to Stop Advertising on Twitter Has Resulted in 'a Massive Drop in Revenue,' Musk Says: 'They're Trying to Destroy Free Speech in America.'" *Business Insider*, November 3, 2022. https://www.businessinsider.com/activists-urging-brands-stop-ads-twitter-massive-drop-revenue-musk-2022-11.

Tarasov, Katie. 2021. "Why Content Moderation Costs Billions and Is so Tricky for Facebook, Twitter, YouTube and Others." *CNBC*, February 27, 2021. https://www.cnbc.com/2021/02/27/content-moderation-on-social-media.html.

Teh, Cheryl. 2022. "Joe Rogan Slams Social Media Platform Gettr, Calling It 'f—Ery' and 'Fugazi' Just Days after Joining." *Business Insider*, January 11, 2022. https://www.businessinsider.com/joe-rogan-slams-gettr-calling-it-fuckery-and-fugazi-2022-1.

Todd, Cherie. 2015. "COMMENTARY: GamerGate and Resistance to the Diversification of Gaming Culture." *Women's Studies Journal* 29 (1): 64–67.

Tufekci, Zeynep. 2011. "Why the 'How' of Social Organizing Matters and How Gladwell's Latest Contrarian Missive Falls Short." *Technosociology* (blog). February 4, 2011. https://technosociology.org/?p=305.

Twitter. 2021. "Hateful Conduct Policy." Twitter. 2021. https://help.twitter.com/en/rules-and-policies/hateful-conduct-policy.

Twitter. n.d. "How to Use Hashtags." Accessed November 30, 2022. https://help.twitter.com/en/using-twitter/how-to-use-hashtags.

Vernick, Gillian. 2022. "EU Poised to Impose Sweeping Social Media Regulation with Digital Services Act." *The Reporters Committee for Freedom of the Press* (blog). May 9, 2022. https://www.rcfp.org/eu-dsa-social-media-regulation/.

Voué, Pierre, Tom De Smedt, and Guy De Pauw. 2020. "4chan & 8chan Embeddings." *ArXiv:2005.06946 [Cs]*, April. http://arxiv.org/abs/2005.06946.

WELT. "Profile." Twitter, 2007. https://twitter.com/welt.

WELT. "Wenn Der Muezzin "Bleibt Zu Hause!" Ruft Http://To.Welt.de/9CJqJ5g," March 22, 2020. https://twitter.com/welt/status/1241707015325523974.

Westfalen1670. 2020a. "@tagesschau Wer Den Import von Antisemiten Befördert Und Aufkommenden #Antisemitismus Dazu Benutzt Den Politischen Gegner Der #Bundesregierung Zu Diskreditieren, Der Ist Eine Marionette Und Keine Vertretung Seiner Gemeinde. @ZentralratJuden #Islamisierung Https://T.Co/M8E4YLWSQZ." Twitter. July 21, 2020. https://twitter.com/Westfalen1670/statuses/1285840090472873984.

Westfalen1670. 2020b. "'Eine Teil Des Textes Aus Einem Artikel von Boris @reitschuster Über #Beirut. In 30 Jahren Braucht Der Leser Nur Noch '"Libanon'" Streichen Und " 'Deutschland'" Einfügen. Dank #SPD #Merkel & Der @cducsubt. #Migranten #Islamisierung Https://T.Co/WzZqGA5Ro7.'" Twitter. August 7, 2020. https://twitter.com/Westfalen1670/statuses/1291718407293935616.

Wilson, Richard A, and Molly Land. 2021. "Hate Speech on Social Media: Content Moderation in Context." *Connecticut Law Review* 52 (3): 1029–76.

Zannettou, Savvas. 2021. "'I Won the Election!': An Empirical Analysis of Soft Moderation Interventions on Twitter." In *Proceedings of the International AAAI Conference on Web and Social Media*, 15:865–76. https://doi.org/10.1609/icwsm.v15i1.18110.

Zannettou, Savvas, Tristan Caulfield, Emiliano De Cristofaro, Nicolas Kourtelris, Ilias Leontiadis, Michael Sirivianos, Gianluca Stringhini, and Jeremy Blackburn. 2017. "The Web Centipede: Understanding How Web Communities Influence Each Other through the Lens of Mainstream and Alternative News Sources." In *Proceedings of the 2017 Internet Measurement Conference*, 405–17. IMC '17. New York, NY, USA: Association for Computing Machinery. https://doi.org/10.1145/3131365.3131390.

Zurth, Patrick. 2020. "The German NetzDG as Role Model or Cautionary Tale? Implications for the Debate on Social Media Liability." *Fordham Intellectual Property, Media & Entertainment Law Journal* 31 (4): 1084–1153.

Chapter VI
Islamophobia & the Crisis of Conspiracy

Introduction

On December 12th, 2022, Elon Musk tweeted "Follow [rabbit emoji]" (Gilbert 2022). Which, in 7 characters broadcast to his 139.8 million Twitter followers and the broader public an implicit promotion of the Q Anon conspiracy theory. Or perhaps this was just another example of the world's richest man engaging in typical shit-posting (Frenkel, Gómez, and Koeze 2023). But if Musk's position was unclear, he clarified the next day Tweeting that "[t]he woke mind virus is either defeated or nothing else matters" (Goldsmith 2022). Musk's recent flirtation with the Q Anon conspiracy theory has accompanied a larger societal interest in and concern over the proliferation of conspiracy theories and (mis)information on digital platforms.

The Q Anon conspiracy theory, in particular, with its myriad, bizarre iterations has been the subject of increasing scholarly research and public commentary (Bloom and Moskalenko 2021; Hoback 2021). Composed of a series of lurid allegations, Q Anon illustrates the way in which even the most disturbing and outlandish discourse from extreme corners of the Internet can materially manifest in real life; at Trump rallies, on bumper stickers, and at the January 6 Insurrection. But the Q Anon conspiracy theory is just one of the latest and most neatly packaged far-right, digital-born conspiracy theories, frequently which are defined by Islamophobic underpinnings, and are formed off-platform and re-circulated on Twitter to a new mainstream audience (Kalmar, Stevens, and Worby 2018; Tuters, Jokubaus-kaitė, and Bach 2018).

While Twitter may not be the origin source of digital conspiracy theories, as a staging ground for public political communication and news dissemination it performs an important function in the larger Internet ecosystem, essentially serving as the setting for extreme far-right actors to broadcast conspiracies in the digital public square. Conspiracy theories play a critical role in far-right political communication as a means of "affective radicalization" of individuals whereby the "corporeal intensity" of paranoid digital content becomes the triggering factor more than the persuasiveness or logic of a narrative (Johnson 2019, 2). Conspiracy theories are a particular mode or style of communication (Johnson 2019), and for far-right communities, they are a weapon of "informational war" that is actively being waged on platforms like Facebook, Instagram, and Twitter (Hannah 2021).

https://doi.org/10.1515/9783111032887-006

As such, this chapter examines the role conspiracy theories play on Twitter as an informational weapon wielded by far-right groups against Muslim communities, but also a range of other marginalized groups and state actors. Concluding with a deep-dive on conspiracy theories knits together a multi-scalar study of the networked contours of far-right publics, the composition of these communities, and processes of content transmission. Conspiracy theories are both a method of communication and a genre of content traded by far-right actors. They are also, or have been until recently at Twitter, a subject that necessitated content moderation.

As such, examining the role conspiracy theories play in far-right networked publics and their composition provides a corollary to the previous discussion of platform governance and content moderation and presents a case study of the way in which far-right actors capitalize on state and global crises. All this heralds what Matthew Hannah calls an "informational dark age" (2021), or what we might call a digital crusade led by an army of social media users. And this global digital crusade serves as an ideological inflection point for the further transnationalization of far-right Islamophobic political coalitions and the actualization of anti-state political violence.

While conspiracy theories have figured centrally into American and German far-right politics throughout various periods (Uscinski and Parent 2014; Snyder 2016), as well as contemporarily in Indian and Nigerian anti-Muslim political discourse (Bukarti 2018; Basit 2021, 7), they are not exclusive to a singular national context, historical era, or communicative medium. In their most basic definition, conspiracy theories are "explanations of events or phenomena that challenge established accounts and instead refer to the machinations of powerful actors or secret societies" (Zeng, Schäfer, and Oliveira 2022, 929). However, increasingly far-right conspiracy theories target marginalized groups alongside powerful or elite institutions or figures.

Today, conspiracy theories spread at lightning speed on social media platforms similar to Richard Dawkins' theorization the "idea-meme" (Cannizzaro 2016, 568), or an object replicated to a new mind through viral imitation. Conspiracy theories now extend beyond isolated, fringe enclaves infecting everyday users through endless, seamless imitation. It is unlikely Musk was explicitly referencing Dawkins' theory of the "idea-meme" when he mentioned the "woke-mind virus," but his phrasing hints at the way in which political communication and ideologies in digital contexts function like a virus, and far-right politics can be understood as a chronic social disease. And while conspiracy theories are traded by online communities of a variety of political persuasions, today extremist right-wing beliefs are correlated with an embrace of conspiracy theories (van Prooijen, Krouwel, and Pollet 2015).

As Richard Hofstadter discussed ruminating on the persistent "paranoid style" that characterizes American political thought (1996), what renders this conspiratorial political pathology dangerous is the way which it may be "directed against a nation, a culture, a way of life, whose fate effects not himself alone but millions of others," whereby conspiratorial thinking becomes patriotic, righteous, and moral (1996, 4). Examining conspiracy theories as a specific style of communication also reveals the way in which the brand of American paranoid thinking and American digital-born conspiracies are exported, exchanged, and transnationalized across global contexts through the medium of Twitter.

Conspiracy theories are articulated on 8kun and polished and refined on sites like *Journalistenwatch*, then they are spread to Twitter to more mainstream users. Twitter is an effective platform for transmission because unlike comparable sites like Facebook which invite a siloing structure of private groups, it promotes open vertical and lateral communication amongst users. Content which is produced on external sites can be easily shared on platforms like Twitter to reach a level of public salience whereby it then loops back to traditional media outlets and even offline conversations. Some of the most viral and infamous conspiracies of the last ten years, including the racist, Islamophobic birtherism conspiracy theory that former President Barack Obama was not an American citizen and a practicing Muslims was circulated and shared on Twitter, by former President Donald Trump (Barkun 2017).

As such, this final chapter explores conspiracy theories circulated by far-right Islamophobic digitally networked communities and their paranoid preoccupation with topics of the family and the state, concluding with a discussion of the COVID-19 pandemic and its effects on political communication in digital spaces. Ultimately, it is the circulation of conspiracy theories on mainstream platforms like Twitter that illustrates how the "Overton window" of political discourse has shifted, with paranoid thinking mainstreamed as a constitutive aspect of contemporary politics that increasingly encourages extremist off-platform political violence (Astor 2019).

While each far-right conspiracy is unique, they are all fundamentally similar in their targeting of institutionalized groups such as national governments, major political parties, or cultural elites, for example, Hollywood stars. Far-right groups accuse these institutions and individuals as engaged in various shades of nefarious activity, but they also scapegoat Muslim communities as well as other marginalized groups. The individual conspiracy theories circulated by far-right users on Twitter are designed to advance a larger conspiracy and world-view—that racially, religiously homogenous national communities are under attack, whether the specifics of the in-group in question resonate as Christian white, ethnic German, Hindu Indian, or Igbo.

And in a moment of global crisis where for a period of time much social life and political communication shifted entirely online (Lakin 2020), far-right actors and fringe news outlets took advantage of public anxieties to situate the pandemic as a dress rehearsal for Islamization, and deployed affective symbols and narratives concerning women, children, and the family to provoke an emotional response from socially conservative users (Johnson 2018). Far-right groups play upon historic racialized suggestions of Muslim men as sexual predators and anxieties over the visible presence of Muslim religiosity in public spaces (Betz 2013; Rettberg and Gajjala 2015), all to advance notions of civilizationalist conflict which feeds into a larger conspiratorial world view.

As we have seen with the rise of Q Anon related violence, anti-lockdown protests led by vaccine skeptics, high-profile instances of political assaults such as the attack on former Democratic Speaker of the House Nancy Pelosi's husband, and the attempted coup by the German far-right extremist Reichsbürger movement (Beauchamp 2022; Lin, Hernandez, and Castleman 2022; Staiano-Daniels 2022), we must recognize it is impossible to address digital-born conspiracy theories and far-right political communication without considering their off platform implications. Not only are groups such as Muslim communities at risk of violence, but threats of violence are spreading, targeting other vulnerable groups imagined as implicated in these conspiracy theories; Jewish communities, queer and trans individuals, and increasingly, the state itself or individual government officials.

Far-right Islamophobic actors on Twitter circulate racialized, paranoid content that initially targets Muslim communities that resonates with a range of users who then become primed to consume and engage with increasingly more extreme conspiracies. Conspiracy theories are one such way to bring everyday users into the extremist fold and to mainstream paranoid thinking, which then informs the articulation of tangible political policies. We have seen this occur with Trump's embrace of Islamophobic conspiracy theories that influenced his passage of the 2017 "Muslim Ban" (Hauslohner 2016). What far-right actors seek to suggest, through the circulation of conspiracy theories, is that Muslims, alongside other imagined enemy actors and groups; Jews, the queer community, feminists, the Black community, cultural elites, and the state, are colluding together to both "destroy" Western civilization and the hetero-patriarchal family structure. This is the complex ideological leap that functions to tie together a host of seemingly unrelated and outlandish claims which we may scroll past on our feeds until piqued by one Tweet or link.

Twitter as a platform is defined by its disembedded, flattened structure that offers the possibility for any one actor, should the conditions be right, to reach a mainstream global audience, and mimetically reproduce sweeping, paranoid ideological narratives that historically would have been dismissed in earlier media environments (Hannah 2021). Far-right actors target and organize on mainstream platforms because there is no informational war to be waged on normies, "liberal cucks," or "femoids" on 4chan or 8kun, or even on alt-tech platforms like Gab or Parler (Krishan 2021). Rather these are the strategic base camps for the movement. To wage the war, far-right actors must operate on mainstream platform like Twitter, either to spread the "dark enlightenment" to radicalize new adherents (Land, n.d.), or to harass and attack their target subjects. As follows, we trace the way in which conspiracy theories are refined and traded across Twitter to radicalize socially conservative mainstream audiences focusing on topics of the family and the state, before concluding with a reflection on how the crisis of the COVID-19 pandemic created new conditions for far-right extremist content to fester and metastasize across a variety of users and national borders.

Affective Symbols: Women, Children, and the Paranoid Patriarchy

For far-right communities, women, children, and the hetero-patriarchal family unit are imagined as both representing and a means to achieve the larger idealized, racially, and religiously homogenous state. Annie Kelly notes that for far-right political communities, gender figures centrally into their worldviews, and into the conspiracies they circulate, with these groups situating "traditional patriarchal masculinity as having been subverted, not just demeaned, thereby seriously weakening the nation-state" (2017). This misogynistic framework increasingly appeals to men across racial boundaries, hence the warm reception of far-right, masculinist nationalistic rhetoric across the globe (HoSang and Lowndes 2019). These beliefs in reactionary gender roles also fit neatly into post-9/11 discourses of homeland securitization where the individual home and family emerge as a crucial site to be protected against emerging global threats, specifically the specter of Islamic terrorism (Fixmer-Oraiz 2019).

Conspiracy theories that center women and children in some sort of danger, of sexual violence, human trafficking, forcible conversion, etc., are visible as a familiar strategy to racialize and Other Muslims, going back to the Crusades (Said 1979). These conspiracies tap into a deep historical well of constructed Western cultural representations of Muslims, and the East more broadly, and thus are useful tools with which to engage and radicalize mainstream socially conservative users, particularly socially conservative women. Gendered anxieties and notions of "maternal duty" can be played upon to encourage everyday users into supporting and circulating increasingly more extreme, racist, and outlandish content (Bracewell 2021). Despite different national contexts, American and German far-right Islamophobic users re-mix historic Western, Orientalist narratives targeting Muslim men and reprise Islamophobic, gendered fears concerning practices of veiling. For far-right groups, Islamization is both an existential civilizationalist and individualized, gendered threat.

Anti-Muslim conspiracy theories situate women as vulnerable victims and comparatively suggest far-right groups are the authentic defenders of women's rights and proponents of addressing violence against women. Often more damaging than explicitly extreme content that mainstream users can identify and reject, is the circulation of conspiracy-lite content that more subtly advances the notion of coordinated, nefarious action by Muslims as a homogenized group. Such as content from users like @PatriotPetition, who Tweets *"#Imam von #Bergamo: "#Christliche-Frauen sind unsere #Beute!...#Islamisierung stoppen! Jetzt aktiv werden und #Petition unterzeichnen..."* (PatriotPetition 2020), which translates to "#Imam from Bergamo. Christian women are our #loot. Stop Islamization! Take action now and sign our #petition," producing affective, politically mobilizing content.

Here the user links out to a far-right German website *Unsere Mitteleuropa*, which discusses how an imam from the Bergamo region in Italy allegedly decreed that *"Ungläubige Frauen, die im Dschihad (heiligen Krieg) gefangen genommen werden, gelten als Beute und daher können die Mudschaheddin (islamische Kämpfer) mit ihnen tun, was sie wollen"* or "Infidel women, are captured in Jihad (holy war) and therefore the Mujahideen (Islamic fighters) can do whatever they want with them" (Vox News 2020). Associating Muslims broadly with the sensationalized case of Hafiz Muhammad Zulkifal who was arrested in Italy in 2015 as part of a counter-terrorism operation serves to suggest that Muslim men are agents of sexual violence and white, European women are victims; Orientalist rhetoric that reprises Crusade-era language of Muslim invasion as both threatening the female body and the European body politic (Fernandez 2009; Marino 2020).

This type of content is representative of a broader conspiratorial racialization of Muslim immigrants and refugees in Europe and US whereby "the myth of the immigrant rapist...reduces immigrants from a wide range of cultural, economic, and religious backgrounds to a singular entity: the violent, misogynist brown man," while also strategically eliding systemic instances of gendered and political violence as perpetuated by white men (Carroll 2017). And while @PatriotPetition has since been suspended, their website is still actively extolling visitors to follow on Facebook, Gab, and Telegram. Among far-right digitally networked communities, "gender issues are absolutely central for racist and authoritarian demands and right-wing mobilizations" and serve as a means by which to expand their co-alitions (Berg 2019, 80), and specifically to appeal to the affective, gendered anxieties of socially conservative women.

As *PatriotPetition.org* suggests, the hetero-patriarchal family unit in the far-right imaginary is directly conceived of as a mirror to the nation, whether in Germany or the US, explicitly stating that *"[d]ie Familie ist der Grundbestandteil des Volkes, das wiederum nichts anderes ist, als unsere "größere Familie,"* or "[t]he family is the basic component of the people, which is in turn nothing else but our 'larger family'" (PatriotPetition.org 2021). For far-right users and political groups, the "ethnicist concept of 'the people' [is] conveyed through the family" (Berg 2019, 81). And it is the small, perhaps easily dismissed conspiracy-lite theories, like the decontextualized story of the imam in Bergamo that undergird the articulation of more extreme gendered conspiracy theories that move beyond singular cases towards the suggestion of coordinated plots and more violent content designed to provoke stronger reactions across national contexts.

For German and American far-right groups, Islamophobic conspiracy theories that center women and stories of gender-based violence are a key part of emerging Transatlantic far-right connections. Purported lurid stories reach an American audience through Twitter and then become codified into news by alt-right digital publications like *Breitbart*, showing the interplay between user-generated content on social media platforms and formal news content from digital publications or outlets. For example, @LGcommaI Tweets: "NOT an #AprilFools: The German #women's magazine 'illu der Frau' (issue 04/2019) published #advice on how to treat knife|stab-wounds...#BRD #Deutschland:#Germany #Islamization" (Information 2020), alongside an alleged screen-shot from the mainstream German women's magazine *illu der Frau.*

The provocative image is framed by hashtags including *Multikulti*, or multiculturalism, an attempt to suggest that rising rates of knife-based assaults are related to the presence of immigrants in Germany, even though the actual text of the article does not mention immigration. This type of (mis)information feeds into a larger mediated effort by far-right groups to draw attention to high-profile cases of gender-based violence such as the Cologne New Year's Eve mass sexual harassments or the murder of Mia Kandel by her former boyfriend, an Afghan asylum-seeker, in order to situate male Muslim immigrants as agents of violence threatening white ethnic German women (Bennhold 2018; Boulila and Carri 2017), a strategy not unique to Germany.

Demonstrating the ideological symbiosis between far-right German and American audiences in the larger media ecosystem, *Breitbart* in fact ran a story discussing the piece, attempting to strengthen the association between knife attacks and immigration stating "[w]hile attacks and murders using knives have often become major headline stories – particularly those which involve migrants stabbing young German women to death, such as the cases of 15-year-old Mia in the town of Kandel in 2017 – actual reliable statistics on knife crime are sketchy at best in Germa-

Figure 1: How do I treat a stab wound?

ny" (Tomlinson 2019). Even as *Breitbart* reporter Chris Tomlinson recognizes that there is a lack of substantive data on knife attacks in Germany, he connects the *illu der Frau* article to the highly publicized case of Mia Kandel (Bennhold 2018).

This type of content does not explicitly suggest there is a secret plot afoot, and thus may not be immediately categorizable as forwarding a conspiracy theory, however, as a rhetorical strategy it takes individualized cases or pieces of information and deploys them to implicitly implicate Muslims globally, and in Germany specifically, as part of a nefarious plot to violate white European women, whereby users become primed to accept beliefs that targeted out-groups are engaged in some ambiguous yet evil action (Douglas et al. 2019; Furnham 2013, 4). As such, we see that for far-right communities, it is a conspiratorial tone or "feeling" which characterizes far-right political communication, and thus this type of content is supremely effective as a tool of "affective radicalization" (Johnson 2019). Particularly in a platformed digital landscape where "vibes" rather than facts increasingly reign supreme.

Vibes can be understood as a "a medium for feeling, the kind of abstract understanding that comes before words put a name to experience," they also possess a "pre-linguistic quality [which] makes them well suited to a social-media landscape" (Chayka 2021). While vibes are more often correlated with a series of ever-proliferating niche and mainstream consumeristic aesthetics, this concept helps illuminate the way in which far-right rhetoric makes use of conspiracies to evoke and sublimate feelings—feelings of racial or ethnic grievance—not into consumptive practices but into political mobilization. As such, this *feeling* of white European and American women as being imperiled evokes not just engagement on Twitter but serves to justify restrictive and racially discriminatory immigration policies as well as to homogenize, racialize, and criminalize Muslim communities as threatening the domestic security of the nation, state, and the family. Feelings trump facts.

While far-right users may capitalize on more free-floating types of conspiratorial communication, these groups also traffic in re-purposed historic conspiracy theories that take on new resonance in a variety of national contexts, such as the Great Replacement theory, still focusing on themes of family and gender. While the Great Replacement may be recognized as an American white nationalist conspiracy theory that posits that the white population of the nation is being "replaced" demographically with immigrants of color and Jews (Shakir 2019), most infamously circulated during the 2017 Neo-Nazi, white supremacist "Unite the Right Rally" in Charlottesville, VA when protestors chanted "Jews will not replace us" referencing the Great Replacement (Green 2017), it has a longer ideological history directly connected to European Islamophobia. While the basic contours of the Great Replacement have been spreading for quite some time in online spaces (Bjørgo and Ravndal 2019), writer and proponent of the French Identarian movement Renaud Camus coined the term initially using it as the title of one of his books (Ekman 2022), spreading its popularity and salience within German far-right circles and the AfD.

In the German context, the Great Replacement is understood as *Bevölkerungs-austausch*, which means population exchange, a phrase that has since become part of German far-right digital parlance (ISD 2020, 23; Tresckow Morley 2021, 35). This notion of *Bevölkerungsaustausch* appears centrally in far-right German conspiratorial discourse where everyday users deploy hashtags and commentary to take the raw material of factual news and spin it for their own ideological aims. For example, @ThomasRettig10 Tweets *"Bremen: Zu wenig Kindergartenplätze wegen der rasant steigenden Zahl von Migranten-Kindern (Weser-Kurier 26.06.20): #Bevölkerungsaustausch #Ersetzungsmigration #Migrationspakt #Resettlement #Replacement #Islamisierung #Masseneinwanderung #Massenmigration"* which translates to "Bremen; too few kindergarten places because of the rising number of migrant-children. Population Exchange. Replacement migration. Migration pact. Resettlement. Replacement. Islamization. Massive immigration. Mass migration" (Rettig 2020).

In this Tweet, @ThomasRettig10 discusses how allegedly there are not enough kindergarten spots for ethnic German children because of the growing number of "migrant children," suggesting that immigrants have no place in Germany society and should not have access to the same social services as ethnic German children, but also explicitly intimating that this is evidence of the, coordinated replacement of ethnic German children. The content of the Tweet includes a screen shot of news story from the newspaper *Weser-Kurier*, a regional newspaper in the Bremen area. The actual newspaper article discussing this lack of kindergarten sports in the Bremen area does not even address migration, rather the issue of a lack of kindergarten spots is reported as due to a structural lack of investment in early childhood education in the city (Faltermann 2020). However, with a few quick modifications, suddenly the headline of the story, *"In Bremen fehlen mehr als 1000 Kita-Plätze,"* becomes transformed into evidence of the Great Replacement in Germany.

For the far-right, the social reproduction of racially homogamous nations is tied to the physical reproduction of children. Alexandra Minna Stern notes this particular emphasis within both American and European far-right groups on procreation whereby the domestic-sphere is a key battleground to achieve racial-political domination (2019). The rise of far-right white influencers taking on the seemingly apolitical label of "crunchy" moms to then peddle white nationalist ideology alongside homeschooling tips and cleaning hacks on personal blogs, alt-tech platforms, and Tik Tok illustrates the centrality of gender reactionaryism and white natalism among far-right groups (Leidig 2023). And increasingly conspiracies like the Great Replacement figure centrally into recruitment and mobilization efforts targeting white women on social media platforms (Shafrir 2022).

Not only do the aesthetics and vibes of the message matter, but messengers matter too. Far-right communities do not simply re-dress hard-core white supremacist, fascist Islamophobic conspiracies on Twitter and immediately win new adherents; for extreme beliefs and conspiracies to successful undergo "normiefiction" (Zeeuw et al. 2020), a different user, the mom-next-door instead of the shitposter, must become the mediator. We see this dynamic whereby users like mom and neighbor @TheDeliaAspect situate children as in danger not only of conversion but full-blown brainwashing: "[t]his is why parents will end up home schooling their kids/let them skip college to protect them from teachers/professors that'll brainwash/mind program them to hate:America/Americans/it's culture,incite racial devide/violence,promote #Socialism/#Islamization,erase/rewrite history" (Del!a [diamond] 2020).

Far-right, and increasingly socially conservative users, articulate a series of paranoid linkages imagining Islamization and Socialism as concurrent processes and make use of innocuous messengers to propagate these the theories and build complex political coalitions. Amongst the far-right, there is a belief that Leftist and Islamist groups are in collusion to destroy Western civilization not only through immigration, but through the manipulation of history and fomentation of civil strife, and discussion of public schooling on social media has emerged as a key topic in this informational war. And in an absence of real evidence of collusion, for far-right German and American communities, conspiratorial thinking is the only way in which it is possible to justify and rationalize this imagined sense of victimization of conservative, Christian, white communities as under threat.

The concept of Islamization, for far-right digitally networked communities, is itself fundamentally a conspiracy, but a particularly effective and affective one that motivates users and excuses far-right violence. With women and children situated as in need of protection either from the "mama-bear" protecting her children from the dangers of multiculturalism in public schools or through the creation of paramilitary white supremacist and fascist organizations like the Proud Boys or the Reichsbürger, confronted with a state either unwilling or in collusion with enemy forces, then multiple levels of activism and violence become not just possible but required within this worldview.

Increasingly we are witnessing instances of "spontaneous" violence carried out by individuals adhering to this collection of "Racialist, Anti-Federalist, and Christian Fundamentalist" ideologies (Sweeney and Perliger 2018, 52). Separate instances of far-right extremist violence which are not coordinated—the Reichsbürger attempted coup in Germany, the Escondido, California Mosque arson in the US, and the 2017 Alwar mob lynching and murder of Pehlu Khan in India—occur in the larger global context of rising Islamophobia, emboldened far-right electoral political influence, and the dominance of digital platforms as organizing tools which serve as a means of affective radicalization.

And in our current socio-political context, instances of far-right individual spontaneous violence are not often viewed by the public "as politically-motivated violence, even given their apparent targeting of a particular ethnic demographic and/or specific religious or political groups" (Sweeney and Perliger 2018, 66), here, Muslim communities. And while high-profile attacks like the attempted murder of Nancy Pelosi's husband (Lin, Hernandez, and Castleman 2022), or the Reichsbürger's planned violent Day of X to overthrow the German government (Bennhold and Solomon 2022), are slowly being recognized as a societal threat, attention remains on the end product. This is to say, focus has remained on assessing radicalization forensically *after* the fact, rather than taking digital far-right discourse in online spaces seriously *before* violence occurs. These events ultimately are examples of far-right stochastic terrorism, carried out by lone wolves and groups, which may be understood as inspired by the extremist rhetoric of politicians (Ioanes 2022), and critically, their compatriots or fellow soldiers on social media. And this flood of violent, far-right content continues to be publicized on Twitter in an increasingly unregulated platform environment.

For far-right groups, specifically those peddling explicitly in Islamophobia, the joint emphasis on a cultural and civilization war, and the radical, extremist rhetoric and conspiracies circulated on Twitter are not only inseparable from instances of off-platform violence, but directly encourage it. If politics are down-stream from culture, then digital hate-speech is downstream from far-right political violence. While it is difficult to identify which users promoting Islamophobic conspiracy theories may be radicalized into committing violence, it is clear we are in a "vibe shift" where previous exceptional advocations of Islamophobia and other far-right extremist positions in mainstream political discourse has become commonplace. And as Elon Musk, Twitter CEO, appears eager to amplify far-right gendered conspiracy theories through his own posting activity (Hurley 2022), we are now in a situation where not only political institutions and leaders are key amplifiers of far-right conspiracies, but where one crucial Big Tech platform appears positioned not only to elide dealing with this crisis, but is interested in creating a welcoming atmosphere for extremist content. As far-right Islamophobic conspiracies about women and children continue to spread unchecked, far-right users are also suggesting there is a bigger plan afoot: the supposed Islamification of the state.

The Imagined "Islamification" of the State

Islamophobic conspiracy theories are multi-scalar in their articulation (Zia-Ebrahimi 2021), transforming the mundane into evidence of larger, structural plots. Naturally, for far-right digital communities carrying out a strategy of paranoid communication, the state, as in the local, regional, and federal state along with major political parties, figure as subjects of suspicion and agents of collaboration with other shadowy forces. Mistrust of the state and allegations of corrupt activity are historically part of conspiratorial thinking (Zeng, Schäfer, and Oliveira 2022). What is different now is how groups articulate paranoid linkages between the state, Muslim communities, and a range of other actors as colluding to take over the country and the world.

For far-right German communities, there is a sense of an alleged, sinister alliance between the German federal government, Left-leaning national political parties, and Muslim communities. There is a symbiosis between individual users and outlets like *Journalistenwatch* in circulating content that allege wild claims like the mainstream Left-leaning parties such as the Sozialdemokratische Partei Deutschlands (SPD) and the Die Grünen are actively seeking to Islamize the country, such as through their support of the equitable right to worship (Vercingetorix 2020).

Far-right users and far-right publications like *Journalistenwatch* situate Left-leaning parties as supporting *Weltoffenheit* or cosmopolitanism (DM 2020). And it is through this critique of multiculturalism or cosmopolitanism by far-right communities that in the German context Muslim communities and Leftists parties become implicated as linked in a form of collusion. Any group who does not conform to ethnic German, Christian, socially conservative positions or identity categories becomes suspect and a potential enemy of the state.

In a viral article discussing supposed collusion, *Journalistenwatch* states *"[w]ährend Kirchenglocken ein rein akustisches Signal ohne inhaltliche Botschaft sind, werden beim muslimischen Gebetsruf religiöse Inhalte und Botschaften verkündet, denen sich niemand entziehen kann"* which translates to "[w]hile church bells are a purely acoustic signal without meaningful message, the Muslim call to prayer contains religious message and meaning no one can escape" (DM 2020). Here, *Journalistenwatch* asserts that Christianity in German is not religious—it is rather part of the secular culture of the nation—and Islam is a foreign religious presence threatening the public with messages "no one can escape." This fear of creeping cosmopolitanism in the form of Islamization is also imagined as being carried out by enemies *within* the German state—the SPD and Die Grünen—*and outside*—Muslim immigrants.

In the German context, this critique or emphasis on cosmopolitanism as a political threat to the state and society is reminiscent of Nazi-era political discourse which positioned Jews as explicitly threatening cosmopolitans seeking the "'destruction' of national, ethnic and religious communities" (Schoeps and Rensmann 2011, 35). While Neo-Nazi parties such as the NDP have revived such antisemitic anti-cosmopolitan discourses (Rensmann 2011, 138), the AfD has centralized an anti-cosmopolitan message within its political program alongside virulent Islamophobia (Klikauer 2018). Historically fascist discourse is actively being repurposed among far-right digitally networked Islamophobic German communities to target not only Jews, but Muslims, Leftist parties, and a multitude of other groups whereby cosmopolitanism speaks to a notion of a more fragmented, diffuse threat to the national, ethnic, and religious imagined German community. But far-right communities go beyond general supposed allusions that mainstream parties are advancing unformed religious plots. Increasingly far-right users advance apocalyptic conspiracy theories that allege partisan opponents want to destroy society.

Far-right users knit together existing conspiracies like the Great Replacement with new allegations that mainstream political parties are involved in making this a reality, made visible here in this post: *"[w]en überrascht das noch? #Hofreiter ist wie viele #Gruene offensichtlich ein ideologisch gestörter Deutschlandhasser, der die #Islamisierung schnellstmöglich umsetzen möchte...[eye rolling face] #antonhofreiter #DieGruenen #Unterwerfung #Houellebecq #ReplacementMigration"* which translates to "[w]ho is still that surprised? Hofreiter like many Greens is likely an ideologically disturbed, German-hater who wants Islamization as fast as possible. #antonheifter #TheGreens #Submission #Houellebecq #ReplacementMigration" from user @mginberlin (Right 2020). @mginberlin refers to Anton Hofreiter, politician and member of the German Die Grünen party (Deutscher Bundestag 2021), and French writer Michel Houellebecq, author of the novel *Submission* (Houellebecq 2015), a book which imagines an Islamized France achieved through an alliance between Islamic fundamentalist groups and Socialists in 2022. For far-right communities, reality and fiction are collapsed together as evidence or prophecy.

While the ideological positions of Islamic fundamentalists and Socialists are outwardly divergent, in fact their supposed similarity is a foundational part of a far-right conspiratorial worldview, with far-right Germans alleging *"...das #deutsche Volk in eine #linke und #islamische Diktatur gezwungen werden soll..."* or "the German people will be forced into a Leftist and Islamic dictatorship" (mgeurope1984 2020). Far-right communities, while adopting positions of authoritarianism politically and patriarchal arrangements personally, suggest that both Muslims and Leftists, Socialists or Communists, in fact hold autocratic ideological positions (Betz 2016). And who is to address this dangerous collusion? For conspiratorial far-right communities—former President Trump is situated as the singular savior: *"#Trump #Meinungsfreiheit #Demokratie #Sozialismus #Kommunismus #Islamisierung Niemals vergessen, wenn Präsident Trump fällt, fällt die gesamte westliche Welt in die Hände von Linksextremisten, Kommunisten und Islamisten !!!"* which translates to "#Trump #FreedomofThought #Democracy # Socialism #Communism #Islamization Never forget when President Trump falls, the entire world falls into the hands of Leftist-extremists, Communists, and Islamists" (FrankWienand1 2020).

Part of what makes far-right conspiracy theories so effective, along with the affect they garner, is that they offer users multiple points of entry into a more extreme program of radicalization unique to a user's identity and national historical context. Socialism and Communism may have returned as in vogue in the US as a call-back to the Cold War era, but for German and European digital denizens already critical of immigration or of a socially conservative, religious bent, in a post-9/11 national security context, Islamization serves as compelling shorthand to beckon users into a far-right conspiratorial community. Far-right groups are able to engage in a form of storytelling that offers simple yet compelling explanations for complex structural global events and processes that also provides a sense of racialized and religious kinship to users—particularly appealing during the socially isolating height of the COVID-19 pandemic when events like societal collapse or the unprecedented expansion of state power were not necessarily paranoid delusions but realities. And Twitter, as a critical medium of digital communication and connection during the pandemic became a platform to foster these paranoid, conspiratorial connections to a new, more receptive audience.

For far-right users across national contexts during the pandemic era things started to "come together" in the form of a global plot that extended beyond borders: "*[i]rgendwie gehört das alles zusammen. #Migrationspakt #Islamisierung #Antifa #BlackLivesMatterGermany #Merkel usw. Deutsch/Deutschsein/Weiße, dafür gibt es nur noch Verachtung, Hass und natürlich Geldforderungen. Jetzt sollen wir beim bezahlen noch niederknieen. Und schweigen,*" or "[s]omehow it all makes sense. #Migration pact #Islamization #Antifa #BlackLivesMatterGermany #Merkel usw. German/being German/white, there is only hatred and request for money. Now we're supposed to kneel down while paying and be silent" (JaNuWatn 2020), accompanied by a meme in *Figure 2*.

To make these seemingly disparate claims hang together requires the invocation of Islamophobia. Turkish immigration, veiling, and an assertion that Islam is a seeking to "take-over" the globe is positioned as undergirding the larger rise of European multilateralism, alongside the "alt-Left boogeyman" of Antifa, and American-born Black Lives Matter movement (Love and Karabinus 2020).

Indeed, these hashtags, #Migrationspakt #Islamisierung #Antifa #BlackLivesMatterGermany #Merkel illustrate how far-right communities form an understanding of the world as defined by racialized and religious conflict. For far-right German users, immigration and Islam are fundamentally linked because of the country's long history of Turkish Muslim immigration. Antifa and Black Lives Matter Germany, which is not a formal organization but may refer to Black German solidarity protests in the summer of 2020 (Safronova 2020), suggest a far-right German fear of "foreign" American Leftist social organizations focused on issues of race and racial justice—supposedly imported problems in an imagined ethnically homogenous German society. Finally, hashtagging #Merkel emphasizes

Figure 2: Somehow it All Makes Sense.

the persistent far-right German suspicion of the German state as collaborating with outside interests.

It is necessary for far-right users to couch Islamophobic, conspiratorial claims within a global context to heighten the affective threat, as well as to situate these amorphous conspiracies within a localized, national context to become legible to fellow Germans or American counterparts. We see here we are operating in a digital platformed ecosystem not only dominated by American corporate interests but by American conspiracy theories and far-right rhetoric which has become transnationalized and incorporated into the global marketplace of far-right ideas.

And of course, the most successful American far-right product to circulate on social media to a global audience is the Q Anon conspiracy theory. For far-right American users, like their German counterparts, the threat to the imagined Christian, conservative, white community is both external and internal, with Democratic figures and groups imagined as conspiring to threaten the nation internally, and external "foreign" groups such as Muslims or Jews collaborating from the outside. This type of emphasis on internal and external enemies feeds into the far-right victimhood narratives which undergird fantasies and actualizations of violence (Marcks and Pawelz 2022).

Holger Marcks and Janina Pawelz in discussing this victimization narrative trend among far-right groups note that these communities "employ myths of victimhood that serve as an emotional foundation for radical action," with victim narratives inspiring "fantasies of violence" that increasingly become actualized (2020, 2, 14). Notions of global conspiracy are thus a crucial form of rhetoric that not only define Islamophobic digitally networked communities in the US and Germany, but herald future political mobilizations and possibly violence. These conspiratorial narratives of victimization create an ideological structure whereby when the "national collective [is depicted] as the victim, individuals have the chance to be heroes" (Marcks and Pawelz 2020, 14). To be a hero and "save" the nation from the grasping hands of a global cabal can mean a multitude of things for different individuals but can range from increased far-right electoral political mobilizations, to engagement in increasingly radical online far-right platforms and websites, to plots to overthrow the state.

For far-right users, the seeds of social conservativism grow into a support of a violent, conspiratorial worldview that can only be realized through conflict, here a form of discursive, cultural warfare—with everyday Twitter users becoming digital soldiers. Far-right users, whether adopting the explicit language of being part of Q's army, or more nuancedly situating themselves as fighting for their kids, their home, their country, draw back to notions of civilizationalist cultural conflict between an alleged non-white regressive, Muslim East and a socially conservative, Christian, white West (Brubaker 2017). And as the COVID-19 pandemic began in 2020, this global crisis created a social context that encouraged apocalyptic thinking and shifted social connectivities online, opening up a new front in informational war.

Quarantine or "Quran-time?": COVID-19 and Islamophobic Digital Discourse

The COVID-19 virus that began in Wuhan, China reached the level of a global pandemic March 11, 2020 and subsequently transformed social and economic life for citizens across the globe (Cucinotta and Vanelli 2020). What was not unique about the pandemic, however, was the way in which it revived historic patterns of scapegoating historically marginalized communities and spurred the circulation of racialized conspiracies similar to past public health crises (Dionne and Turkmen 2020). And while the COVID-19 pandemic saw an explosion of Sinophobia and targeting of Asian communities in the West (Tahmasbi et al. 2021), Muslim communities in Europe, the US, and India were also implicated by far-right actors and news outlets as either contributing to the spread of the virus (Amarasingam, Umar, and Desai 2022; Chandra et al. 2021), or, in coordination with the state and other groups using the pandemic as a cover to Islamize society.

In Germany, exemplifying broader European far-right trends, Muslims communities were accused of being given special political treatment by an alleged Islamophilic German government or were situated as taking advantage of exceptional COVID-19 rules to "Islamize" neighborhoods and schools. In the US, other Islamophobic conspiracies dominated, particularly around the cultural flashpoint of masking (Lupton et al. 2021), a position that quickly became adopted by Germans. American far-right actors alleged that the public health practice of masking was a cover to encourage the practice of veiling, signaling the first step of the Islamization of society. Ultimately, COVID-19 served as a strategic theme and communicative condition whereupon far-right groups were able to deploy racialized rhetoric targeting Muslim communities by focusing on a seemingly "color-blind" issue of public health.

While in-person religious gatherings during the COVID-19 pandemic were a topic of concern in the early days of the pandemic (Badshah and Ullah 2020), the historic far-right preoccupation with Muslim displays of aural religiosity became re-mixed into a suggestion that Muslim communities, here in collusion with the state, and were taking advantage of pandemic exceptions to unduly monopolize the public sphere by performing the call to prayer (Ewing 2000; Joppke 2013). Whether Duisburg or Miltenerg, far-right communities suggested that the call to prayer was increasingly performed due to "exceptions" articulated during the early pandemic, with one AfD representative asking *"[w]ill man heimlich den Ausnahme- zum Dauerzustand machen? NEIN ZUR #ISLAMISIERUNG!!! #Covid_19 #CoronavirusPandemic,"* or, "[d]oes one want to make this exceptional state permanent? NO TO #ISLAMIZATION! #Covid_19 #CoronavirusPandemic" (AfD Walldürn 2020). It is precisely the COVID-19 pandemic and the "states of exception" it fostered in society which allowed for far-right German digital news outlets and users to re-frame the topics of the muezzin with greater visibility and salience.

The COVID-19 pandemic as a public health crisis has been defined by unprecedented levels of governmental intervention into daily life through the implementation of lockdowns, curfews, mandated school and business closures, and required masking, testing, and vaccination requirements. However, for far-right users, these new forms of state action were imagined as a malevolent pretense to "re-order" society (GhaneaBassiri 2012), with this rhetoric of re-ordering a traditional far-right conspiracy. As Giorgio Agamben has noted, the unprecedented nature of the global pandemic provided a social context whereby governments were able to justify and expand "exceptional measures" of their power:

> ...the state of fear, which in recent years has diffused into individual consciousnesses and which translates into a real need for **states of collective panic**, for which the epidemic once again offers the ideal pretext. Therefore, in a perverse vicious circle, the limitation of freedom imposed by governments is accepted in the name of a desire for safety, which has been created by the same governments who now intervene to satisfy (2020).

Agamben, here, emphasizes the cyclical nature of public crises and increasing governmental encroachments on freedom and tendencies towards re-creating "states of exception" to deprive citizenry of their rights, deprivations that are accepted in exchange for stability. However, Agamben's core argument, identifying a dynamic of the hallowing out of social and individual life and liberties in an era of overlapping political, health, and environmental crises (Agamben 2021), has dovetailed to anti-state political arguments made by far-right politicians and actors during the pandemic and been situated as the intellectual evidence to support their anti-establishment position (Kotsko 2022). Rather than considering the cyclical nature of crises and subsequent governmental overreach as affecting the entire public, far-right communities imagine themselves as the exceptionally targeted ones, or the primary victims. And the individual panic or anxiety experienced by far-right groups cannot be satisfied by existing governmental action in this scenario but rather through a different intervention—the ascendency of an ethnonationalist government led by the AfD, Trump's second term in office, or in the extreme, the creation of ethnically and racially homogenous nation-states.

The emphasis on supposed governmental encroachments upon basic freedoms by far-right groups in Germany has paralleled an explosion of pandemic related far-right conspiracies and far-right activism in the US that has asserted that the pandemic and governmental health restrictions, specifically masking, are part of a plot to restrict individual freedoms and began an Islamic-Leftist take-over of society (Charlsens 2020). Not only are Muslim communities imagined as taking advantage of these states of exception but Left-leaning parties like the Democrats, are positioned as partners. This dynamic is neatly captured here in this meme, which suggests that liberals in the US, who during the pandemic were more supportive of public health measures like masking (Lizza and Lippman 2020), pushed this measure as a means to encourage practices of veiling.

Figure 3: The Goal of the Left (jeezyjeezy1 2020).

For far-right users the factuality of the information they circulate is irrelevant, as is the fact that as of 2023 we have seen widespread global relaxation of pandemic era restrictions such as masking and other governmental interventions (Stokel-Walker 2022). To fill this need for a feeling of collective panic and subsequent interventions (Agamben 2020), far-right groups continue to circulate paranoid, affective content, playing upon the historic cultural flashpoint of veiling in order posit their own fascist political interventions.

Conclusion: Digital Soldiers Waging Informational War

Conspiracies theories are a critical vernacular required to ascertain the lexical undercurrents of far-right political movements. They are dangerous not only in so far as they undergird and spur expressions of organized and individual instances of stochastic terrorism, but also in the way in which, overtime, they contribute to the radicalization of users. The extremity and ever-evolving nature of conspiracy theories "ensures that each claim and counterclaim can never be individually assessed" and thus individuals become habituated to far-right rhetoric and an ever more extreme constellation of beliefs (Munn 2019), with Islamophobia a crucial point of entry into this process.

The approval and support of far-right conspiracy theories and memes from Twitter CEO Elon Musk and the platform's relaxing of its previous ban on political cause-based advertisements only suggests that the site (Conger 2023), operationally speaking, is fostering the material conditions that have signaled to extreme off-platform communities and far-right groups that Twitter is a hospitable environment to spread their message as part of the informational war being waged online. And they will reach a more mainstream global public than 8kun or Truth Social would allow. Far-right German and American groups have found great success in re-purposing historic and contemporary conspiracy theories and deploying gendered rhetoric to affectively market far-right politics to sympathetic audiences. Critically, the COVID-19 pandemic created both a situational opportunity for far-right groups and a new topic with which to fill a discursive vacuum and repurpose existing allegations targeting Muslim communities during the public health crisis.

It has been this state of exception of the early COVID-19 pandemic that allowed users to articulate and tie together a broad range of conspiracy theories implicating various actors from Muslim communities to Left-leaning parties as involved in a global plot to re-order society. The COVID-19 pandemic indelibly informed the way in which German and American far-right, Islamophobic digitally networked communities mediated this concept of a state of exception whereby internal and external "enemies" colluded to allegedly realize an authoritarian take-over of society, with Christian, socially conservative white or ethnic Germans the victims of this imagined conspiracy. And this state of exception has increasingly bolstered exceptional measures of violence and anti-democratic far-right political movements.

As Twitter has yet to collapse, far-right groups will continue to find that the platform has become a more fertile terrain to produce and circulate conspiracy theories, virally infecting global audiences across the Atlantic. Whether the platform remains operational in the future is a subject for speculation. What *is* clear is that conspiracy theories as a mode of communication and means of radicalization remains affective and effective in reaching a range of users.

References

AfD Walldürn. 2020. "Muezzinrufe in Unserer Bayerischen Nachbarstadt #Miltenberg! Liegt Es an Den '"Ausnahmeregelungen"' Wegen Des #Coronavirus? Will Man Heimlich Den Ausnahme-Zum Dauerzustand Machen? NEIN ZUR #ISLAMISIERUNG!!! #Covid_19 #CoronavirusPandemic (SB 2020)"." Twitter. April 5, 2020. https://twitter.com/afd_wallduern/status/1246874815144886273.

Agamben, Giorgio. 2020. "Lo Stato d'eccezione Provocato Da Un'emergenza Immotivata." *Positions Politics* (blog). February 26, 2020. http://positionspolitics.org/giorgio-agamben-the-state-of-exception-provoked-by-an-unmotivated-emergency/.

Agamben, Giorgio. 2021. *Where Are We Now?: The Epidemic as Politics*. Lanham, MD: Rowman & Littlefield Publishers. https://rowman.com/ISBN/9781538157602/Where-Are-We-Now-The-Epidemic-as-Politics.

Amarasingam, Amarnath, Sanober Umar, and Shweta Desai. 2022. "'Fight, Die, and If Required Kill': Hindu Nationalism, Misinformation, and Islamophobia in India." *Religions* 13 (5): 380. https://doi.org/10.3390/rel13050380.

Astor, Maggie. 2019. "How the Politically Unthinkable Can Become Mainstream." *The New York Times*, 2019. https://www.nytimes.com/2019/02/26/us/politics/overton-window-democrats.html.

Badshah, Syed Lal, and Asad Ullah. 2020. "Spread of Coronavirus Disease-19 among Devotees during Religious Congregations." *Annals of Thoracic Medicine* 15 (3): 105 – 6. https://doi.org/10.4103/atm.ATM_162_20.

Barkun, Michael. 2017. "President Trump and the 'Fringe.'" *Terrorism and Political Violence* 29 (3): 437 – 43.

Basit, Abdul. 2021. "Conspiracy Theories and Violent Extremism: Similarities, Differences and the Implications." *Counter Terrorist Trends and Analyses* 13 (3): 1 – 9.

Beauchamp, Zack. 2022. "The Bizarre Far-Right Coup Attempt in Germany, Explained by an Expert." *Vox*, December 9, 2022. https://www.vox.com/2022/12/9/23500307/germany-coup-prince-heinrich-qanon.

Bennhold, Katrin. 2018. "A Girl's Killing Puts Germany's Migration Policy on Trial." *The New York Times*, January 17, 2018. https://www.nytimes.com/2018/01/17/world/europe/germany-teen-murder-migrant.html?_r=0.

Bennhold, Katrin, and Erika Solomon. 2022. "Far-Right Group Suspected in German Plot Gained Strength From QAnon." *The New York Times*, December 8, 2022, sec. World. https://www.nytimes.com/2022/12/08/world/europe/germany-plot-qanon.html.

Berg, Lyn. 2019. "Between Anti-Feminism and Ethnicized Sexism. Far-Right Gender Politics in Germany." In *Post-Digital Cultures of the Far Right*, edited by Maik Fielitz and Nick Thurston, 79 – 92. Bielefeld: transcript-Verlag.

Betz, Hans-George. 2013. "Mosques, Minarets, Burqas and Other Essential Threats: The Populist Right's Campaign against Islam in Western Europe." In *Right-Wing Populism in Europe: Politics and Discourse*, edited by Ruth Wodak, Majid KhosraviNik, and Brigitte Mral, 71 – 87. London: Bloomsbury Publishing.

Betz, Hans-George. 2016. "Against the 'Green Totalitarianism': Anti-Islamic Nativism in Contemporary Radical Right-Wing Populism in Western Europe." In *Europe for the Europeans : The Foreign and Security Policy of the Populist Radical Right*, edited by Christina Schori Liang, 33 – 54. London and New York: Routledge.

Bjørgo, Tore, and Jacob Aasland Ravndal. 2019. "Extreme-Right Violence and Terrorism:" The Hauge: International Centre for Counter-Terrorism.

Bloom, Mia, and Sophia Moskalenko. 2021. *Pastels and Pedophiles: Inside the Mind of QAnon.* Stanford: Stanford University Press.

Boulila, Stefanie C, and Christiane Carri. 2017. "On Cologne: Gender, Migration and Unacknowledged Racisms in Germany." *European Journal of Women's Studies* 24 (3): 286 – 93. https://doi.org/ 10.1177/1350506817712447.

Bracewell, Lorna. 2021. "Gender, Populism, and the QAnon Conspiracy Movement." *Frontiers in Sociology* 5: 1 – 4.

Brubaker, Rogers. 2017. "Between Nationalism and Civilizationism: The European Populist Moment in Comparative Perspective." *Ethnic and Racial Studies* 40 (8): 1191 – 1226. https://doi.org/10.1080/ 01419870.2017.1294700.

Bukarti, Audu Bulama. 2018. "How Fake News in Nigeria Compounds Challenges to Co-Existence." Commentary. Tony Blair Institute for Global Change. https://institute.global/policy/how-fake-news-nigeria-compounds-challenges-co-existence.

Cannizzaro, Sara. 2016. "Internet Memes as Internet Signs: A Semiotic View of Digital Culture." *Sign Systems Studies* 44 (4): 562 – 86. https://doi.org/10.12697/SSS.2016.44.4.05.

Carroll, Caitlin. 2017. "The European Refugee Crisis and the Myth of the Immigrant Rapist." Europe Now. 2017. https://www.europenowjournal.org/2017/07/05/untitled/.

Chandra, Mohit, Manvith Reddy, Shradha Sehgal, Saurabh Gupta, Arun Balaji Buduru, and Ponnurangam Kumaraguru. 2021. "'A Virus Has No Religion': Analyzing Islamophobia on Twitter During the COVID-19 Outbreak." arXiv. http://arxiv.org/abs/2107.05104.

Charlsens, Dick. 2020. "Und Demnächst Wird Uns Erzählt, Dass Es Jetzt, Wo Wir Uns Alle an Die Masken Gewöhnt Haben, Auch Keinen Grund Mehr Gibt, Die Vollverschleierung Abzulehnen. #Islamisierung #Covid_19." Twitter. April 26, 2020. https://twitter.com/co_faktor/statuses/ 1254305788241346560.

Chayka, Kyle. 2021. "TikTok and the Vibes Revival." *The New Yorker*, April 26, 2021. https:// www.newyorker.com/culture/cultural-comment/tiktok-and-the-vibes-revival.

Conger, Kate. 2023. "Twitter to Relax Ban on Political Ads." *The New York Times*, January 3, 2023, sec. Technology. https://www.nytimes.com/2023/01/03/technology/twitter-political-ads.html.

Cucinotta, Domenico, and Maurizio Vanelli. 2020. "WHO Declares COVID-19 a Pandemic." *Acta Bio-Medica: Atenei Parmensis* 91 (1): 157 – 60. https://doi.org/10.23750/abm.v91i1.9397.

Del!a [diamond]. 2020. "This Is Why Parents Will End up Home Schooling Their Kids/Let Them Skip College to Protect Them from Teachers/Professors That'll Brainwash/Mind Program Them to Hate:America/Americans/It's Culture,Incite Racial Devide/Violence,Promote #Socialism/ #Islamization,Erase/Rewrite History Https://T.Co/Gy8bgIWP9x." Twitter. July 15, 2020. https:// twitter.com/TheDeliaAspect/statuses/1272456929969942529.

Deutscher Bundestag. 2021. "Dr. Anton Hofreiter, Bündnis 90/Die Grünen." 2021. https:// www.bundestag.de/abgeordnete/biografien/H/hofreiter_anton-520476.

Dionne, Kim Yi, and Fulya Felicity Turkmen. 2020. "The Politics of Pandemic Othering: Putting COVID-19 in Global and Historical Context." *International Organization* 74 (S1): E213 – 30. https:// doi.org/10.1017/S0020818320000405.

DM. 2020. "Muezzin-Ruf in Bielefeld Trotz Gerichtsverbot: Islamisierung Hat Für SPD Und Grüne Höchste Priorität." *Journalistenwatch*, May 31, 2020, sec. Frontpage. https:// www.journalistenwatch.com/2020/05/31/muezzin-ruf-bielefeld/.

Douglas, Karen M., Joseph E. Uscinski, Robbie M. Sutton, Aleksandra Cichocka, Turkay Nefes, Chee Siang Ang, and Farzin Deravi. 2019. "Understanding Conspiracy Theories." *Political Psychology* 40 (S1): 3 – 35. https://doi.org/10.1111/pops.12568.

Ekman, Mattias. 2022. "The Great Replacement: Strategic Mainstreaming of Far-Right Conspiracy Claims." *Convergence* 28 (4): 1127–43. https://doi.org/10.1177/13548565221091983.

Ewing, Katherine Pratt. 2000. "Legislating Religious Freedom: Muslim Challenges to the Relationship between 'Church' and 'State' in Germany and France." *Daedalus* 129 (4): 31–54.

Faltermann, Pascal. 2020. "In Bremen Fehlen Mehr Als 1000 Kita-Plätze." *Weser-Kurier*, June 26, 2020, sec. Stadt. https://www.weser-kurier.de/bremen/bremen-stadt_artikel,-in-bremen-fehlen-mehr-als-1000-kitaplaetze-_arid,1920387.html.

Fernandez, Sonya. 2009. "The Crusade over the Bodies of Women." *Patterns of Prejudice* 43 (3–4): 269–86. https://doi.org/10.1080/00313220903109185.

Fixmer-Oraiz, Natalie. 2019. *Homeland Maternity: US Security Culture and the New Reproductive Regime*. Urbana, Chicago, and Springfield, IL: University of Illinois Press.

FrankWienand1. 2020. "#Trump #Meinungsfreiheit #Demokratie #Sozialismus #Kommunismus #Islamisierung Niemals Vergessen, Wenn Präsident Trump Fällt, Fällt Die Gesamte Westliche Welt in Die Hände von Linksextremisten, Kommunisten Und Islamisten !!!" Twitter. August 21, 2020. https://twitter.com/FrankWienand1/statuses/1296747220390285312.

Frenkel, Sheera, Martín González Gómez, and Ella Koeze. 2023. "Dissecting Elon Musk's Tweets: Memes, Rants, Private Parts and an Echo Chamber." *The New York Times*, January 31, 2023. https://www.nytimes.com/interactive/2023/01/31/technology/elon-musk-tweets.html.

Furnham, Adrian. 2013. "Commercial Conspiracy Theories: A Pilot Study." *Frontiers in Psychology* 4: 1–5.

GhaneaBassiri, Kambiz. 2012. *A History of Islam in America From the New World to the New World Order*. Cambridge, MA: Cambridge University Press.

Gilbert, David. 2022. "Elon Musk Is Now Promoting QAnon." *Vice*, December 13, 2022. https://www.vice.com/en/article/y3pjkw/elon-musk-is-now-promoting-qanon.

Goldsmith, Jill. 2022. "Elon Musk Tweets 'The Woke Mind Virus Is Either Defeated Or Nothing Else Matters' After Being Booed At A Dave Chappelle Show." *Yahoo*, December 12, 2022, sec. Entertainment. https://www.yahoo.com/entertainment/elon-musk-tweets-woke-mind-182522320.html.

Green, Emma. 2017. "Why the Charlottesville Marchers Were Obsessed With Jews Anti-Semitic Logic Fueled the Violence over the Weekend, No Matter What the President Says." *The Atlantic*, August 15, 2017. https://www.theatlantic.com/politics/archive/2017/08/nazis-racism-charlottesville/536928/.

Hannah, Matthew. 2021. "QAnon and the Information Dark Age." *First Monday*, January. https://doi.org/10.5210/fm.v26i2.10868.

Hauslohner, Abigail. 2016. "How a Series of Fringe Anti-Muslim Conspiracy Theories Went Mainstream – via Donald Trump." *Washington Post*, November 5, 2016, sec. National. https://www.washingtonpost.com/national/how-a-series-of-fringe-anti-muslim-conspiracy-theories-went-mainstream–via-donald-trump/2016/11/05/7c366af6-8bf0-11e6-bf8a-3d26847eeed4_story.html.

Hoback, Cullen, dir. 2021. *Q: Into the Storm*. Documentary Series. HBO. https://www.hbo.com/q-into-the-storm.

Hofstadter, Richard. 1996. "The Paranoid Style in American Politics." In *The Paranoid Style in American Politics and Other Essays*, 3–40. Cambridge, MA: Harvard University Press.

HoSang, Daniel Martinez, and Joseph E. Lowndes. 2019. *Producers, Parasites, Patriots Race and the New Right-Wing Politics of Precarity*. Minneapolis, MN: University of Minnesota Press. https://www.upress.umn.edu/book-division/books/producers-parasites-patriots.

Houellebecq, Michel. 2015. *Submission*. London: Macmillan.

Hurley, Bevan. 2022. "Elon Musk, Who Has a Trans Daughter, Likes Anti-Trans Tweet from Notorious Right Wing Account | The Independent." *The Independent*, December 27, 2022, sec. Americas. https://www.independent.co.uk/news/world/americas/elon-musk-anti-trans-twitter-libs-of-tiktok-b2251975.html.

Information, Logic Geometry. 2020. "'NOT an #AprilFools: The German #women's Magazine "'Illu Der Frau'" (Issue 04/2019) Published #advice on How to Treat Knife|stab-Wounds. Even More Remarkable Is the Picture Which Makes Women Associate Short #skirts with Phalloid #danger. #BRD #Deutschland:#Germany #Islamization Https://T.Co/AeBbi6uXGd.'" Twitter. April 1, 2020. https://twitter.com/LGcommaI/statuses/1245307899095769088.

Ioanes, Ellen. 2022. "An Atmosphere of Violence: Stochastic Terror in American Politics." *Vox*, November 5, 2022. https://www.vox.com/2022/11/5/23441858/violence-stochastic-terror-american-politics-trump-pelosi.

ISD. 2020. "Trans-Atlantic Journeys of Far-Right Narratives Through Online-Media Ecosystems." London: Institute for Strategic Dialogue. https://www.isdglobal.org/wp-content/uploads/2020/12/TransAtlanticJourneysofFar-RightNarratives_v4.pdf.

JaNuWatn. 2020. "Deutsch/Deutschsein/Weiße, Dafür Gibt Es Nur Noch Verachtung, Hass Und Natürlich Geldforderungen. Jetzt Sollen Wir Beim Bezahlen Noch Niederknieen. Und Schweigen. Https://T.Co/VEbO3ZB1LK". Twitter. June 12, 2020. https://twitter.com/JaNuWatn/statuses/1270962465258573825.

jeezyjeezy1. 2020. "This Is What Liberals Are Pushing for When They Try to Force Us to Wear Face Masks. #islamization #islam #islamisation #liberals #democrats #DemocratsAreMarxistsDestroyingAmerica #DemocratsAreDestroyingAmerica #Covid19 #WuhanVirus #ChinaVirus #ChineseVirus #Covid19Hoax #Corona Https://T.Co/HIr8619pnU." Twitter. July 28, 2020. https://twitter.com/jeezyjeezy1/statuses/1288164603151745025.

Johnson, Jessica. 2018. "The Self-Radicalization of White Men: 'Fake News' and the Affective Networking of Paranoia." *Communication, Culture and Critique* 11 (1): 100–115. https://doi.org/10.1093/ccc/tcx014.

Johnson, Jessica. 2019. "Affective Radicalization and White Masculinity." *Feminist Media Studies* 19 (2): 297–99. https://doi.org/10.1080/14680777.2019.1573533.

Joppke, Christian. 2013. "Islam in Europa – Integration Durch Recht Und Ihre Grenzen." *KZfSS Kölner Zeitschrift Für Soziologie Und Sozialpsychologie Volume* 65: 409–35.

Kalmar, Ivan, Christopher Stevens, and Nicholas Worby. 2018. "Twitter, Gab, and Racism: The Case of the Soros Myth." In *Proceedings of the 9th International Conference on Social Media and Society*, 330–34. SMSociety '18. New York, NY, USA: Association for Computing Machinery. https://doi.org/10.1145/3217804.3217939.

Kelly, Annie. 2017. "The Alt-Right: Reactionary Rehabilitation for White Masculinity." Eurozine. September 15, 2017. https://www.eurozine.com/the-alt-right-reactionary-rehabilitation-for-white-masculinity/.

Klikauer, Thomas. 2018. "Germany's New Populist Party The AfD." *German Politics and Society* 36 (4): 78–97.

Kotsko, Adam. 2022. "What Happened to Giorgio Agamben?" *Slate*, February 21, 2022. https://slate.com/human-interest/2022/02/giorgio-agamben-covid-holocaust-comparison-right-wing-protest.html.

Krishan. 2021. "Challenge for Conservative Social Media Platforms: Attracting 'libs' to Own." *Washington Examiner*, July 15, 2021, sec. News. https://www.washingtonexaminer.com/news/challenge-conservative-social-media-platforms-attracting-libs-own.

Lakin, Max. 2020. "Social Lives Are Moving Online as the U.S. Adjusts to the Coronavirus." *The New York Times*, March 17, 2020, sec. U.S. https://www.nytimes.com/live/2020/coronavirus-covid-19-03-17.

Land, Nick. n.d. "The Dark Enlightenment." http://keithanyan.github.io/TheDarkEnlightenment.epub/TheDarkEnlightenment.pdf.

Leidig, Eviane. 2023. *The Women of the Far Right: Social Media Influencers and Online Radicalization.* New York: Columbia University Press.

Lin, Summer, Salvador Hernandez, and Terry Castleman. 2022. "Accused Pelosi Attacker David DePape Spread QAnon, Other Far-Right, Bigoted Conspiracies." *Los Angeles Times*, October 28, 2022, sec. California. https://www.latimes.com/california/story/2022-10-28/pelosi-attack-suspect-david-depape-shared-conspiracy-theories.

Lizza, Ryan, and Daniel Lippman. 2020. "Wearing a Mask Is for Smug Liberals. Refusing to Is for Reckless Republicans," May 1, 2020, sec. Coronavirus. https://www.politico.com/news/2020/05/01/masks-politics-coronavirus-227765.

Love, Patrick, and Alisha Karabinus. 2020. "Creation of an Alt-Left Boogeyman: Information Circulation and the Emergence of 'Antifa.'" In *Platforms, Protests, and the Challenge of Networked Democracy*, edited by John Jones and Michael Trice, 173–98. Rhetoric, Politics and Society. Cham: Springer International Publishing. https://doi.org/10.1007/978-3-030-36525-7_10.

Lupton, Deborah, Clare Southerton, Marianne Clark, and Ash Watson. 2021. *The Face Mask In COVID Times: A Sociomaterial Analysis. The Face Mask In COVID Times.* Berlin: De Gruyter. https://doi.org/10.1515/9783110723717.

Marcks, Holger, and Janina Pawelz. 2022. "From Myths of Victimhood to Fantasies of Violence: How Far-Right Narratives of Imperilment Work." *Terrorism and Political Violence* 34 (7): 1415–32. https://doi.org/10.1080/09546553.2020.1788544.

Marino, Francesca. 2020. "Tablighi Jamaat, an 'antechamber of Terrorism' in Europe?" *ANI News*, April 2, 2020, sec. World. https://www.aninews.in/news/world/europe/tablighi-jamaat-an-antechamber-of-terrorism-in-europe20200402214459/.

mgeurope1984. 2020. "Es Ist Offensichtlich, Dass Das #deutsche Volk in Eine #linke Und #islamische Diktatur Gezwungen Werden Soll…Schutz Durch #Polizei Und #Militär Wären Dann in Der Tat Überflüssig [Eye Rolling Face] #Unterwerfung #Islamisierung #Merkel #ReplacementMigration Https://T.Co/NtAibVcXvz." Twitter. June 30, 2020. https://twitter.com/mgeurope1984/statuses/1278078723275796488.

Munn, Luke. 2019. "Alt-Right Pipeline: Individual Journeys to Extremism Online." *First Monday* 24 (6). https://doi.org/10.5210/fm.v24i6.10108.

PatriotPetition. 2020. "#Imam von #Bergamo: "#ChristlicheFrauen Sind Unsere #Beute!" Https://T.Co/GHL3y2PdHu #Islamisierung Stoppen! Jetzt Aktiv Werden Und #Petition Unterzeichnen: Https://T.Co/7rgWI10aqt." *Twitter* (blog). July 7, 2020. https://twitter.com/PatriotPetition/statuses/1280370207261782018.

PatriotPetition.org. 2021. "Über Uns." *PatriotPetition.Org* (blog). 2021. https://www.patriotpetition.org/uber-uns/.

Prooijen, Jan-Willem van, André P. M. Krouwel, and Thomas V. Pollet. 2015. "Political Extremism Predicts Belief in Conspiracy Theories." *Social Psychological and Personality Science* 6 (5): 570–78. https://doi.org/10.1177/1948550614567356.

Rensmann, Lars. 2011. "'Against Globalism': Counter-Cosmopolitan Discontent and Antisemitism in Mobilizations of European Extreme Right Parties." In *Politics and Resentment: Antisemitism and*

Counter-Cosmopolitanism in the European Union, edited by Julius H Schoeps and Lars Rensmann, 117–46. Leiden, Boston: Brill.

Rettberg, Jill Walker, and Radhika Gajjala. 2015. "Terrorists or Cowards: Negative Portrayals of Male Syrian Refugees in Social Media." *Feminist Media Studies* 16 (1): 178–81. https://doi.org/10.1080/14680777.2016.1120493.

Rettig, Thomas. 2020. "Bremen: Zu Wenig Kindergartenplätze Wegen Der Rasant Steigenden Zahl von Migranten-Kindern (Weser-Kurier 26.06.20): #Bevölkerungsaustausch #Ersetzungsmigration #Migrationspakt #Resettlement #Replacement #Islamisierung #Masseneinwanderung #Massenmigration Https://T.Co/QmgKC2117I." Twitter. June 26, 2020. https://twitter.com/ThomasRettig10/statuses/1276495330914287617.

Right, M.G. 2020. "Wen Überrascht Das Noch? #Hofreiter Ist Wie Viele #Gruene Offensichtlich Ein Ideologisch Gestörter Deutschlandhasser, Der Die #Islamisierung Schnellstmöglich Umsetzen Möchte...[Rolling Eye Face] #antonhofreiter #DieGruenen #Unterwerfung #Houellebecq #ReplacementMigration Https://T.Co/208deN5S1z." Twitter. March 21, 2020. https://twitter.com/mgeurope1984/status/1241414778662408198.

Safronova, Valeriya. 2020. "Black Germans Say It's Time to Look Inward." *The New York Times*, October 4, 2020. https://www.nytimes.com/2020/10/04/style/black-germans-say-its-time-to-look-inward.html.

Said, Edward W. 1979. *Orientalism*. New York, NY: Vintage Books.

Schoeps, Julius H, and Lars Rensmann. 2011. "Politics and Resentment: Antisemitism and Counter-Cosmopolitanism in the European Union." In *Politics and Resentment: Antisemitism and Counter-Cosmopolitanism in the European Union*, edited by Julius H Schoeps and Lars Rensmann, 3–82. Leiden, Boston: Brill.

Shafrir, Doree. 2022. "The Whiteness of Sad Beige." Substack newsletter. *Now We're Talking with Doree Shafrir* (blog). August 24, 2022. https://doree.substack.com/p/the-whiteness-of-sad-beige.

Shakir, Kevin Hayder. 2019. "Dissecting Myths of a Great Replacement A Critical Discourse Analysis of the Christchurch Terror Attack Manifesto." Bachelor's, Denmark: Roskilde University. https://rucforsk.ruc.dk/ws/portalfiles/portal/64897639/kevin_shakir_bachelor_thesis.pdf.

Snyder, Timothy. 2016. *Black Earth: The Holocaust as History and Warning*. London: Bodley Head.

Staiano-Daniels, Lucian. 2022. "The Far-Right Has Turned East Germans Against Vaccines." *Foreign Policy*, February 12, 2022.

Stern, Alexandra Minna. 2019. "Alt-Right Women and the 'White Baby Challenge.'" *Salon*, July 19, 2019. https://www.salon.com/2019/07/14/alt-right-handmaidens-and-the-white-baby-challenge/.

Stokel-Walker, Chris. 2022. "COVID Restrictions Are Lifting – What Scientists Think." *Nature* 603 (7902): 563–563. https://doi.org/10.1038/d41586-022-00620-7.

Sweeney, Matthew M., and Arie Perliger. 2018. "Explaining the Spontaneous Nature of Far-Right Violence in the United States." *Perspectives on Terrorism* 12 (6): 52–71.

Tahmasbi, Fatemeh, Leonard Schild, Chen Ling, Jeremy Blackburn, Gianluca Stringhini, Yang Zhang, and Savvas Zannettou. 2021. "'Go Eat a Bat, Chang!': On the Emergence of Sinophobic Behavior on Web Communities in the Face of COVID-19." In *Proceedings of the Web Conference 2021*, 1122–33. WWW '21. New York, NY, USA: Association for Computing Machinery. https://doi.org/10.1145/3442381.3450024.

Tomlinson, Chris. 2019. "German Women's Magazine Gives Tips on Treating Stab Wounds." *Breitbart*, April 25, 2019, sec. Crime. https://www.breitbart.com/europe/2019/04/25/german-womens-magazine-gives-tips-stab-wounds/.

Tresckow Morley, LoLo. 2021. "Immigration, Social Media, and the Far-Right: A Twitter Study of the Political Communication of Alternative für Deutschland Following Terrorist Events." Master's Thesis, Chapel Hill, NC: University of North Carolina at Chapel Hill.

Tuters, Marc, Emilija Jokubauskaitė, and Daniel Bach. 2018. "Post-Truth Protest: How 4chan Cooked Up the Pizzagate Bullshit." *M/C Journal* 21 (3). https://doi.org/10.5204/mcj.1422.

Uscinski, Joseph E., and Joseph M. Parent. 2014. *American Conspiracy Theories*. Oxford: Oxford University Press.

Vercingetorix. 2020. "#MuezzinRuf in Bielefeld Trotz Gerichtsverbot: #Islamisierung Hat Für @spdde Und @Die_Gruenen Höchste Priorität Https://T.Co/JfaKCPuvpn via @jouwatch." Twitter. June 1, 2020. https://twitter.com/Vercing61979660/statuses/1267343379567951879.

Vox News. 2020. "Imam von Bergamo: "Christliche Frauen Sind Unsere Beute!"." *Unser MittelEuropa*, June 23, 2020. https://unser-mitteleuropa.com/imam-von-bergamo-christliche-frauen-sind-unsere-beute/.

Zeeuw, Daniel de, Sal Hagen, Stijn Peeters, and Emilija Jokubauskaite. 2020. "Tracing Normiefication: A Cross-Platform Analysis of the QAnon Conspiracy Theory." *First Monday*, October. https://doi.org/10.5210/fm.v25i11.10643.

Zeng, Jing, Mike S Schäfer, and Thaiane M Oliveira. 2022. "Conspiracy Theories in Digital Environments: Moving the Research Field Forward." *Convergence* 28 (4): 929 – 39. https://doi.org/10.1177/13548565221117474.

Zia-Ebrahimi, Reza. 2021. *Antisémitisme et islamophobie. Une histoire croisée*. Amsterdam: Contreparties. https://journals.openedition.org/lectures/51992.

Chapter VII
Conclusion: Digital Soldiers & Cultural Warfare

Our platformed digital society is defined by constant stimulation, distraction, and an endless stream of content (Smith 2023). In a period where we have unprecedented access to information via the continuous flood of the digital news era, historical events like the War on Terror, the 1979 Iranian hostage crisis, much less the Crusades seem impossibly far away. Even recent occurences like the 2015 Syrian Refugee Crisis or the 2017 Muslim Ban seem remote and forgettable in our cultural landscape. It often feels like our individual and collective memories are slipping, and information is "memory-holed" (Tiffert 2019), not merely by powerful interests but by far-right digital coalitions who make use of social media platforms to continuously reinvent reality and history. And in digital spaces, far-right political subcultures, discourse, and groups move at lightning speed and often disappear without leaving a trace. In fact, the centrality of Islamophobia to far-right politics in Germany and the US appears quickly supplanted by emergent attacks on queer and trans communities.

In studying any digital political movement, the sheer torrent of data and rapidity of rhetoric can make it difficult not only to reconstruct and make sense of how political coalitions evolve and operate, but the very ephemerality of digital political discourse can present fundamental challenges to sustained scholarly investigation, particularly on Twitter which is structured to present a continuous stream of content mimicking the transitoriness of more extreme sites like 4chan (Bernstein et al. 2011). However, this makes it all the more necessary to engage not only in a bracketed study of these communities, but to adopt a strategy of slow, feminist data-driven investigation to make sense of this phenomenon. In this investigation, this book has looked at the role played by an influential subset of Islamophobic far-right actors, micro-influencers, digital news outlets, and garden variety online digital denizens, as a case study to explore the larger far-right ecosystem.

Giorgia Lupi and Stefanie Posavec as feminist information designers have championed a model of a "slow/small" data visualization, analysis, and capture that emphasizes bodies, localities, and temporalities (Kienle 2019; Lupi and Posavec 2016), and it is precisely this slowness of feminist data-driven investigation which asserts the importance of partiality, smaller n-counts, and multiplicitous perspectives (D'Ignazio and Klein 2020; Leurs 2017). What this slow and targeted inquiry into far-right Islamophobic coalitions on Twitter reveals is in fact a larger story about the way in which far-right groups are able to seamlessly organize, communicate, and radicalize out in the open on digital platforms reaching global audien-

https://doi.org/10.1515/9783111032887-007

ces on Twitter, one of the most influential news and political communication sites on the Internet.

Digital Islamophobia, ultimately, is both a strategy of communication and a form of hate-speech (Vidgen and Yasseri 2020), which signals a more epistemic technocultural crisis of violent discourse on social media platforms like Twitter, YouTube, Facebook, and Tik Tok. Platforms which increasingly struggle or decline to manage this type of content underscore the systemic global crisis of resurgent racialized and ethnic nationalism. And these resurgent forms of racialized, ethnic, and religious revanchist political movements are visible on our physical and digital streets not only in Germany and the US, but also in India and Nigeria. As Islamophobia has increasingly been recognized as a form of religio-racism outside of Western contexts that drives political policies in states like India (Sikka 2022, 477), like all other far-right political subcultures it is mediated, expressed, and disseminated on social media platforms.

And digital Islamophobia has been neatly packaged in former President Trump's anti-Muslim screeds posted to Twitter (Khan et al. 2021), recognizable in the AfD's strategic use of Tweets to spread Islamophobic political messaging (Maza 2018). But underneath the surface of this viral, high-level conversation, something more durable and disturbing was being built, often shielded from regular media and scholarly attention because of the seeming banality and inconsequence of rank-and-file accounts, who, post by post, @ by @, and hashtag by hashtag, were strategically building at times temporary but elastic, global, multi-racial coalitions. And this work has been carried out not only by high-profile users, but by everyday suburban white American moms, Indian American Hindu nationalists, German AfD supporters, and Biafran IPOB micro-influencers. These seemingly disparate users have constructed conspiratorial informational flows, forged discursive ties, and radicalized sympathetic new adherents. Long after Twitter trends are forgotten are the real users, the real people, behind the screens who become invested in and generative of projects of racialized nationalism.

As a sustained study of recent digital history, this book has reconstructed from bits and pieces of trace data a complex global network of micro-influencers, dubious digital outlets, and everyday users for whom Islamophobia is a shared grammar and point of entry into an increasingly more radical far-right media ecosystem that extends beyond Twitter to external news sites like *Breitbart* or *Journalistenwatch*, to private Telegram channels, to alt-tech platforms like Gab and Telegram. Twitter may be the primary platform examined in this book, but, like the hashtags #Islamization and #Islamisierung, it is merely the portal into the technosocial space of fractious, circulating far-right counter publics which come in and out of visibility (Florini 2019; Shahin and Dai 2019; Squires 2002).

Twitter as a mainstream micro-blogging site, unlike other comparative social media platforms or less trafficked extremist message and image boards, has, in the case of far-right and seemingly mundane socially conservative users, served as a global digital town square where far-right rhetoric can be hawked to new audiences or buyers and digital Islamophobia can be mainstreamed (Habermas 1991; Winter 2019). Digital Islamophobia is not simply increasingly a constitutive aspect of the larger amorphous, digital far-right, but it is a strategic and useful communicative strategy to radicalize socially conservative users who support more rhetorically subtle forms of anti-Muslim, gender reactionary, and white supremacist ideologies. It is Islamophobia that brings together a range of actors from AfD German supporters to Trump-voting moms in the suburbs, to Hindu nationalist Indian Americans, to anti-Muslim IPOB activists united by a range of distinct yet complimentary goals—an anti-Muslim vision of nationalism that is religiously, racially, and ethnically exclusionary, dependent on national historical context.

Twitter has facilitated the building of these affective networked coalitions of hate across the Global North and South. And while contemporary expressions of Islamophobia are indelibly informed by global structures of race and racism which eminent from interlocking Western structures of settler colonialism, racial capitalism, and racialized and ethnic nationalism (Leroy 2016), activists and actors in Nigeria and India are increasingly the leading forces in refining, producing, and spreading Islamophobic digital discourse, inspired and aided by their American allies.

In states like India which have been defined by an increasingly radical rightward political shift exemplified by the successful elections of politicians like Prime Minister Modi and the right-wing Hindu nationalist Bharatiya Janata Party (BJP), Islamophobic activism and rhetoric on Twitter has paralleled the articulation of exclusionary legal acts like the CAA-NRC and increased instances of state-sponsored and extra-legal violence targeting Muslims (Amarasingam, Umar, and Desai 2022; Bhatia and Gajjala 2020; Butler 2022; Griswold 2019). If the War on Terror and subsequent programs of domestic surveillance and harassment can be understood as the political nadir of the Muslim experience in the West (Abbas 2021), we are now witnessing the digital nadir of the Muslim experience online with record levels of hate-speech and paranoid content produced and shared on major platforms like Twitter.

Just as contemporary offline expressions of Islamophobia in political policy and rhetoric are informed by Western structures of race and racism, Twitter's platformed structure and its very algorithms are informed by similar racialized logics which we can understand as a form of platformed racism (Matamoros-Fernández 2017), designed to encourage extreme speech. More broadly, digital platforms like Twitter continue to operate influenced by an American "Wild West" model of free speech which lends itself towards corporate strategies of content moderation which both superficially adhere to an imaginary post-racial vision the web and also function to reproduce white supremacy (Jereza 2022). Users on Twitter make use of this chaotically regulated digital environment to build far-right networks and instrumentalize Twitter's disembedding, flattening affordances to build affective coalitions.

Twitter, in its structuration facilitates the collapsing of local, regional, and national boundaries, disembedding content from its original context and encouraging the user-directed decontextualization of information. While the underlying historical dynamics of Islamophobia are historically and socially specific in Germany, the US, Nigeria, and India, on Twitter these histories disintegrate into a steady stream of emotive content. Twitter has been a powerful platform in terms of digital political communication and social movement building, particularly in the way in which it has facilitated the building of transnational political linkages via affective networked connections which translate into tangible political publics (Papacharissi 2015a; 2015b; Papacharissi and Trevey 2018).

And we can point towards instances where progressive transnational political coalitions have used Twitter to push back against anti-Muslim political movements, looking at deployments of the hashtags like #womenofshaheenbagh that went global and turned a feminist, working-class Muslim protest in Delhi into an international movement and moment supported by allied groups and users in the US, UK, and beyond (Bhatia and Gajjala 2020; Gajjala et al. 2023; Edwards et al. 2020). Using Twitter's affordances both activists and average users can deploy hashtags which garner affective intensities and foment tangible, offline political action, peaceful protest or violence.

This book has emphasized how far-right Islamophobic groups deploy networked, technological, and rhetorical strategies to expand their own coalitions and agitate for far-right policies or even conspiracies, slowly but surely shifting the Overton window of discourse closer and closer to an acceptance of anti-Muslim hate-speech (Astor 2019). Far-right Islamophobic groups on Twitter are actively engaging in "informational war" (Hannah 2021), advancing racist, religiously exclusionary forms of nationalism which seek to obliterate Muslim communities from inclusion in the past, present, and future of American, German, Indian, and Nigerian societies. And while there are vibrant and powerful progressive political movements online, lately the balance in digital environments, specifically on Twitter, has been tipped in favor of far-right interests since Elon Musk's take-over.

Twitter, despite its uneasy status as a major social media platform compared to its competitors in terms of total number of users (Odabaş 2022), has had an outsized influence on news and politics (Parmelee and Bichard 2013). And since Elon Musk's acquisition of the platform, while Twitter has not imploded like its detractors have prophesied (McNamee 2022), it has entered a period of slow decline. Its bare-bones workforce increasingly confronts technical challenges to carry out maintenance and the implementation of new features (Holt 2023), corporate bills and employee salaries have gone unpaid (Iovine 2023; Stokel-Walker 2022), advertisers have fled choking the platform of limited revenue (Tabahriti 2022), hate-speech has surged (Frenkel and Conger 2022), and Musk has carried out a management style driven by vanity and a belief in conspiracy theories (Conger, Mac, and Isaac 2022).

Twitter may be but one platform in the archipelago of social media sites that constitute our platformed digital media ecosystem, but it has been a crucial staging ground for far-right communities to wage informational war and for progressive coalitions to hit back. As Musk has increasingly signaled his own personal belief in far-right, racist conspiracies and political ideology made visible in his own posting behavior and sharing of memes (Frenkel, Gómez, and Koeze 2023), on the level of corporate policy implementation, Musk has made tangible changes to the way in which Twitter engages in content moderation and deals with (mis)information that have rendered the platform more welcoming to extreme speech (Gilbert 2022).

Over the course of this book, these six chapters have looked at the extreme speech of digital Islamophobia as a means to make sense of how far-right actors connect, how networks are built, and what type of content affectively animates these emerging transnational coalitions. Even as it is critical to recognize the indelible American influence in terms of racism, legal frameworks like Section 230, and the exportation of American digital cultural products like conspiracy theories upon our digital environment, far-right political ideology is today a global racial project. Ungoverned American technology platforms have fostered an environment where an American affinity for religio-racial ethno-nationalist politics, anti-Muslim Hindu nationalism, resurgent far-right German anti-immigrant populism, and a fractured Nigerian democratic civil society all converge and collide on Twitter.

The scale of the crisis of digital Islamophobia may seem impossible to address, built into the very structure of Twitter which relies upon user-generated content and the ability to modify information and disembed content to make connections. To "bring people together." But if the fundamental structure of Twitter does not change, and the company is unable or uninterested in moderating content, then as scholars and policy makers we must be more creative in addressing this crisis. This can mean tangible changes to Twitter's content moderation policies which require the platform to take down hate-speech or (mis)information within a certain period of time as NetzDG stipulates (Griffin 2022). Or, this could mean that the impending Digital Services Act from the EU must be aggressively implemented and financial penalties expressly carried out (Vernick 2022). Ensuring these policy interventions are enforced, would, on a case-by-case basis create some reduction in the amount of hate-speech and (mis)information on the platform, which means less harm, and would reduce the influence of these higher profile (mis)information spreading accounts. However, hard moderation has its limits even when a company is interested in implementing it, much less when it is legally compelled to do so (Wilson and Land 2021).

As with the conversation regarding the social media app Tik Tok and the American and European impulse to ban the Chinese-based company due to purported data privacy and national security concerns (Maheshwari and Holpuch 2023; Laslo 2023), it is naïve to think that any singular national governmental action alone can completely re-shape the digital ecosystem. Even as China's "Golden Shield" approach to Internet censorship has been successful in blocking citizen access to foreign platforms (Chandel et al. 2019), users continue to iterate and innovate in accessing banned content using VPNs and spreading anti-state messages using creative means of digital activism such as during the recent Blank Paper Protest (Westfall 2022). Users still find ways to communicate and connect for both progressive and reactionary aims.

Furthermore, with much of the far-right content on Twitter originating from dubious digital news platforms and fringe message and image boards, users will continue to surface extremist content. As Twitter remains a key mainstream platform for digital news dissemination and political communication, the far-right can instrumentalize the platform to spread their message. Even as conditionally effective as "hashtag revolutions" have been (Gladwell 2010), a digital culture war, unlike a revolution, does not necessarily have to call for specific policies, but rather it is a war of position (Gramsci 1976). It is the advancement of a far-right, racially and religiously exclusionary political culture that Islamophobic coalitions and groups seek to advance and embed in our discourse.

When we look at digital Islamophobia, a myriad of other political problems come into focus. Anti-Muslim rhetoric about veiling turns into anti-science conspiracies about masking. Allegations of public-school conversions evolve into suggestions that states are planning authoritarian take-overs. Fears of sexual violence collapse into well-worn Orientalist rhetoric. And so on. And this type of racialized, Islamophobic paranoid thinking is uniquely suited to expression on digital platforms, and particularly on Twitter. But even as disturbing or dismissible as such activity is on mainstream platforms, what we are witnessing are merely the superficial symptoms of religio-racial nationalisms.

So, what is to be done if strategies of corporate content moderation are unlikely to succeed and governmental policies regulating social media platforms are limited in their efficacy? It is difficult as individual scholars, activists, and even policymakers to address the deluge of far-right hate-speech and political content online, but this is precisely the goal of far-right digitally networked groups; to produce an overwhelming amount of content that plays on anxieties, re-casts histories, and further infects the body politic.

Elon Musk's acquisition of Twitter has thrown into stark relief that the status quo of how social media platforms operate is increasingly untenable. Political institutions have recognized this, with the case of Twitter v. Taamneh (2023) concerning whether algorithmic recommendation systems of digital platforms and failures to moderate could be situated as platforms becoming culpable for abetting the circulation and hosting of terroristic content (Millhiser 2023). But in this era of multiple, overlapping crises, we are also confronting a crisis of imagination—of how to regulate and remake our digital ecosystem, and with that, to reimagine national democratic political communities that unbundle historic associations between race, religion, ethnicity, and national identity. Which is to say, to address the root causes of religio-racial nationalisms rather than simply the symptoms of digital hate-speech as they appear.

With a functioning but limited technocratic EU, a Supreme Court reaffirming Section 230, and a far-right sympathizer as current CEO of Twitter, we are at an inflection point. It behooves us not merely as researchers or activists, but as citizens, not to be paralyzed by these crises but to approach them with a sense of possibility. If the nation is being reclassified in civilizationalist terms by the far-right, then it is also possible to reimagine what new, progressive affective coalitions look like that re-cast the nation in other modes of community. Samuel Huntington articulated his "clash of civilizations" thesis in response to Francis Fukuyama's positing of the "end of history" in the post-WWII democratic liberal order (Fukuyama 2006; Huntington 1993). We have not so much seen the end of history, as rather its disembedding in an age of algorithmic platformed technologies. The far-right does not seek to go back in historical time, but to remake it, alongside the nation. It is time for those invested in a different digital future to offer an alternative of our own.

References

Abbas, Tahir. 2021. "Reflection: The 'War on Terror', Islamophobia and Radicalisation Twenty Years On." *Critical Studies on Terrorism* 14 (4): 402–4. https://doi.org/10.1080/17539153.2021.1980182.

Amarasingam, Amarnath, Sanober Umar, and Shweta Desai. 2022. "'Fight, Die, and If Required Kill': Hindu Nationalism, Misinformation, and Islamophobia in India." *Religions* 13 (5): 380. https://doi.org/10.3390/rel13050380.

Astor, Maggie. 2019. "How the Politically Unthinkable Can Become Mainstream." *The New York Times*, 2019. https://www.nytimes.com/2019/02/26/us/politics/overton-window-democrats.html.

Bernstein, Michael, Andrés Monroy-Hernández, Drew Harry, Paul André, Katrina Panovich, and Greg Vargas. 2011. "4chan and /b/: An Analysis of Anonymity and Ephemerality in a Large Online Community." In *Proceedings of the International AAAI Conference on Web and Social Media*, 5:50–57. https://ojs.aaai.org/index.php/ICWSM/article/view/14134.

Bhatia, Kiran, and Radhika Gajjala. 2020. "Examining Anti-CAA Protests at Shaheen Bagh: Muslim Women and Politics of the Hindu India." *International Journal of Communication* 14: 6286–6303.

Butler, Umar. 2022. "Islamophobia in the Digital Age: A Study of Anti-Muslim Tweets." Victoria: Islamic Council of Victoria. https://doi.org/10.25916/GC0A-X327.

Chandel, Sonali, Zang Jingji, Yu Yunnan, Sun Jingyao, and Zhang Zhipeng. 2019. "The Golden Shield Project of China: A Decade Later—An in-Depth Study of the Great Firewall." In *2019 International Conference on Cyber-Enabled Distributed Computing and Knowledge Discovery (CyberC)*, 111–19. https://doi.org/10.1109/CyberC.2019.00027.

Conger, Kate, Ryan Mac, and Mike Isaac. 2022. "Elon Musk Fires Twitter Employees Who Criticized Him." *The New York Times*, November 15, 2022, sec. Technology. https://www.nytimes.com/2022/11/15/technology/elon-musk-twitter-fired-criticism.html.

D'Ignazio, Catherine, and Laura F. Klein. 2020. *Data Feminism*. Cambridge: MIT Press.

Edwards, Emily, Oladoyin Olubukola Abiona, Sarah Ford, Olayombo Tejumade Raji-Oyelade, Radhika Gajjala, and Riddhima Sharma. 2020. "Shaheen Bagh: Making Sense of (Re)Emerging 'Subaltern' Feminist Political Subjectivities in Hashtag Publics (Through a Mess of Computational Humanities Data Analyses)." In. Virtual.

Florini, Sarah. 2019. *Beyond Hashtags: Racial Politics and Black Digital Networks*. New York: New York University Press.

Frenkel, Sheera, and Kate Conger. 2022. "Hate Speech's Rise on Twitter Is Unprecedented, Researchers Find." *The New York Times*, December 2, 2022, sec. Technology. https://www.nytimes.com/2022/12/02/technology/twitter-hate-speech.html.

Frenkel, Sheera, Martín González Gómez, and Ella Koeze. 2023. "Dissecting Elon Musk's Tweets: Memes, Rants, Private Parts and an Echo Chamber." *The New York Times*, January 31, 2023. https://www.nytimes.com/interactive/2023/01/31/technology/elon-musk-tweets.html.

Fukuyama, Francis. 2006. *The End of History and the Last Man*. New York: Simon & Schuster. https://www.simonandschuster.com/books/The-End-of-History-and-the-Last-Man/Francis-Fukuyama/9780743284554.

Gajjala, Radhika, Emily Lynell Edwards, Debipreeta Rahut, Ololade Margaret Faniyi, Bedadyuti Jha, Jhalak Jain, Aiman Khan, and Saadia Farooq. 2023. "Transnationalising Dadis as Feminist Political/Activist Subjects." *Feminist Encounters: A Journal of Critical Studies in Culture and Politics* 7 (1): 08. https://doi.org/10.20897/femenc/12886.

Gilbert, David. 2022. "Elon Musk Is Turning Twitter Into a Haven for Nazis." *Vice*, November 29, 2022. https://www.vice.com/en/article/n7zm9q/elon-musk-twitter-nazis-white-supremacy.

Gladwell, Malcolm. 2010. "Small Change." *The New Yorker*, September 27, 2010. https://www.newyorker.com/magazine/2010/10/04/small-change-malcolm-gladwell.

Gramsci, Antonio. 1976. *Selections from the Prison Notebooks of Antonio Gramsci*. Edited and translated by Quintin Hoare and Geoffrey Nowell-Smith. London: Lawrence & Wishart.

Griffin, Rachel. 2022. "New School Speech Regulation as a Regulatory Strategy against Hate Speech on Social Media: The Case of Germany's NetzDG." *Telecommunications Policy* 46 (9): 102411. https://doi.org/10.1016/j.telpol.2022.102411.

Griswold, Eliza. 2019. "The Violent Toll of Hindu Nationalism in India." *The New Yorker*, March 5, 2019. https://www.newyorker.com/news/on-religion/the-violent-toll-of-hindu-nationalism-in-india.

Habermas, Jürgen. 1991. *The Structural Transformation of the Public Sphere An Inquiry into a Category of Bourgeois Society.* Translated by Thomas Burger. Cambridge, MA: MIT Press.

Hannah, Matthew. 2021. "QAnon and the Information Dark Age." *First Monday* 26 (2). https://doi.org/10.5210/fm.v26i2.10868.

Holt, Kris. 2023. "Twitter Was Broken Due to an API Issue (Updated)." *Engadget*, March 6, 2023. https://www.engadget.com/every-link-on-twitter-is-broken-right-now-165929931.html.

Huntington, Samuel P. 1993. "The Clash of Civilizations?" *Foreign Affairs* 72 (3): 22–49. https://doi.org/10.2307/20045621.

Iovine, Anna. 2023. "Twitter Hit with New Lawsuits for Not Paying Bills." *Mashable*, February 25, 2023, sec. Tech. https://mashable.com/article/twitter-non-payment-lawsuits.

Jereza, Rae. 2022. "'I'm Not This Person': Racism, Content Moderators, and Protecting and Denying Voice Online." *New Media & Society*, September, 14614448221122224. https://doi.org/10.1177/14614448221122224.

Khan, Mohsin Hassan, Farwa Qazalbash, Hamedi Mohd Adnan, Lalu Nurul Yaqin, and Rashid Ali Khuhro. 2021. "Trump and Muslims: A Critical Discourse Analysis of Islamophobic Rhetoric in Donald Trump's Selected Tweets." *SAGE Open* 11 (1): 1–16. https://doi.org/10.1177/21582440211004172.

Kienle, Miriam. 2019. "Dear Data: Feminist Information Design's Resistance to Self-Quantification – ProQuest." *Feminist Studies* 45 (1): 129–58, 264.

Laslo, Matt. 2023. "The Push to Ban TikTok in the US Isn't About Privacy." *Wired*, February 23, 2023. https://www.wired.com/story/us-congress-tiktok-ban-privacy-law/.

Leroy, Justin. 2016. "Black History in Occupied Territory: On the Entanglements of Slavery and Settler Colonialism." *Theory & Event* 19 (4). https://muse.jhu.edu/pub/1/article/633276.

Leurs, Koen. 2017. "Feminist Data Studies: Using Digital Methods for Ethical, Reflexive and Situated Socio-Cultural Research." *Feminist Review* 115: 130–54.

Lupi, Giorgia, and Stefanie Posavec. 2016. *Dear Data.* Princeton, NJ: Princeton Architectural Press. http://www.dear-data.com/thebook.

Maheshwari, Sapna, and Amanda Holpuch. 2023. "Why Countries Are Trying to Ban TikTok." *The New York Times*, March 3, 2023, sec. Technology. https://www.nytimes.com/article/tiktok-ban.html.

Matamoros-Fernández, Ariadna. 2017. "Platformed Racism: The Mediation and Circulation of an Australian Race-Based Controversy on Twitter, Facebook and YouTube." *Information, Communication & Society* 20 (6): 930–46. https://doi.org/10.1080/1369118X.2017.1293130.

Maza, Cristina. 2018. "Twitter, Facebook Scrub German Party's Anti-Islam Posts." *Newsweek*, January 2, 2018, sec. World. https://www.newsweek.com/twitter-facebook-anti-muslim-posts-germany-afd-767869.

McNamee, Roger. 2022. "Twitter Is Collapsing, and Nothing Can Replace It." *Time*, November 18, 2022. https://time.com/6234759/nothing-can-replace-twitter-roger-mcnamee/.

Millhiser, Ian. 2023. "The Supreme Court Hears Two Cases That Could Ruin the Internet." *Vox*, February 16, 2023. https://www.vox.com/policy-and-politics/2023/2/16/23582848/supreme-court-internet-section-230-terrorism-cases-gonzalez-google-twitter-taamneh.

Odabaş, Meltem. 2022. "10 Facts about Americans and Twitter." Social Media. Pew Research Center. https://www.pewresearch.org/fact-tank/2022/05/05/10-facts-about-americans-and-twitter/.

Papacharissi, Zizi. 2015a. "Affective Publics and Structures of Storytelling: Sentiment, Events and Mediality." *Information, Communication & Society* 19 (3): 307–24. https://doi.org/10.1080/1369118X.2015.1109697.

Papacharissi, Zizi. 2015b. *Affective Publics: Sentiment, Technology, and Politics.* Oxford, UK: Oxford University Press.

Papacharissi, Zizi, and Meggan Taylor Trevey. 2018. "Affective Publics and Windows of Opportunity: Social Media and the Potential for Social Change." In *The Routledge Companion To Media And Activism,* edited by Meikle Graham. London: Routledge.

Parmelee, John H., and Shannon L. Bichard. 2013. *Politics and the Twitter Revolution: How Tweets Influence the Relationship between Political Leaders and the Public.* Lanham, MD: Rowman & Littlefield Publishers. https://rowman.com/ISBN/9780739165010/Politics-and-the-Twitter-Revolution-How-Tweets-Influence-the-Relationship-between-Political-Leaders-and-the-Public.

Shahin, Saif, and Zehui Dai. 2019. "Understanding Public Engagement With Global Aid Agencies on Twitter: A Technosocial Framework." *American Behavioral Scientist* 63 (12): 1–24.

Sikka, Sonia. 2022. "Indian Islamophobia as Racism." *The Political Quarterly* 93 (3): 469–77. https://doi.org/10.1111/1467-923X.13152.

Smith, Dana G. 2023. "Concentration Tips: How to Focus Like It's 1990 – The New York Times." *The New York Times,* January 9, 2023. https://www.nytimes.com/2023/01/09/well/mind/concentration-focus-distraction.html.

Squires, Catherine R. 2002. "Rethinking the Black Public Sphere: An Alternative Vocabulary for Multiple Public Spheres." *Communication Theory* 12 (4): 446–68. https://doi.org/10.1111/j.1468-2885.2002.tb00278.x.

Stokel-Walker, Chris. 2022. "Twitter Is Now Having Trouble Paying Some Employees on Time." *Ars Technica,* November 28, 2022. https://arstechnica.com/tech-policy/2022/11/twitter-missed-payroll-for-some-european-staff-this-month/.

Tabahriti, Sam. 2022. "Elon Musk Says Activist Pressure on Twitter Advertisers Is an Attempt to 'Destroy Free Speech in America.'" *Business Insider,* November 4, 2022, sec. Tech. https://www.businessinsider.com/elon-musk-says-twitter-activist-groups-trying-destroy-free-speech-2022-11.

Tiffert, Glenn D. 2019. "Peering down the Memory Hole: Censorship, Digitization, and the Fragility of Our Knowledge Base." *The American Historical Review* 124 (2): 550–68. https://doi.org/10.1093/ahr/rhz286.

Vernick, Gillian. 2022. "EU Poised to Impose Sweeping Social Media Regulation with Digital Services Act." *The Reporters Committee for Freedom of the Press* (blog). May 9, 2022. https://www.rcfp.org/eu-dsa-social-media-regulation/.

Vidgen, Bertie, and Taha Yasseri. 2020. "Detecting Weak and Strong Islamophobic Hate Speech on Social Media." *Journal of Information Technology & Politics* 17 (1): 66–78. https://doi.org/10.1080/19331681.2019.1702607.

Westfall, Sammy. 2022. "How Blank Sheets of Paper Became a Protest Symbol in China." *Washington Post,* November 29, 2022. https://www.washingtonpost.com/world/2022/11/28/china-sheet-paper-blank-protest-covid/.

Wilson, Richard A, and Molly Land. 2021. "Hate Speech on Social Media: Content Moderation in Context." *Connecticut Law Review* 52 (3): 1029–76.

Winter, Aaron. 2019. "Online Hate: From the Far-Right to the 'Alt-Right' and from the Margins to the Mainstream." In *Online Othering,* edited by K Lumsden and E Harmer, 39–63. Palgrave Studies in Cybercrime and Cybersecurity. Cham, Switzerland: Palgrave Macmillan.

Index

https://doi.org/10.1515/9783111032887-008

www.ingramcontent.com/pod-product-compliance
Lightning Source LLC
Chambersburg PA
CBHW062055270326
41931CB00013B/3087